The Last Voyage of Drake & Hawkins

Edited by

KENNETH R. ANDREWS

CAMBRIDGE

Published for the Hakluyt Society

AT THE UNIVERSITY PRESS

1972

Published by the Syndics of the Cambridge University Press
Bentley House, 200 Euston Road, London NW1 2DB
American Branch: 32 East 57th Street, New York, N.Y.10022

© The Hakluyt Society 1972

Library of Congress Catalogue Card Number: 70–154509

ISBN: 0 521 01039 X

Printed in Great Britain
By Robert MacLehose & Co. Ltd
The University Press, Glasgow

Contents

CONTENTS

vi

CONTENTS

Plates

Maps

Preface

This book is a sequel to Miss I. A. Wright's and my own volumes on English voyages to the West Indies. Miss Wright gave me a flying start by handing on to me the various references she had collected to relevant material in Seville and at an early stage Professor Engel Sluiter of Berkeley, California, gave me further valuable leads to the Spanish archives, including microfilms and transcripts of certain documents. To these two scholars I owe the greatest debt. I am also much indebted to Dr H. A. Lloyd of Hull University, who brought to my notice the Baskerville material in the Harleian MSS and supplied further information about Baskerville and others of Essex's followers. Professor D. B. Quinn directed my attention to the Adams Journal and encouraged my efforts by his unfailing interest. I am much obliged to the museum experts who have taken trouble over my problems, especially Sr Julio Marrero Nuñez of the San Juan National Historic Site, Puerto Rico, Beverley C. Williams of the Canal Zone Library Museum and Mr E. Gaskell of the Wellcome Institute of the History of Medicine. I am grateful to Mlle de la Roncière for paving my way in the Bibliothèque Nationale and to the late R. A. Skelton for introducing me to her and generally assisting in the launching of this project. In its later stages I have relied heavily on the patience and helpfulness of the honorary secretaries of the Hakluyt Society. Finally I am very pleased to welcome the contribution of Commander D. W. Waters to this book.

I wish to thank the University of Hull and the British Academy for financing my second stay in Spain in 1966; Lord Salisbury for permission to print various documents from the Hatfield collection; the Bibliothèque Nationale, Paris, for the photographs of the Paris Profiles reproduced herein; the Bayerische Staatsbibliothek, München, for permission to reproduce f. 13v. of the Munich log; the Director of the Archivo General de Indias,

PREFACE

Seville, for permission to reproduce the two plans of the Morro at
Puerto Rico; and the Director of the Archivo General de
Simancas for permission to reproduce Casola's sketch of the
Canaries action. The maps of San Juan and the Panama Isthmus
were drawn on my instructions by Mr A. F. Herzer.

Hull, 1970   K. R. A.

xii

Notes on Presentation

Accents
Accentuation was not used in sixteenth-century Spanish and is therefore not used here in direct quotation from contemporary sources. Where the documents, however, appear in modern translation, accents have been supplied, except in cases where, as in 'Panama', there is a different English usage.

References to Publications
Unless otherwise stated, the place of publication is London, England.

Abbreviations
A. de I.: Archivo General de Indias.
A.O.: Audit Office.
A.P.C., N.S.: J. R. Dasent (ed.), *Acts of the Privy Council, New Series*.
B.M.: British Museum.
C.: Chancery.
Cal. S.P.D.: Calendar of State Papers Domestic.
Cal. Hatfield MSS: Calendar of the Manuscripts of the Marquess of Salisbury.
E.: Exchequer.
E.H.R.: English Historical Review.
H.A.H.R.: Hispanic American Historical Review.
H.C.A.: High Court of Admiralty.
Munich Log: Bayerische Staatsbibliothek, München, Codex Anglicus: 2.
Paris Profiles: Bibliothèque Nationale, Paris, Manuscrits Anglais: 51.
P.C.C.: Prerogative Court of Canterbury.
Principal Navigations: Richard Hakluyt, *The Principal Navigations, Voyages Traffiques & Discoveries of the English Nation.*
P.R.O.: Public Record Office.
S.P. 12: State Papers Domestic, Elizabeth.

NOTES ON PRESENTATION

S.T.C.: A. W. Pollard and G. R. Redgrave, *A Short-Title Catalogue of Books Printed in England, Scotland and Ireland . . . 1475–1640.*

For abbreviations of the titles of the English narratives of the expedition see the introduction to Chapter III.

Introduction

The West Indian expedition of 1595–6 was a miserable failure, in which Drake, Hawkins and many others died. In crude outline the facts of the story have long been known, but it is hardly surprising that they have attracted far less attention than happier episodes in Drake's career. The best studies of the voyage, those by Corbett[1] and Oppenheim,[2] are highly condensed interpretations, based on a rather limited range of sources, particularly on the Spanish side, and few students of maritime history can have had the opportunity to study enough of the relevant material to form considered judgements of the issues involved. It is the belief that such an exercise may be rewarding, in terms of a better understanding of the Elizabethan sea war, that has inspired the present work. Its object is not to offer another interpretation, but to provide those interested with representative documents and associated information from which they may draw their own conclusions. The editor's opinions on particular matters are expressed throughout, but no summary exposition of the events and circumstances has been attempted. Those who prefer to begin with a general narrative can turn to Maynarde (document 18 herein) or to the journal published by Hakluyt.[3]

In selecting these documents from the much larger mass of material available, I have preferred manuscripts to printed items, except in two cases of important pieces which have appeared only in Spanish (documents 26 and 37), three cases of especially relevant matter published at the time (documents 31, 40 and 41) and three that have been published more recently, but with serious textual deficiencies (documents 18, 19 and 29). Perhaps the most arresting items in the present collection are the letters written by

[1] J. S. Corbett, *Drake and the Tudor Navy* (1893), II, 402–37.
[2] M. Oppenheim (ed.), *The Naval Tracts of Sir William Monson*, I (1902), 312–40.
[3] See the introduction to Chapter III and document 41.

Baskerville and Conabut, respectively commanders of the English and Spanish troops, immediately after the battle of Capirilla (documents 36 and 35). Such direct products of the action itself have had high priority, as have the recorded depositions of English prisoners (documents 22 and 33) and various other documents which report prisoners' statements directly or indirectly. Letters and narratives by participants constitute the bulk of the material chosen. The chief aim in selection has been to present a variety of aspects and viewpoints. Accordingly one of the main features of this volume is the juxtaposition of English and Spanish evidence, more or less evenly balanced in quantity. The purpose of this is not merely to do justice to both sides. The interest of the Spanish evidence lies partly in the light it throws on the Spaniards themselves and their defences, but equally in what it says and implies about the English. Thus one Spanish document alone gives Drake's instructions to the *Francis,* his letter to the governor of Puerto Rico and a convincing picture of his reaction to the repulse at San Juan, matters on which the English sources are either reticent or mute. Moreover it is only when the statements of the contestants are set side by side that the sequence and timing of events can be fully understood; only when the mutual knowledge, half-knowledge or ignorance of the parties are compared that their efforts can be properly judged; only when two dimensions, as it were, can be related that the third dimension of circumscribing conditions can be discerned and the recurrent irony of the drama appreciated. Finally, the selection has been influenced by the conviction that the events do not explain themselves, but make sense only in terms of the political, strategic, financial, personal and, in the broadest sense, logistic factors on both sides. Hence the inclusion of considerable detail on the background and preparation of the voyage in the first two chapters; and the attention to background in the introductions to Chapters IV, V and VI.

On the English documents nothing need be added here to the individual accounts of each given in the chapters below. The only English evidence that is new, in the sense of not having been used by those who have written about this voyage hitherto, is the Baskerville material, including the 'discourse' of the voyage (document 20; and see also documents 8, 16, 17, 28, 36, 44, 45, 46 and 47). The exchequer accounts of the expedition (document 14) were used, though not extensively, by Oppenheim, and are surprisingly little known considering their potential interest to the naval historian. Of the items not reproduced here, the various English narratives are described in Chapter III below; two minor contemporary publications, Fitzgeffrey[1] and Roberts,[2] proved of limited value.

The Spanish documents require more comment. Spanish contemporary publications are, with the exception of Avellaneda's report (document 40), of little value in comparison with the manuscript material. Lope de Vega's epic poem, *La Dragontea*,[3] is a frankly romantic treatment, founded but precariously on the facts. Francisco Caro de Torres' account of the deeds of Don Alonso de Sotomayor, although written by a participant, is too inaccurate and eulogistic to be regarded as a reliable source.[4] Herrera's[5] and Pedro Simón's[6] histories are essentially secondary works. With the one exception mentioned, therefore, the Spanish items produced here represent manuscripts: letters from individuals (usually addressed to the king or to Juan de Ibarra, secretary of the council of the Indies); formal *relaciones*; and extracts from

[1] Charles Fitzgeffrey, *Sir Francis Drake, His Honorable lifes commendation, and his Tragicall Deathes lamentation* (Oxford, 1596).

[2] H.R. [Henry Roberts], *The Trumpet of Fame: or Sir F. Drake's & Sir J. Hawkins' Farewell* (1595).

[3] Lope de Vega Carpio, *La Dragontea* (Valencia, 1598). Ed. V. Fernández Asís, 2 vols (Madrid, 1935).

[4] Francisco Caro de Torres, *Relacion de los Servicios que hizo a Su Magestad del Rey Don Felipe Segundo y Tercero, don Alonso de Sotomayor del Abito de Santiago* [etc.] (Madrid, 1620).

[5] Antonio de Herrera y Tordesillas, *Historia General del Mundo*, III (Madrid, 1612), 587 ff. This is based in part on primary sources, though it contains errors.

[6] Pedro Simón, *Noticias historiales de las Conquistas de Tierra Firme en las Indias Occidentales*, V (Bogotá, 1892), 126–46. Simón is inclined to romanticize and is not necessarily reliable even when he claims personal knowledge. For example, he says that the governor of Puerto Rico in 1595 was Juan Fernández Coronel, whom he knew well. In fact the governor was Pedro Suárez Coronel. Lope de Vega made the same mistake.

informaciones. Each type must be treated with special caution. Nearly all the Spanish letters mentioned in this volume were written by officials to people of higher authority whom they wished to influence. *Relaciones,* or reports, would be made by individuals to higher authorities for the same purpose, and are not free from similar suspicion when compiled by or on behalf of an official body, as in the case of the *audiencia* of the Canary Islands (see Chapter IV). The same warning might apply, of course, to any letter or report, but axe-grinding does seem to be remarkably common and blatant in the bureaucratic context of Spanish-American affairs. As for the *informaciones,* there hardly exists a more suspect type of historical evidence. For these were essentially testimonials, legally drawn up and designed to secure the subject a reward (or *merced*) for services rendered to the crown, a reward often exactly specified – usually promotion to a more lucrative office. A petition stating the services would be followed by the testimony of numerous witnesses, mechanically and repetitiously confirming the claimant's story. Occasionally a deposition may enlarge upon a point with circumstantial detail, but the context is hardly such as to encourage belief in these elaborations, particularly because they may contradict other depositions, just as *informaciones* on behalf of different individuals frequently contradict each other. Accordingly the use of these voluminous materials has been reduced to a minimum here, extracts being taken from petitions and not from depositions. The character of the Spanish evidence generally, it must be said, makes it difficult to judge issues which were then subjects of controversy, such as the state of the defences of San Juan de Puerto Rico. Fortunately, on many of the significant issues the evidence is not seriously conflicting. For example, the course of the Panama campaign is made perfectly clear in spite of the bitter factional quarrels among Spanish participants claiming credit for the victory.

While it is not intended here to formulate an integrated interpretation, it may be helpful to consider certain lines of perspective and certain obscurities. In the first place the problem of the aims of the expedition is of primary importance for our understanding of the course of events. The evidence discussed in

Chapter I below suggests that the original aim may have been not merely to sack Panama, but to hold it and thus secure a stranglehold upon Spain's main treasure route. At a very late stage in the preparations, however, there was some change of plan, and when the fleet finally left England its mission was simply to capture treasure and return within nine months, though now it was also expected to tackle Puerto Rico on the way to Panama. The developments and arguments which resulted in this curious abortion should of course be viewed in the large context of Elizabethan strategic thought.[1] The idea that Spain could be brought to her knees by intercepting her supplies of treasure from America was then commonplace. Contemporary Englishmen tended to overestimate the importance of this revenue to Spain and to underestimate the difficulty of intercepting it, for the judgement of all concerned – not least the queen herself – was naturally influenced by the prospect of millions of silver. And of the various schemes for achieving this object, those which proposed the establishment of a base at or near the sources of the treasure had, despite their disregard of logistics, a strong appeal to the more imperialistically minded of Elizabeth's men of war. In 1595 the English possessed the initiative for the first time since 1589, free of the threat from Brest and confident in the ability of the French and the Dutch to deal with Spain's armies. The earl of Essex's influence was now strong and he was presumably already revolving the ideas of offensive strategy which he was later to express with remarkable cogency.[2] Essex was an old ally of Drake's and, as our documents show beyond reasonable doubt, a prime mover in the Panama project. Later, it is true, he came to regard a transatlantic strategy as impracticable, but it seems not unlikely that in 1594 he favoured it. Such are the general considerations (as distinct from the particulars examined in Chapter I) which tend to support the hypothesis that the queen originally agreed to a plan to secure control of the Isthmus.

[1] The best short treatment is R. B. Wernham, 'Elizabethan War Aims and Strategy', *Elizabethan Government and Society, Essays Presented to Sir John Neale* (eds. S. T. Bindoff, J. Hurstfield and C. Williams, 1961).
[2] L. W. Henry, 'The Earl of Essex as Strategist and Military Organizer, 1596–7', *E.H.R.*, LXVIII (1953), 363–93.

Her strategic thinking in general was nevertheless based upon a profoundly defensive view of the war and upon a severely limited budget. She tended to give low priority to maritime offensives other than privateering ventures likely to yield an immediate profit. The divergence between her own attitudes and those of her 'men of war' had been the main cause of the failure of the Lisbon expedition in 1589, and now, in 1595, she was strongly impressed by Spain's mobilization of an armada which appeared to threaten Ireland, or even England itself, with invasion that year or the next. The exchanges documented in our first chapter thus form a variation on an already familiar theme, as Drake and Hawkins recognized when they referred to 'the Lyke dyscontentment or worse then that of the portyngall viage' (document 7). The queen was perhaps unduly anxious about the dangers of invasion and the suggestions she authorized for a revised plan of the voyage were unrealistic, but there is something to be said for the decision to convert the expedition into a simple privateering venture. If the original plan was indeed to hold the Isthmus, it was fundamentally unsound, whereas the prizes to be had at Puerto Rico and Panama in one voyage could conceivably have made an appreciable difference to the balance of fighting power for two or three years. The serious mistake of the amended plan was the inclusion of Puerto Rico as a preliminary target, but it seems likely that without the promise of treasure at Puerto Rico the fleet might never have crossed the Atlantic.

The apparent coincidence of public and private interests found appropriate expression in the joint stock organization adopted for the venture, a form of enterprise at once financially convenient and militarily pernicious, an epitome of Elizabethan government in general and of its management of sea warfare in particular. Whatever weight may be given, in explanation of the events, to the relationship between the generals, the analysis in our second chapter shows that personalities were bound up with factions, and factions with financial interests. If the fleet was so divided as to be, until the death of Hawkins, virtually two fleets, which very nearly parted company, this was due to structure as much as to personality. Each equipped and provisioned his own squadron, each had

INTRODUCTION

his own financial and shipowning associates, each his personal following of kinsmen and clients among the officers. The two squadrons were two interest groups, two factions. When the argument, so fraught with consequences, arose between the two leaders, it was about victualling, manning and plunder – matters of policy which were also matters of interest to those with stakes in the venture. Whether the bad furnishing (if such it was) of Drake's squadron was a vital factor in the fate of the voyage is a question each reader may judge for himself; what is of deeper significance, perhaps, is that the organizational form, itself characteristic of the society and its methods of warfare, gave the project a built-in liability to factional disputes, inadequate victualling and unwise diversions in pursuit of profit. Unfortunately the evidence relating to private subscriptions is too scrappy to establish how and when the generals raised their shares of the joint stock. Further information on this might throw some light on the otherwise inexplicable delays in the preparation of the voyage down to July 1595, delays which gravely prejudiced the success of the enterprise. Apparently Drake and Hawkins had nothing to gain and much to lose by postponing their departure, but the queen blamed them to their faces for it, as if their responsibility was self-evident. The answer may be that they found it difficult to raise the necessary funds from private sources.

In their assessments of the performance of the English force modern historians have differed sharply. Some have emphasized the strengthening of Spanish forces since the defeat of the Armada. Corbett, for example, wrote: 'In the failure to grasp that Spain had become a great sea power with a fleet in a constant state of mobilisation and admirals well practised in handling and protecting large numbers of ships, lay the fatal misconception that overhung the whole expedition.'[1] With respect to the Caribbean in particular it is commonly held that 'The débacle of Drake and Hawkins in 1595 . . . illustrates the growing power of Spanish forces in the region.'[2] Fernández Duro, on the other hand, con-

[1] *Drake and the Tudor Navy,* II, 402–37.
[2] R. D. Hussey, 'Spanish Reactions to Foreign Aggression in the Caribbean to about 1680', *H.A.H.R.,* IX (1929), 286–302.

cluded that the Spanish defences were slight and weakly manned at every point attacked. He, like Oppenheim, was strongly critical of the conduct of the expedition.[1] Cheyney's verdict was that 'failure as the expedition certainly was, it owed this failure not to the strength of the Spaniards but to its own misfortunes and mistakes'.[2]

Unless the campaign is examined in detail, it is tempting to make the easy assumption that the side which won was fundamentally the stronger, and then to seek evidence of its strength, including the fact that it won. But much of the contemporary comment is of dubious value. How much weight should be given to those English statements which, after the event, stressed the formidableness of the opposition? Can Baskerville's reports, for example, be taken at their face value? If we look for confirmation to the other side, we find for the most part, before the enemy's arrival, charges and counter-charges of incompetence, corruption and neglect of the most elementary precautions or defence-works; and, after the victories, except at Puerto Rico, frequent reference to miracles, providence and divine intervention. These, however, are usually no more than thinly disguised and scarcely disinterested reflections upon the conduct of specified human beings, opinions as much to be trusted as Baskerville's excuses. Nor is it sufficient to refer to the programme of fortification initiated by Juan de Tejeda and Bautista Antoneli in the later eighties. At the Panama Isthmus Antoneli's work, which was confined to Porto Belo, proved irrelevant to the defence and was heavily set back by the destructive efforts of the raiders. At Puerto Rico the fort in construction played its part in the battle, but it is doubtful how much more effective it was in 1595 than it might have been in 1591, had an attack occurred then. In reality San Juan in 1595 owed its strength to somewhat fortuitous circumstances, which are considered in Chapter V below.

As for Spanish naval power, the failure of Avellaneda's

[1] C. Fernández Duro, *Armada Española desde la Unión de los Reinos de Castilla y de Aragón*, III (Madrid, 1897), 106–15.

[2] E. P. Cheyney, *A History of England from the Defeat of the Armada to the Death of Queen Elizabeth*, I (1914), 549.

armada must be set off against the success of Pedro Tello's frigates. In respect of naval organization, too, the dispatch of the frigates was creditable, but that of the armada hardly so. Nor was the performance of Spain's naval intelligence system anything like so impressive as a cursory glance at the course of events might suggest. In some cases there were extraordinary delays in the transmission of vital news – the news of Sancho Pardo's arrival in Puerto Rico, for example. In others the Spaniards owed more to luck than to good judgement: Pedro Tello's capture of the *Francis* and Avellaneda's sighting of Baskerville's fleet are instances of this. Not seldom the Spaniards misconstrued or failed to act upon information received. Whether Spain's naval record, taking the campaign as a whole, bears out Corbett's view is debatable.

Whatever conclusions may be reached, however, concerning Spain's power to defend her empire at this time, it may well be that the English, or some of them, underestimated it. The ease with which Drake had taken Santo Domingo and Cartagena in 1585–6 was impressive, and the freedom and success of privateering operations in the Caribbean since seemed to confirm aggressors and victims alike in the view that the whole area was extremely vulnerable. It was perhaps a mistake to imagine that major targets would be as easy prey to a large force as minor ones were to ordinary privateers, but it was a mistake easily made by a man with Drake's experience of the Caribbean. Even after Puerto Rico one Spaniard reported Drake to be 'extremely conceited and confident' (document 30) and his contemptuous attitude towards the enemy is reflected in prisoners' statements (Chapter IV and document 33). Many of the features of the expedition suggest over-confidence: the casual inclusion of Grand Canary and Puerto Rico as extra targets, the leisurely approach to both, the delay at Río de la Hacha, the hasty thrust across the Isthmus, to mention only a few. In one respect, however, conventional judgements on this issue appear, in the light of our evidence, to be misplaced. The generals were not so careless in matters of security as has usually been thought. The Spaniards did not, before the voyage, obtain from England itself any precise knowledge of the English destination. Somehow (probably with difficulty) they discovered from prisoners taken at

Grand Canary that the first target was Puerto Rico; the men of the *Francis*, though put to torture, could reveal no more than this, and it was not until after the repulse at Puerto Rico that the authorities there gathered the English intention to make for Panama.

Apart from over-confidence, personality obviously played a major part in deciding the fate of the voyage. Maynarde's account of the quarrels between Drake and Hawkins cannot be bettered. Their temperaments, the anger of their disputes and the unfortunate consequences thereof are brilliantly drawn. Nor is Maynarde so familiar with the common pattern of interest, faction and leadership that he fails to perceive it. Troughton's intense involvement and Baskerville's discreet silence equally bear out the essential truth of Maynarde's picture. It is not clear however, why Drake and Hawkins shared the command, for Maynarde's suggestion that the queen insisted is no more than a guess, plausible enough, but evidently made in ignorance of the origins of the project in early 1593, when the two leaders were already jointly associated with it. In this connection and throughout it can hardly be forgotten that both were old men. A Spanish version of an English prisoner's statement actually refers to Drake as *el viejo* (document 22) and Hawkins was considerably older. Long denied an important rôle in action, they may have allowed eagerness to overbear their better judgement in accepting the division of the command. Age may in part explain their inability to collaborate or adapt to each other, and their set habits of thought, which in Hawkins produced a plodding caution, in Drake a careless and eventually wild opportunism. Each is said to have died of 'grief': in Hawkins' case no specific illness is mentioned, and it is credible that despair brought on or hastened his decline; in Drake's the physical cause was dysentery, and whether his evident state of desperation had any relevance to his death is a matter for speculation. It is probable that he died knowing he had failed.

Had they attempted to hold Panama (assuming that this was the original plan) the results for them would have been disastrous. In its revised form the venture might have had, if successful, some limited effect upon the war. Its actual effect was negligible. It would be mistaken to say the same of the entire maritime effort of

the English after 1588, but this expedition reveals some characteristic features of the Anglo-Spanish contest and is worth studying
for that reason alone. It was, moreover, a significant event in the
history of the West Indies, deserving comparison with the expeditions of 1585 and 1655.

I. *The Preliminaries*

According to Sir Richard Hawkins, a project for a voyage to Panama was afoot in the six months preceding March 1593[1] and it was presumably for this purpose that Drake and Sir John Hawkins were authorized in January 1592/3 to use three of the queen's and twenty private ships.[2] Nothing came of this, but in June 1594 the scheme was again discussed[3] and on 4 December the exchequer was ordered to make certain sums available for an expedition to be led by Drake and Hawkins,[4] who were jointly commissioned by letters patent on 29 January 1595/6.[5] By the beginning of March they had spent £22,000 and reports of their preparations had reached Spain.[6] For the most part these greatly exaggerated the size of Drake's force and were vague about its objectives. The best of the informants avowed 'that the English themselves say that the truth about this fleet is impossible to ascertain, because although various hints are made, the queen's intention remains secret'. Since the Indies were mentioned, and particularly Havana, an alert dated 26 February/8 March was dispatched to those parts, being received in Santo Domingo on

---

[1] 'Although it [his own South Sea venture] lay six moneths & more in suspence, partly, upon the pretended Voyage for *Nombrededios* and *Panama,* which then was fresh a foote; and partly, upon the *Carracke* at *Dartmouth,* in which I was imployed as a Commissioner: but this Businesse being ended, and the other pretence waxing colde, the fift of March [1592/3] I resolved with the iourney' (J. A. Williamson (ed.), *The Observations of Sir Richard Hawkins* (1933), p. 10).

[2] W. Murdin (ed.), *A Collection of State Papers . . . left by William Cecill, Lord Burghley* (1759), p. 800.

[3] Maynarde (document 18).

[4] Document 14. An estimate of costs was made out on 24 October 1594 (P.R.O., S.P. 12/250, no. 16 (f. 111)).

[5] P.R.O., C.66/37 Eliz., pt. 14, m. 18. Printed in R. G. Marsden (ed.), *Documents relating to the Law and Custom of the Sea,* 1 (1915), 284–7.

[6] Museo Naval, Colección Sanz Barutell, 2, ff. 662–4 (art. 6, nos. 153, 154, 155); Simancas, Estado Inglaterra, 433 (28 February 1595).

21 April/1 May[1] and in Panama on 10/20 June.[2] Portugal, however, was also mentioned and such was the anxiety in Lisbon during March and April, according to an English intelligence agent, that at least eight or nine thousand people fled the city.[3] Towards the end of April an Englishman recently returned from Spain declared that the king was worried chiefly about the returning Indies treasure fleet, recognizing the threat to Lisbon, but regarding it as secure.[4] But during May Spanish intelligence appears to have gained the clear impression that Drake's target was in general terms the West Indies.[5] A second alert was therefore dispatched on 4/14 June.[6] As the queen pointed out to Drake and Hawkins (document 4), it was their delay in setting forth that enabled the Spaniards to discover their purpose. At one stage they were expected to leave on 1/11 May and originally the departure was planned for an even earlier date (document 3). The information the Spaniards gathered after 1/11 May derived from a variety of sources and represented common knowledge rather than direct access to precise and secret plans.[7] They did not know which

[1] Lope de Vega Portocarrero to the king, 20 May 1595 (A. de I., Santo Domingo, 51).

[2] Dr Juan del Barrio to Ibarra, 24 January 1596 (A. de I., Santo Domingo, 81). The message reached Havana by 28 May/7 June: letters of Don Juan Maldonado, 7 and 8 June 1595 (A. de I., Santo Domingo, 128).

[3] 'Advertisements delivered by one lately come from Lisbon', 9 June 1595 (P.R.O., S.P. 12/253, no. 58); cp. William Holliday to Burghley, 3/13 June 1595 (B.M., Cotton MSS, Titus, B. VIII, ff. 176–7).

[4] Examination of Thomas Richardson, *Cal. Hatfield MSS,* V, 186.

[5] Reports of 10/20 May, 13/23 May, 23 May/2 June 1595 (Museo Naval, Colección Sanz Barutell, 2, ff. 666–7 (art. 6, nos. 159, 160, 161)); report from Funchal, 31 May/10 June 1595 (A. de I., Santo Domingo, 81).

[6] The message was received in Panama on 13/23 August 1595: Dr Juan del Barrio to Ibarra, 24 January 1596 (A. de I., Santo Domingo, 81).

[7] It was suspected that Netherlanders in London were passing information to Antwerp via Middelburg: Edward Palmer to the lord admiral, 23 July/2 August 1595 (P.R.O., S.P. 12/253, no. 32). Later it was alleged that full details of the fleet had been forwarded by one Nuñez Velho, a prisoner of the earl of Cumberland's: William Holliday to Cecil, 25 September/5 October 1595 (P.R.O., S.P. 12/254, no. 7) and intelligence reports of 2/12 September and 8/18 October by a Flemish merchant in Plymouth were said to give the same kind of information

particular West Indian places Drake intended to raid, because different reports mentioned different objectives. Havana, for example, was mentioned more often than Panama. During the summer and autumn, however, the Spanish authorities seem to have realized with increasing clarity that Panama was the likeliest target.

This conclusion was based, at least in part, on information obtained in Trinidad by Antonio de Berrío, the explorer of the Orinoco, from Sir Walter Raleigh, and in La Margarita by Pedro de Salazar, governor of that island, from some of Raleigh's men held prisoner by him. Salazar's relation,[1] dated June 1595, represented his prisoners as saying that 'Francis Drake was in London and Plymouth preparing an armada of forty big ships, and would be coming to this area in August to winter in the Indies with ten thousand men and many munitions of war. His plan was to take Puerto Rico, Santo Domingo and Cartagena, but his chief intention was to go direct to Panama, for they saw many flat-bottomed boats being made, which he will take with him in order to go up the river; and this they certify beyond any doubt.'

Berrío, in a careful report to the king[2] of his dealings with Raleigh, wrote, on 11 July: 'From this English general I had account of the plan of Francis Drake and John Hawkins, who are both coming, in joint and equal command, bringing twenty large galleons of the queen of England and forty others of smaller size, not counting a further number of privateers consorted with them. In these ships they carry many flat boats in addition to those normally required for service. They have orders to go, without

(A. de I., Contratación, 5169, lib. IX, f. 439). Even at these late dates, however, the Fleming's intelligence of English intentions consisted of 'what he could gather of their designs'.

[1] 'Relacion de lo sucedido en la ysla de Trinidad' by Pedro de Salazar, governor of La Margarita (A. de I., Santo Domingo, 180).

[2] Antonio de Berrío to the king, 11 July 1595 (A. de I., Santo Domingo, 179 (formerly 180)). I am much indebted to Professor P. Lefranc for bringing this document to my notice and sending me a microfilm of it. It is printed in Pablo Ojer, *Don Antonio de Berrío, Gobernador del Dorado* (Burgos, 1960), p. 203. Berrío wrote from La Margarita, after being released by Raleigh, who had captured him in Trinidad. He would therefore presumably have compared notes with Salazar.

touching at any inhabited part of the Indies, direct to the River Chagre, where they are to launch the boats with 2,000 soldiers and to make for Panama as secretly as possible. All the rest of the ships are to put in to the city of Nombre de Dios, the plan being to cause warning to be sent of their presence there, reinforcements to be dispatched thither, and the defence of the river to be neglected. They intend, if they take Panama, to fortify it in order to gain control of the South Sea and, this done, to sack Cartagena and demolish it and to winter in the Indies, destroying all the maritime places they can. This is the account related to me by General Guatarral, who is captain of the queen of England's guard.'

The differences between the two reports are not significant. They agree in overestimating Drake's strength, in identifying his first and main target as Panama, in indicating the Chagre as his approach route, and in emphasizing his intention to winter in the Indies and to attack further Caribbean ports, including Cartagena. It is clear that Raleigh and his companions disclosed the heart of the matter to the Spaniards.[1] It follows, although accuracy in respect of quantities is not to be expected in the context, that the other agreed points carry a considerable weight of credibility. The conclusion that the original intention was not merely to raid Panama but to hold it for some time receives some support from Monson's statement that the generals' object was to take that city 'and, if they saw reason for it, to inhabit and keep it',[2] as well as from Maynarde's phrase 'if for two or three yeeres a blowe were given him there' (document 18), which perhaps implied an occupying force maintained by annual expeditions. Baskerville's letter

[1] It is likely that Raleigh spoke freely to Berrío because he intended to take him to England and that it was only in order to redeem his own men (including John Gilbert and Henry Thynne) that he was obliged to release him. I am indebted to Professor Lefranc for this suggestion.

[2] Oppenheim, *Monson's Tracts*, 1 (1902), 313. Although Monson apparently had nothing to do with this expedition, it was early in 1596 (or possibly a little earlier still) that he became a close and trusted adherent of Essex, being appointed the latter's flag-captain in the Cadiz voyage. He was thus well placed to learn about the true purposes of Drake and Hawkins and it is unlikely that he was mistaken on this point, even though his account of the course of the voyage is inaccurate.

to Essex (document 8), objecting to a time limit of six months with the plea that 'to undertake to performe matters of so greatt Importe In so shorte a tyme is Impossible' and referring to 'the first platte, which I fear is or wilbe wholy alterid', also suggests that something more than a raid was planned.[1] The strength of the expedition and the allocation of six of the queen's best warships (a far greater contribution than the two she supplied in 1585) point to the same conclusion, but perhaps the most impressive indication of a strategic purpose is the active interest of the earl of Essex in the project. Essex was now the chief exponent of offensive strategy and it seems most likely that he played the decisive part in securing the adoption of the project. It is just possible that at one stage he contemplated participating personally.[2] The commander and the second-in-command of the land-force, Sir Thomas Baskerville and Sir Nicholas Clifford, were fully committed Essex men and owed their involvement in the venture (which they regarded with mixed feelings) to him (documents 8 and 13). Several of the other land captains were Essex men.[3] In letters to

[1] A Spanish intelligence report of 23 May/2 June 1595 had already suggested that the English intended to winter in the Indies (Museo Naval, Colección Sanz Barutell, 2, ff. 666–7 (art. 6, no. 161)). The *relaciones* of Sotomayor and Ruiz Delduayen (documents 33 and 32) refer, in spite of prisoners' statements to the contrary, to an intention to occupy, though almost certainly any such intention had long since been abandoned.

[2] On 1 January 1594/5 Sir Henry Davers wrote to Essex that he was secretly informed that the earl intended a journey in the spring. He expressed his loyalty and his desire 'to give a blow wherein you may equalize your fortune to your worth' (*Cal. Hatfield MSS*, v, 77–8). In a letter attributed to February 1594/5 Essex wrote to Cecil: 'Sir, I told you too day whither I was goinge and how the queen had aunswered me. I must acquaint you further, thatt the queen offring to talke with me this morning about sea causes, I told her my lord Admirall was in the house and Sir Francis Drake and Sir John Hawkins were in the towne' (Hatfield MSS, 25, no. 29). In May 1595 Anthony Standen wrote to Anthony Bacon, concerning Essex: 'I learn that he hath given out speeches at Walsingham that he will to the Indies. It is too much compassion to see how they set him on the tenter-hooks' (Thomas Birch, *Memoirs of the Reign of Queen Elizabeth* (1754), I, 245). In the absence of further evidence it is not established that Essex at any time seriously intended to join the expedition.

[3] See pp. 45–8 and, for further indications of Essex's interest in the voyage, pp. 27–9, 34, 253–4.

him Drake, Hawkins and Baskerville wrote freely of their discontents and clearly looked to him as their chief spokesman at court (documents 7 and 8).

It is not clear why the preparations took so long. Both the queen and the lord admiral blamed the generals (documents 3 and 4). The threat or counter-threat of Spanish naval action did not appear until June and therefore cannot explain the previous delay. Baskerville's commission was not issued until 22 May[1] and only after that date were the land forces assembled. The official accounts (document 14) show that many important items were not nearly ready at the end of May. Mobilization then apparently accelerated, but at the same time the news from Spain was arousing misgivings in London,[2] and Sir Thomas Gorges' first visit to Plymouth in mid-July was clearly concerned with more than a view of the fleet (documents 1, 2, 13). The Spanish raid on Cornwall followed, but whether it seriously affected the government's attitude to the Panama project is to be doubted.[3] The episode is not mentioned in the course of the argument which developed towards the end of July and lasted until about 18/28 August (documents 2–12).

Although certain untraced items are missing, this discussion of the strategic issues is full enough to make extensive comment unnecessary here. Sir Thomas Lake pithily sums it up (document 12). It is worth noting, however, that Cecil's representation of the venture as a move to divert Spain's offensive finds no explicit support elsewhere and should be read strictly in its context (document 39). The effects of the exchanges appear to have been the imposition of a time-limit upon the expedition and the sacrifice

---

[1] *Cal. S.P.D., 1595–7,* p. 43. The statement that 'the conditions of the venture as between the Queen and the Admirals were not settled until June' (Oppenheim, *Monson's Tracts,* I (1902), 322) is incorrect, being based on a misdated document.

[2] William Holliday to Burghley, 3/13 June 1595 (B.M., Cotton MSS, Titus, B. VIII, ff. 176–7); document 4.

[3] Four galleys from Blavet in Brittany landed a small force at Mousehole on 23 July/2 August. Mousehole, Newlyn, Penzance and some nearby villages were burnt and the Spaniards departed on 25 July/4 August (*Cal. S.P.D., 1595–7,* pp. 77–9). Baskerville sent some troops from Plymouth, but they failed to contact the enemy (*Cal. Hatfield MSS,* v, 290, Sir Nicholas Clifford to Essex, 26 July 1595). The alarm in London appears to have been shortlived.

of any important strategic purpose, whether offensive or defensive.[1] It is likely that the disagreements were finally resolved only by the news from Puerto Rico (document 10), which no doubt considerably inflated that 'hope of Treasure, which is our greatest desire and want' (document 12).

The argument also involved a further loss of precious time. The fleet was evidently ready to sail in the early days of August,[2] but did not leave until 28 August/7 September. The Puerto Rico news probably reached Spain in July and on 13/23 August Don Pedro Tello de Guzmán was formally instructed to lead five frigates of war to Puerto Rico to collect the treasure.[3] On 11/21 September Spanish fishing vessels returning from Newfoundland sighted Drake's fleet off Cape Finisterre and the report of this event by the Casa de la Contratación contained the additional news that Pedro Tello had left the Guadalquivir on 15/25 September. The comment of the Contratación officers was that even if the English were making for Puerto Rico, Pedro Tello would arrive first.[4] In fact the English anchored off Grand Canary on 26 September/6 October, whereas Pedro Tello did not reach Alegranza (Canary

---

[1] At some stage, probably in the early summer, Drake and Hawkins apparently promised to co-operate with Captain Robert Crosse in an attempt to waylay the East India carracks off the coast of Portugal. Crosse, in command of the queen's ships *Swiftsure* and *Crane* and of a flyboat, returned empty-handed and complained to Cecil on 1/11 October of the generals' failure to keep 'their determined appointment' (*Cal. Hatfield MSS*, v, 395). Henry Roberts' suggestion that Crosse was to take part in the main expedition was probably mistaken (H.R., *The Trumpet of Fame* (1595)).

[2] Drake and Hawkins wrote to Burghley on 21/31 July that they expected to be ready to sail by the end of the month (P.R.O., S.P. 12/253, no. 24). On 29 July/8 August Drake wrote to Burghley asking for instructions and assuring him that 'our desyre is to make all haste awaie' (P.R.O., S.P. 12/253, no. 42). Sir Thomas Gorges wrote to Cecil on 13/23 August concerning the 'companie of gallant gentlemen' at Plymouth: 'I assure you their longe staie doth breede discontent amongst them' (Hatfield MSS, 34, no. 22).

[3] A. de I., Indiferente General, 2496, lib. VII, f. 132.

[4] A. de I., Contratación, 5169, lib. IX, f. 413. On 17/27 September the council of the Indies informed the king of news received from Guipúzcoa that Drake had left England for the Indies on 29 August/8 September with 26 ships (B.M., Additional MSS, 36316, f. 166).

Is.) until 28 September/8 October (document 26). Drake lost his two days' lead by pausing to attempt Las Palmas.

1. *Sir Thomas Gorges to Cecil, 16 July 1595*[1]

Sir, havinge such oportunytie, as by this bearer, I thought yt not amysse to advertise you, of my being at Plymouthe, whether I came, on Satterday the xij[th] of this monthe. Since my beinge here, I have viewed most of the Shipps, which I find to be in very good sorte. Sir John Hawkins, I dowbt not but you knowe to be a man exellent in these things, and at this time one, that hath a speciall Care to see all things don in good order him selfe. Sir frauncis Drake since my being here, hath bin Lyttle in the Towne, for that he is so buysied about provicion in the Country, which with all dilligence, is donne, for the spedier dispatche of their viage. Towching my Instruccions, I Cannot yet certify you anie thinge, because Sir Tho. Baskerfield is not come to Plymouth, but daily expected. My comminge did greatly amase them at first, for feare I had bin sent to have staid them, but when they knewe the Contrary, none so ioyfull as they, that yt would please her Highnes to send one downe to viewe their bravery, which I do thinke wilbe such, as I have not yet seene. I dowbt not, but my comminge wilbe to great effect, concerninge the buysines her Majesty sendeth me about. It wilbe fourteene daies at the Least, or they shalbe reddy to departe, by reason of some pynnaces they have alonge with them, which Cannot be furnished sooner. So remembringe my dewty unto yow, I humbly take my Leave, and Comytt you to the almighty. Plymouth this xvj[th] of July 1595

     your honours to Comaund
     Thomas Gorges

[1] P.R.O., S.P. 12/253, no. 19. Endorsed: 'To the right honorable Sir Robert Cicill knight one of her Majesties most honorable Privie Councell. 16 July 1595. Sir Thomas Gorges to my master. From Plymmoth.' Gorges (1536–1610) was a groom of the privy chamber and keeper of the robes, a trusted and influential courtier and man of affairs. He had strong associations with Devon. Though his nephew Arthur was a literary friend of Raleigh's, and another nephew, Ferdinando, became a follower of Essex, Sir Thomas does not seem to have adhered to any particular faction.

2. The queen to the generals by Sir Thomas Gorges, 1 August 1595[1]

Wee have returned you this gentleman with asmuch expedition as yᵉ consideracion of such an affaire would permytt us, with some Instructions in writing signed by our Counsell agreable to our directions which our pleasure is should be followed by you for yᵉ presente Action, requiring yow both in theise and all other thinges which he shall imparte unto yow to give him full and ample credyt. By which this our sending one so nere unto us thus soddenly after his former painfull Jorny (to whom you are not a Litle beholding for his Report of yᵉ exceeding care and paines of yow and our servant Baskervyle for all thinges belonging to our service) wee trust yow can very well conceave that wee are full of care for you as persons to whom we wishe all happie and prosperous successe not doupting but yow will thincke that if we did not much Rely uppon your faiths valour and Judgment wee would not commyt to you so great a charge and especially in such a tyme considering yᵉ Nature of this Action where matter of mony is one of our Least adventures in comparison of yᵉ rest. And therfore be thus perswaded that our extraordinary expirience of your former meryttes is the only and chiefest cause of this so extraordinary an Affiance in those Courses to which yow have conducted [us][2]

3. The lord admiral to Cecil, 8 August 1595[3]

Sir I received your letter of the 7. this day being the 8 at 2. of the cloke in the afternoone at my house of blechyngly with the inclosed from the Two generals. And for my openyon I dow not see they cane

---

[1] Hatfield MSS, 33, no. 68. Endorsed: 'Primo August. Copy of her majesties lettre to the generalls by Sir Thomas Gorges'.

[2] The remaining few lines are formal.

[3] Hatfield MSS, 33, no. 101. Endorsed: 'To My especyall good frend Sir Robert Cecyll. 8 August 1595. Lord Admiral to my master.'

alter from ther course of ther voyage but that the wholl charge must be her *Majesties* . . . I did not thynke ther was any menynge that they should with ther flet ronne into St gorges chanell but alongst the cost to cape cleer, wyche wold not have ben out of ther way muche whatsoever they wryte. And to you in pryvat they neded not to take suche exceptions for going so lytell out of ther way, when they have retarded ther going so long as they have done promising they wold have departed the fyrst of May ye sonner at the fyrst. . . .[1]

    C. Howard

4. *The queen to Drake, Hawkins, Gorges and Baskerville, 11 August 1595*[2]

Trustie & wellbeloved we greet you well. By your lettres of the first of this moneth we have perceaved the aunswere that you have

---

[1] The rest of the letter is brief and unrelated to this context.

[2] P.R.O., S.P. 12/253, no. 76. Endorsed: '1595 11 August. Copie of hir *Majesties* lettre to *Sir Francis* Drake, *Sir John* Hawkins, *Sir Thomas* Gorges, *Sir Thomas* Baskevyle at Plymmouth.' An earlier draft of this, dated 9 August and endorsed as 'altered by *Robert* Cecill' (P.R.O., S.P. 12/253, no. 70) is identical in wording down to 'attempted about June or July'. From that point it reads as follows (in modernized spelling): 'And therefore except we might think it either certain or probable that you might return hither with your navy before the end of May, whereof even now at your departure you did assure us, so as your shipping might be refreshed and put in good order after your coming home, which you know would require one month's space, we would not assent to your going forward in this voyage, though we presume the same voyage might be never so profitable as hath been hoped; but we are moved as is fit in so great a matter to prefer surety before any profit. And therefore we have thus determined that if you should now depart and finding no cause of your stay upon the coast of Spain to withstand their force, and so depart on your voyage, if you can by good reason assure us to return into our realm by the end of April, or by the furthest by the end of May, we then do yield unto you our assent for your proceeding in the voyage, wherein we wish you as good speed as yourselves can desire, not doubting but you will, without respect of the prince's profit intended by this your voyage, either stay upon the coast of Spain to impeach the issue of the Spanish army at this

made to the second *lettres* sent to you from our Councell in our name after the arrivall there of *Sir* Thomas Gorges, whereby you pretend there is no possibillity for you to lynger uppon the Coast of Ireland as you were advised by the sayd second *lettres* for the withstanding of the Spaniardes passing into Ireland. But yet you writte that if in your Course toward the Coast of Spaine, or going alongest the Coast you shall perceave anie strength of shippes bending toward England or Ireland, you doe faithfully assure us to give over all and to follow them referring your selfes for the charge thereof to our dealing with you. Uppon this your aunsweare made we have entered into some deepe consideration of the cause, which we doe impart to you privately not to be communicated to anie others. And uppon such consideration we have resolved what we shall require of you not doubting but you will have regard thereto as in your dewtyes you ought to doe for the State of our Crowne and our Realme. First we have considered uppon the advertysementes we have ought of Spaine continewally renewed by reportes of persons comming from thence that there is preparation made and continewally in making for three Fleetes or Navyes to come to the Sea. The one in the Sowth of Spaine abowt Cales, the other in Lisbone, the third at Farolle the Groigne and other North partes

present, or if there should be no such present occasion, then to proceed and order your whole journey in that sort, without spending your time upon any unnecessary or small attempts, as you might return before the time afore limited. And if by the reason of your long stay contrary to your first determination you should not be able to return by the time afore limited and thereby this your journey should be stayed, whereof we would be very sorry, then we would have you consider like men of knowledge and experience what attempt you could presently make with this force that you have, or with some part thereof, to any part of Spain, especially to the places whence you shall understand their shipping and magazine of victuals is, to destroy either their victuals or their ships, whereby the intention of their next year's attempt might be frustrate, or at the least diminished. And of all this we require you to have due consideration and to advertise us of your resolution and of the time of your departure as you shall determine. And to further your voyage we are content to be at chance with a number of ships to be to those west parts of our realm towards Ireland under the conduct of Sir Henry Palmer to withstand the attempt to be taken in hand with any mean number of ships of Spain against Ireland, or else by pursuit to distress them before their landing.'

of Biscaye. And by some reportes it should seame that with the Fleet from the North of Spaine there should be intended a voyage presently into Ireland and namely to land abowt Tredaghe.[1] But whether the same is presently to be taken in hand now before wynter we cannot certainly understand although we greately doubt thereof. Besides this it is certaine that these preparations made in Spaine are so great as the like were not in the yeare 1588 and it is not to be doubted but that the intention is in the next Summer with the same great armies to invade our Realmes of England and Ireland also. Whereuppon we found it very daungerous to yeald to your departure at this present, specially befor the present attempt for Ireland might be discouvered. But moste of all daungerous if you should not the next Summer in convenient tyme be returned to healpe to doe some service according to the strength of your shippes against the spanish Armye that should attempt the invasion of this Realme, which is to be thought wold be attempted about June or July if not sooner. But forasmuch as we are sufficiently informed both by men of good experience here as also by that assurance which your selfes uppon your departure gave us that you shall not need for anie action of importance to tary out longer then six monthes at the furthest, unlesse you should spend tyme in other unnecessary or vayne attemptes wherein we little doubt of your discretion seing you can well consider that as our affares doe stande, tyme to us is a thing moste precious: we have thought good to lett you knowe that both in regard that your own delayes hath made your iorney and purposes now so notorious (yea in particular to the Spaniard) as they have sufficient warning to provide for your discent, And seing that by one of his Fleetes already being saffe come home his meanes are so increased as if the other be not some way intercepted or diminished he shalbe in better case then ever he was, and we by your absence worse furnished then ever: we must not entertaigne nor so ground all our hopes uppon this single iorney of youres, but that we must enioyne you so to shape your Corse as though the other attemptes be not neglected (which may happely fayle for nothing can be made so sure) yet in the beginning of this your iorney some such Coorse may be taken as may be both security for

[1] Trawenagh Bay, Co. Donegal.

us and not unlikely to prove proffitable if it please God to blesse your entreprise. In which consideration we hold it necessary that First according to your last offer you shape your Corse alongest the Coast of Spaine and there informe your selfes by all possible meanes what is like to be attempted this way, for the resisting whereof we doubt not but you will use all courage, deligence, and iudgement, as that which you doe knowe concerneth chiefly our State and kingdome. Which being don we wold have you then sett some such Coorse as whereby you may be likelyest to intercept his fleet now dayly expected, wherein yf you shalbe so happie to doe some honorable service, as your selfes can well consider that it must needes be proffitable: So shall ye be assured that we shall have cause to accompt it so notable a service, as though all the rest should not succeed; yet for that Action we should thinke both your paines and charge sufficiently requited. These thinges being therefore duely considered with your selfes, both what preiudice it wold be to us to be assailed in your absence, and what losse of honor, hope and proffitte it wilbe if by insisting onely uppon one ground (which may have contrary successe) all the endes both of security and commodity shalbe neglected: We have thought fitt to require your aunsweare to all these pointes with all expedition whereuppon you shall receave such further direction as shalbe thought fitt for us to give, whose interest we thinke you doe conceave to be so great in this Action as none can be more unwilling to disturbe it, nor more carefull to yeald it all furtherance which reason and sound consideration can permitt. Besides we must not forbeare to require you for that this monthe is the likelyest tyme of anie accesse into Ireland, that yf you heare by anie intelligence of anie shippes drawing to that Coast you doe forthwith neglect no tyme of making out of after them to destroy them without tarrying for further direction which may spend tyme to our preiudice seing you doe know that ether by you or by nothing we must offend them. And that you may see that we spare no Cost for the better advancement of this iorney we have appointed our servant Sir Henry Palmer to come to ye Coast to secure it in your absence. And because you may conceave why we accompt y^t your voyage might be finished in five or six monthes, we doe send herewith a note in writing[1] delivered to us by such as have good experience in the voyages therein mentioned So as you may well spare one month or more to attempt the interrupting of the Fleet of the Havana which is certainely looked for to become to the Islandes in September. Given under our Signett at our Manor of Grenwich the xj[th] day of August 1595 in the xxxvij[th] yeare of our Raigne.

5. Drake and Hawkins to Cecil, 13 August 1595[2]

Yt may please your honour we lattely reseavyd a letter from her majestie which we have herewith answeryd[3] & do humbly pray your honour yt may be delyveryd. We have wrytten to my lord your father & my lord admyrall to hellp away her majesties resolucion so we humbly pray your honour hellp allso; and yf her majestie shall determyne any longer to stay us or to allter the Journey first intendyd, that then yt may please her highnes to take the charge hoolely in to her owne hondes & that some order be gyven that mony may be had here to dyscharge the companyes nedefull which groweth very great dayly & that other charges thatt dayly arysethe may be defrayed or ells we are not able any longer to sustayne ytt, & so in all dewty Humbly take our leve from plymothe the xiij[th] of august 1595.

your Honours Humbly to commaund
Fra. Drake.   John Hawkyns

---

[1] Enclosed is a brief statement of estimated sailing times: England to the Canaries, 24 days, so as they proceed after mid-August, for then the winds be most nearly northerly. Canaries to Dominica, 26 days. Cartagena to Nombre de Dios, 5 days. Nombre de Dios to Cartagena and thence to Cape San Antonio, 12 days. Cape San Antonio to England, 70 days. The actual times on this voyage were, respectively, 28 days, 30 days, 5 days, 24 days and between 60 and 70 days. In fact the estimated times were rather optimistic, making no allowance for bad weather. The Dominica–Cartagena leg is omitted and no time is allowed for essential watering and victualling stops or for the land operations.

[2] P.R.O., S.P. 12/253, no. 79. Endorsed: 'To the Ryght honorable Sir Robert Cycyle knyght one of her majesties most honorable prevye cownsell gyve this at the court, in Hast Hast Hast post hast for her majesties specyall service [details of the stages] Receaved the xv[th] of the same at Grenewich.'

[3] See document 6.

we have sene the letter her majestie sent to the generalls & us & were acquayntyd with ther answere.

Thomas Gorges.   Tho. Baskervile.

6. Drake and Hawkins to the queen, 13 August 1595[1]

Our most gracyous and most Soveraygne prynce, we have consyderyd uppon the Latte letters of the xj[th] of august Reseavyd from your heighnes, we have no doupt but your majestie ys most assuredly confyrmyd in a good opynyon of our loyalltie, our fydellytye, and areddynes to spend our lyves and abbylytye to do your heighnes all dewtye and service to the uttermost of our powers, and ever with gods favour shalbe soo, and our indevour allwayes imployed for the good of our contry.

To attend any tyme upon the cost of spayne or the coste of Ireland, ys very perylous for us havyng so great a fleete and so great a company of men, which requyre a very spedy landynge out of the shippes.

To follow the flette which are to come from the havanna, many of our provycions and many of our companyes are superflewus for that purpose, besyede the xx[tye] pynaces that we carry do very myche incomber our shipes & are utterly unfytt for that service.

To promyse any certayntye of our retorne we can nott, but we here take heaven and erthe to wyttnes, that our onely desyre ys to make a spedye retorne withowt any delaye even as we furst dyd sett downe, withowtt thattemptynge of any other enterpryse to impeche yt, for god blessynge us, in whose handes and power the retorne ys to be made spedellye or by his dyspleasure yt ys to be prolonged.

we do here stay your majesties good pleasure, unable to contynew the importyble charge, and in all humble and most dewtyfull manner beseche your heighnes to resollve, that we may depart and brynge to a happye end our first attempt; or ells that your heighnes wyll resolve uppon any entrepryse ells that shalbe sett downe, and

[1] P.R.O., S.P. 12/253, no. 79 (1), enclosed with the above letter to Cecil (document 5). Endorsed: 'To the Quenes moste exellent and sacred majestie gyve this. 13 August 1595. Sir Francis Drake Sir John Hawkins to ye Queenes Majesty.'

we wyll in the best and spedyest sort we may take outte our pynaces, Lessen our companyes and fytt and make free our shippes accordyng to the porpose and service that shalbe sett downe, so as from the begynnynge to thendynge the charge be hoolelye your majesties, all which to a prynce of great abyllytye and power as your majestie ys wylbe a small losse, but to us withowt your most gracious and pryncely favour we are utterly spoyled and undone.

we are lothe to be tedyous knowynge your heighnes dothe myslyke yt, & therfore do referre the consyderacion of this weightye matter to your pryncely Judgment which with our humble prayers to god we wyshe may so direct your royall hart as all may be detremyned to his glory, your majesties Compfort and the benyfytt of your most Royall Kyngdome, & so with all humblenes and dewtye we take our leve from plymouthe the xiij[th] of awgust 1595
your majesties most humble and dewtyfull servauntes
fra: Drake   John Hawkyns

7. *Drake and Hawkins to Essex, 13 August 1595*[1]

Right honerable our especiall good Lordship this mornyng we receaved a Lettre from her majestie in which Lettre we were requyred to geve aunswer presently unto dyvers particuller Servysyes whiche her highnes hathe now comanded us, uppon som intellegence lattly com out of spayne, the whiche Lettre we aunswered, that yf it please her majestie to comand us to any other Servysyes then first was agreed uppon, that it would please her highnes at our most humble suitt, to take uppon her the hooll charge, aswell of the tonnage of the merchant shippes, as of vytualls, and wages, both for land servitors, and maryners.

The charge hathe bene and dothe contynewe very great, and it hathe bene the more, for the kepyng the hooll companyes together, were it knowen to the better, but that ther were any other purpose

---

[1] Hatfield MSS, 34, no. 19. Endorsed: 'To the right Honorable our Synguller good Lord therell of essexe. Sir francis Drak & Sir John Hawkins at Plymmouth. 13 August 1595.'

then the first, they would most a way, althoughe it hath ben very chargeable unto them, which will much dyscontent them.

And for our owne particullers, we humbly besech your good Lordship that yf her majestie doe alter our first agreement, that you stand strongly for us that the hooll charge may be borne by the queene, else Look we for nothing, but the Lyke dyscontentment or worse then that of the portyngall viage. Thus in haste, we most humbly take our Leaves from plymoth this 13th of august 1595.

your good Lordship humbly to be comanded
Fra: Drake   John Hawkyns

8. *Baskerville to Essex, 13 August 1595*[1]

Most Honorable

I would nott have fayled to have wryghten more often to your Lordship If I had the means to have convayed them saflye now I wryght only bycause Itt pleasid yow to taxe me in your laste Letter with nexligence, which thoughe I exscuse nott, yett I humbly desir your Lordship to truste thatt my nott wryghting growes nott by any want of desir to do you servis, for I hope the testymony I have Alredy geven dothe suficiently wittnis howe much I ame yours, and with what Lytell respecte I have esteamid all favors from other menn, keping my self only clear to you, withoutt Ingaging In the Least poynt to any other, with the self same affection I ever bore to your servis, I bear now and ever will withowtt alteracion. Yett cann I nott by any means dryve outt of me the opynyon I have conceavid, thatt your Lordship only hathe bin the ocasion of my going this Jorney of so greatt exspence by which I protest I Am alredy halfe ruinid, and shalbe wholy If the Jorney goe nott forward acording to the first platte, which I fear is or wilbe wholy alterid. Whatt hopes then remayne to bear owtt this myghty Charg I have bin att, Any

---

[1] B.M., Harleian MSS, 4762, f. 12 – a draft, without heading, date or endorsement. The final version sent to Essex is in Hatfield MSS, 34, no. 20; this is endorsed: 'To the right Honorable his very good lord, the Earle of Essex att Courte. Sir Thomas Baskarvil. At Plimmouth 13 August 1595.' The only significant variation from the draft is given in the next note.

thing from her majestie I utterly dispayr of, the exsample of her last refusall is so frech in my memory, and this I know the Least of my enymies Cann Crosse me more then all my grettest frindes Cann do me good. I beseech your Lordship therfor thatt since you are he thatt hath bin the Cause of my going, thatt Itt will pleas you now to second the Jorney In such sorte thatt we maye goe forward in our first Course withoutt Lymyting us so strycke a tyme, wherby we may nott only undo our selfes in our purcis butt allso In our reputacions for who is so unadvisid thatt will undertake to perform such a vyag[1] In six months. If we do nothing with such a fleett and such nombers of gallant menn as we have we may justlye be taxed, and I protest I had rather be buried alyve then any such disgrace shuld happen, butt to undertake to performe matters of so greatt Importe In so shorte a tyme is Impossible for Lengthe of tyme must only make our Jorney fortunatt unto us. I wishe therfor thatt eyther I wer wholy quitt off Itt ore else thatt Itt would pleas her majestie we myght go forward as Itt was first determynyd, or that we myght be apoyntid, being all in her majesties pay, to atend upon the Coste of Spayne the goinge out of the Navye ther providid, butt[2]

[1] From this point the final version reads: 'wherein ther is so greatt expectacions of so great thinges to be donn, In so shorte a tym. for my parte I rather desire to be buried alive then to lyve with disgrace, and thoughe I have the Least parte In this Enterpris, yett know I som parte of the burthen will Lyght upon me. the whole fortune of our Jorney dependes upon the Lengthe of tym, for by tym all thinges are donn and withoutt it nothing can be donn. I wishe therfor thatt I wer well quitt of Itt or else thatt the first determynacion myght stande. I beseche your Lordship to geve me a Lytell Leave to argue the matter more at Large, your Lordship beste knows such forcis as thess cannot be held Longe together withoutt a pryncis pay, or hopes of greatt spoyle, bothe them being taken away of nessesity confusion must grow, our Longe stay hear hathe allredy weryed the most parte, and no dought, If they had butt the Least Inkeling, thatt the course of the Jorney shuld be turnid some other way, they would albe gonn. I besech your Lordship therfor to have a care of us your pore frends and to favore us so farr thatt If her majestie will Alter the first course, thatt we may have from her som means to bear outt the greatnis of my Charg, for I protest ther is in me no Lenger abylyty to Indure Itt and so geving your Lordship Humble thankes for the gracis yow have donn me I Humbly take my Leave plymouthe this 13 of August
        your Lordships servant redy to be comandid
        Tho Baskerville'
[2] The draft ends abruptly here.

9. Burghley's memorandum of a letter from the queen to Drake and Hawkins, 16 August 1595[1]

Trustie & welbeloved. We have received your letters of the xiij[th] wherewith wee are noe waies satisfied for the principall matters whereof wee gave you direction by ours neither for your preventinge to goe uppon the Coast of Spaine to meete with the Spanishe forces that might issue thence neither yet by your refusall to spend a moneth to the meetinge with the Indian Fleete; but thowgh we are content to passe over your awnsweares to those two pointes, yet we cann noe waies allowe your uncertaine and frivolous awnsweare to our motion to have knowledge in what time we might hope of your returne, in that yowe have used wordes altogether uncertaine, withowt awnswearinge ether our opinion accordyng to your owne former promize that the voiadge might be performed in six or seven monethes : and for proof of the probabillitie thereof in our opinion wee sent yowe an informacion given us by men of creditt within what time the voiadge might be reasonablye made with Gods favour, and reasonable windes, whereof you have made noe mention, but passe yt over with all uncertainetye whearein wee have cawse to dowbt whether yowe have taken to hart or had regarde to our former reasons expreslye conteined in our lettres which as duetifull subiectes yowe owght to have done, havinge neither limited any time certen by your owne iudgement nor awnswearinge the times expressed by us : And thowgh yowe maie saie that noe person cann make assurance of such a matter withowt Gods sufferaunce to have winde meete therefore yet yowe might have said that with Gods favour havinge noe lett by winde, yowe had [?][2] wherein to have finished the Journeie within the space of

---

[1] Hatfield MSS, 35, no. 31. Endorsed: '16 August 1595. *Memorandum* of hir *Majesties lettres* to *Sir Francis* Drake. *Sir* John Hawkins.' A draft of this letter, similar in substance but different in wording, in Burghley's hand, was made on the same day but not sent (P.R.O., S.P. 12/253, no. 87. Endorsed: '16 August 1595. A letter devised for *Sir Francis* Drak & *Sir* John Hawkyns, but not sent.').
[2] Word illegible.

six or seven monethes as at the first yowe did promize, or enlarginge your selves with two monethes more, your voiadge might be ended by the ende of Aprill, or at the farthest by middest maie which is nyne monethes.

But consideringe yowe have not hearein awnsweared us, as yowe owght to have done, wee cannot assent to your departure without yowe shall presentlie herein satisfie us in shewinge your intention fullie in what time yowe shall minde to finishe the voiadge, havinge with Gods favour a reasonable winde to further yowe: And so wee charge yowe uppon your Allegiaunce to make us a direct awnsweare, either that yowe minde and purpose by all your meanes possible to finishe your voiadge in the time by us aforementioned, which if yowe shall uppon your allegiaunce assure us that yowe minde so certainely to doe, then wee are content that with the next good winde yowe maie depart, or else make yowe accompt that the journeie shall staie, for the breakinge wheareof the disgrace shall be yours, and to deminishe the losse of the charges susteyned, yowe shall consider howe the chargeable provisions maie be despersed with lest los and the companies discharged so as the losse betwixt us and yowe maie be made as little as can be devised and therein wee charge yowe to so advertise us with speede of your opinion for order to be gyven accordyng.

10. Drake and Hawkins to the queen, 16 August 1595[1]

May yt please your most excellent majestie to be advertysed, that very Lattely a barke of brystow toke a spanyshe fryggatt that came from an Ilond in the west Indyes called porto Rico, & had in her sondry passangers, that came owt of the vyceadmyral a shipp of

[1] Hatfield MSS, 35, no. 30. Endorsed: 'To our most dred Soveraygne the Quenes most excellent majestie. in all possyble Hast Hast post Hast. 16 August 1595. To her majestie From Sir Francis Drake and Sir John hawkins. A Spanishe Frigatt taken by a Bark of Brystoll. Received ye xviij th of ye same at Grenewich.' This disposes of Monson's assertion that the queen notified the generals of the presence of the treasure at Puerto Rico and at the same time ordered the change of plan.

iij^c and L^{ti} ton w*h*ich was of the Latte flett that came into spayne and beynge in dystresse by losse of her maste was forsydd to harborowgh in the port or haven of this Iland of portorico, she had then in her tow myllyons and a hallf of tresure, she lyethe ther unrygged and her ordenance put a shore. yt ys abowt tow monthes past that the maryners that dothe dyscover this came from thence and Left ther ship in that port; w*h*ich cannot come from thence w*ith*owt order from the kynge. we have sent to brystow for the masters mate of the shipe, and a portyngall that hathe dyscoveryd this matter, & do mynd w*ith* gods favour to take that place w*ith* all spede, yt lyethe in our way & wyll no way impeache us.

we do wrytt to none other in this matter, but reserve ytt to yo*u*r heighnes to imp*art* yt to souche of yo*u*r maj*es*ties counsell as shall seme best to your heighnes.

here hathe byne very fowle & tempestyows wether yett all yo*u*r maj*es*ties shipes and the rest are all in good safftye thank*es* be to god & so in most humble and most dewtyfull maner take our leve from plymothe the xvjth day of august 1595.

Your maj*es*ties most Humble and most dewtyfull servaunt*es*

fra: Drake   John Hawkyns

we send yo*u*r maj*es*tie the letter that came from the allderman of brystow & we have confferyd w*ith* the master that toke the frigatt.

11. *Drake and Hawkins to Burghley, 18 August 1595*[1]

Our dewty in most Humble maner rememberyd. Yt may please yo*u*r Lor*d*ship, we have answeryd her maj*es*ties Letter, we hope, to her heighnes contentment,[2] whome we wold nott wetyngly or wyllyngly desplease. [They thank Burhgley for his favour; report

---

[1] B.M., Harleian MSS, 6997, f. 84. They wrote a similar letter to Cecil the same day (*Cal. Hatfield MSS*, v, 332), to which Gorges and Baskerville added a note that they had seen the queen's letter and the generals' reply, 'which we cannot mislike'.

[2] On 20 August Burghley wrote to Cecil (P.R.O., S.P. 12/253, no. 88): 'I am glad ye plymmouth Generalls do content hir Maj*es*ty w*ith* ther answer.'

the loss of a few small vessels on the coast of Spain; looking daily for a good wind, they take their leave.]

12. *Sir Thomas Lake to Sir Robert Sydney,* *22 August 1595*[1]

... We dwell in a most certain expectation of being attempted the next Yeare, ether directly here at Home, or by the Way of Scotland. ... We ground not this our Apprehension onely, uppon the certain Knowledge we have of the Preparations in Spaine, to be farre greater then in the Year 88; but uppon Advertisements of the Purpose for which they were made; from both private Persons and Princes, such as I may not name. The expectation of this Danger bred here great Diversity of Opinions, of the Proceeding of our Sea Voyage. They that wold have it stayd, alleaging the impossibility of their returne in a small Tyme, fitt to serve our Turne, if need required; the hazard of the Losse of so manye Mariners going into hott Cuntryes, the Absence of the Shippes and Ordonance. The other Partie alleaging the Losse of the Queene, and the Adventurers if it brake of, The Dishonnor, because it wold be imputed to feare, and a probability that the return might be tymely enoughe, with hope of Treasure, which is our greatest desire and want. Some Proposition was made by the active Sort (you may ghesse whom) to convert this Fleet, assimbled with some Enforcement, to an offensive Course, uppon the Ports of Spaine; but checked from above, or crossed under Hand, not without a great Distemper of Humures on both Sides, for a few Dayes; yet, in most Mens Iudgements, the likelyest Way to divert our present Feares. But now in the End, they are directed to proceed, and in them resteth much of our Hopes; for it beginneth now to be spoken, that these great Rumors of Preparations are partely for feare of us, and partely to have stayd this Voyage; exitus acta probat. But I am of Opinion, that seing we rest here in these Doubts, you may doe some Service

---

[1] A. Collins (ed.), *Letters and Memorials of State ... collected by Sir Henry Sydney* (1746), I, part 2, 343–4.

to cause such of those Countrey Men as trade to Spayne, to make some speciall Observation . . . From Nonsuch, where this Night we are arrived, this xxijth of August, 1595.

Yours to command,
Tho. Lake

13. Sir Nicholas Clifford to Essex, August 1595[1]

my brother your lordship did mistake my meanynge in my letter, for I hope your lordship shall not fynde me so rashe in my opynion, that I knowe howe my fortune standes with the Queene, and that I did looke for, was from your lordship. I desyer to color, my obscure goinge from the men of warr, for many reasons, of the wich, if it please yowe, in any ocasion to thinke of yt, shall make me fitter hereafter to serve yow. Your lordship doth know our generalls humors, are, to respect none, but those whome they must perforce, and Sir thomas baskervyle, to be, a true lover of him sealf, but I beseech youre lordship to beleeve that in this jorney I will doe nothinge to displease yow, what cause soever shall hapen I am putt out of the Q. shipp wiche was dettermyned of by the lords. It is tould me, it is my lord Admyralls commandment, I could not goe unlesse I had the Captayne lodgd with me, nether could I have my gent. nor provysion, accommodated with me, my lord yt ys a great touch to me, and I do dysdayne it from them, althoughe I have showed noe such thing, but hould my sealf contented with a marchants shipp, wich I goe in, I protest againe unto youre lordship I will carie my self in this jorney accordinge to your desyers, what soever you thinke of me or my mynde. So I rest.

I cannot advertyse your lordship of any procedinge here because I am not acquainted with them.

your Lordships pore kynseman and servant

Ni. Clifford

Sir thomas Gordge brought a comaundement downe to the contrarye as he tould me.

[1] Hatfield MSS, 172, no. 58. Endorsed: 'To my honorable lord of essex. At Plimmouth. August 95.' On Sir Nicholas Clifford, see below, p. 46.

II. *The Expeditionary Force*

THE FLEET LIST
(as at departure)

Ship	Tons	Captain	Master
Defiance	550	Sir Francis Drake	
Garland	660	Sir John Hawkins	Michael Meryall
Hope	600	Gilbert Yorke	Edward Tyllesley
Elizabeth Bonaventure	600	John Troughton	
Adventure	340	Thomas Drake	
Foresight	300	William Wynter	
Concord	330	David Serrocold	Olaf Maister
Amity	200	Henry Savile ?	Benjamin Gonson
Susan Bonaventure	250	Richard Barnard	Rowland Coytmore
Salomon Bonaventure	246	William Myddelton	John Corbin
Saker	246	Alexander Vaughan	Jonas Bonner
Elizabeth	194		
Jewel	130	Edward Goodwin	
Pegasus	80	Timothy Shotten	
Little John	100		
Desire	246	Henry Austen	
Phoenix	80	Bernard Drake	
John Trelawney	150	Richard Gifford	Piers Lemon
Help		Henry Duffield	Anthony Lister
Francis	35	Robert Wignall	
Richard			
Exchange	140		
Delight		Josias Ravenscrofte	
John Bonaventure		James Fenton	
Elizabeth Constant		William Morrice	
Nannycocke			
Blessing			

THE SHIPS

Defiance. 550 tons. Queen's ship, built 1590. Appears to have undergone some major repair or rebuilding shortly before the voyage (p. 68 below).

Garland (or *Guardland*), 660 tons. Queen's ship, built 1590.

Hope. 600 tons. Queen's ship, built 1559.

Elizabeth Bonaventure. 600 tons. Queen's ship, bought 1567, rebuilt 1581. Often called simply the *Bonaventure.*

Adventure. 340 tons. Queen's ship, built 1594.

Foresight. 300 tons. Queen's ship, built 1570.

Concord. 330 tons. A merchantman-privateer of London, owned in 1594 by Oliver and Nicholas Stile, members of the Colthurst partnership. One of their partners, Simon Lawrence, had the *Amity* built in 1593 (P.R.O., S.P. 12/254, no. 33). In 1598 the *Amity* and the *Concord*, commanded respectively by Benjamin Gonson and Olaf Maister, were jointly set forth on a trading-privateering voyage by Oliver Stile, Thomas White (formerly a captain in the service of the Colthurst group) and Lady Margaret Hawkins, Sir John's widow (K. R. Andrews, 'The Economic Aspects of Elizabethan Privateering' (London University Ph.D. thesis, 1951), pp. 351, 353). Two of the witnesses of Sir John's will were Richard Colthurst and Edward Lawrence, who may have been related to members of the Colthurst group. It seems likely that Hawkins, the Stiles and White were joint adventurers in these two ships in 1595 (Henry Colthurst, the chief of the group, died about the turn of the year 1594–5 and Simon Lawrence some months before). For the Colthurst partnership see T. S. Willan, *Studies in Elizabethan Foreign Trade* (1959), pp. 205–11; K. R. Andrews, *Elizabethan Privateering: English Privateering during the Spanish War, 1585–1603* (1964), pp. 100–2.

Amity. 200 tons. Of London. See above note on the *Concord.*

Susan Bonaventure (or *Susan and Parnell*). 250 tons. Of London, a Levant trader and privateer, built after 1582 (P.R.O., S.P. 12/250, no. 33). Served against the Armada (J. K. Laughton (ed.), *State Papers relating to the Defeat of the Spanish Armada*

(1894) II, 328), in the fleet which took the *Madre de Deus* (Oppenheim, *Monson's Tracts,* I, 281), in the Mediterranean 1598 (Andrews, *Elizabethan Privateering,* p. 268), in the West Indies 1602 (P.R.O., H.C.A. 13/104, 8 July 1602). In 1593 this ship had been set forth by John More, Gerard Gore, Richard Gore and others, London merchants (P.R.O., H.C.A. 25/3 (9), 2 March 1592/3).

Salomon. 246 tons. Of London, built 1594 (P.R.O., S.P. 12/251, no. 3). Probably the same as the *Salomon* sailing in company with the *Susan and Parnell* and two other ships in the Mediterranean in 1598, when the merchants interested in prizes included John More, Thomas Cordell and Richard Staper (Andrews, 'Economic Aspects of Elizabethan Privateering', pp. 357–8). In 1595 these two *Bonaventures* probably represent the contribution of a London merchant group including John More and Thomas Cordell, both prominent privateering promoters.

Saker. 246 tons. Of London, built 1594 (P.R.O., S.P. 12/254, no. 33).

Elizabeth. 194 tons. Of London, probably built 1594 (P.R.O., S.P. 12/254, no. 33). Privateering in 1594 (P.R.O., H.C.A. 13/31, 21 November 1594). Scuttled at Porto Belo. Owned by John Watts, merchant, of London (H.R. (Henry Roberts), *The Trumpet of Fame* (1595), pp. 11–12). Watts, the greatest of the London privateering magnates, also contributed the *Jewel,* the *Pegasus* and the *Little John* to this expedition.

Jewel. 130 tons. Of London, owner John Watts. In the West Indies 1594, the Mediterranean 1595 and continued active after returning from Drake's voyage (Andrews, *Elizabethan Privateering,* pp. 106–8).

Pegasus. 80 tons. Of London, owner John Watts. In various privateering expeditions from 1591 (Andrews, 'Economic Aspects of Elizabethan Privateering', p. 261).

Little John. 100 tons. Of London, owner John Watts. Privateering on various occasions since 1585 (P.R.O., H.C.A., 25/1 (4), 15 July 1585; Andrews, 'Economic Aspects of Elizabethan Privateering', pp. 252–4).

Desire. 246 tons. Of London, probably built 1594 (P.R.O., S.P. 12/254, no. 33). Adams Journal (see p. 79 below) says this was a Plymouth ship, but is contradicted by P.R.O., E. 351/2233.

Phoenix (or *Felix*). 80 tons. Of London, a pinnace, owner Richard Drake of Surrey, one of the equerries of the queen's stable, whose adventure in this expedition is mentioned in *Cal. S.P.D., 1598–1601*, p. 507, and whom Drake described in his will as his 'cousin'. The pinnace, still owned by Richard Drake, was privateering in 1598, 1599 and 1600 (Andrews, 'Economic Aspects of Elizabethan Privateering', p. 361; P.R.O., H.C.A. 13/34, 8 July 1600; 13/35, 25–30 May 1601; 13/103, 26 April, 29 July and 4 November 1600; 14/33, nos. 41, 48; B.M., Additional MSS, 12503, ff. 371, 382).

John Trelawney (or *Pulpit*). Of Plymouth, 150 tons. Employed as a supply ship in the 1588 campaign (Laughton, *Defeat*, II, 329) and in this voyage as a victualler. Burned at San Germán Bay, Puerto Rico.

Help. Of London. An entry under date 4 June 1595 in Thomas Myddelton's journal of accounts reads: '*Per* Thaccompt of Shipping Called the Help/ unto Cashe/ iiCLxxxiij^{li}xvj^{s}x^{d}/ and is for my third parte of the good shipp called the help: now ready to go in the voyadge with Sir Frauncis Drake & Sir John hauckins knightes and doth wholly belong unto them & my self by equall thirds cost my part – 283/16/10' ('A jurnal of all owtlandishe accomptes', National Library of Wales). Both the ship's name and the cost of her setting forth suggest this was an auxiliary, probably of not more than 100 tons burden, and may have been the 'caravel' mentioned in VTD (see p. 39, n. 1 below). She was captured by Avellaneda after losing company (documents 18 and 40).

Francis. 35 tons. Of Greenwich. Possibly owned by Drake, but probably not the same as the bark which sailed with him in 1585–6, then described as 'a very proper barke of 70. tunnes' (D. B. Quinn (ed.), *The Roanoke Voyages, 1584–1590* (1955), p. 290). Sunk by Pedro Tello.

Richard. A victualler, of London, scuttled at Guadalupe 'being slugeshe not able to kepe way with us anye longer' (Bodleian

Journal – see p. 79 below). She was bought for the expedition for about £200 (p. 57 below).

Exchange. 140 tons. Of Bristol, owner William Wynter. Privateering in 1592 (K. R. Andrews, *English Privateering Voyages to the West Indies, 1588–1595* (1959), pp. 211, 215). Damaged and therefore sunk near Mona I.

Delight. Of Hampton. Possibly the 50-ton vessel employed in 1588 (Laughton, *Defeat,* II, 326) and/or that set forth by the earl of Cumberland in 1590 (Andrews, 'Economic Aspects of Elizabethan Privateering', pp. 281–2). Described as a pinnace by Troughton. Scuttled at Porto Belo.

John Bonaventure. Of London. Oppenheim (*Monson's Tracts,* I, 316) gives 200 tons, but does not mention the source.

Elizabeth Constant (or *Elizabeth Constance,* or *Elizabeth*). Of Bridgewater (P.R.O., E.351/2233). Part-owned by Michael Meryall. Perhaps formerly the *Elizabeth Fishbourne* of Plymouth, 70 tons, set forth in 1591 by Richard Fishbourne, Thomas Newman and William Morris (P.R.O., H.C.A. 25/3 (9), 25 May 1591). Richard Fishbourne of Plymouth, gent., had commanded John Watts' *Little John* in the Cadiz voyage, when he proved himself Drake's loyal supporter (J. S. Corbett (ed.), *Papers Relating to the Navy during the Spanish War, 1585–1587* (1898), pp. 159, 163–4). He was a privateering promoter throughout the war (e.g., P.R.O., H.C.A. 13/36, 15 July 1603; Andrews, *Elizabethan Privateering,* p. 178). In 1595 he was paid 40/- for some unspecified service in connection with Drake's expedition (P.R.O., E. 351/2233).

Nannycocke. Of Ramsgate, a ketch. Bought for the expedition (p. 57 below).

Blessing. Of Ramsgate, a ketch. Bought for the expedition (*ibid.*).

The caravel sometimes mentioned was probably the *Help.*[1]

---

[1] The contexts of the various references in VTD to the 'caravel' rule out its identification with most of the minor vessels, but not with the *Help.* Adams Journal, moreover, in an otherwise correct fleet list, omits the *Help* and includes 'the Littell Caruell'. It is possible, however, that the caravel was an additional vessel, making 28 in all. The *aviso,* or frigate, captured off Nicaragua, was placed under a Captain Eden, but destroyed at Porto Belo (document 37).

At least 14 pinnaces were taken in parts.[1]

Of the 27 ships that left England, one was captured, one sunk by the enemy and five destroyed by the English themselves.

THE CAPTAINS

Sir Francis Drake. Superseded as commander of the *Defiance* on his death by Jonas Bodenham. The latter was probably Drake's first wife's nephew and became Drake's secretary in or before 1588, when he also served under him in the *Revenge.* He kept Drake's accounts for the voyage of 1595–6 and was sued by Thomas Drake in this connection, being accused of large-scale fraud in his handling of Drake's finances (E. F. Eliott-Drake, *The Family and Heirs of Sir Francis Drake* (1911), I, 142–7). On 27 January 1596, the day before he died, Drake signed a codicil to his will granting Bodenham the manor of Sampford Speney in addition to the sum of £100 bequeathed to him in the will (*ibid.* I, 137–40).

Sir John Hawkins. Superseded as captain of the *Garland* on his death by Humphrey Reynolds, who commanded queen's ships on various occasions from 1594 to 1603 (Oppenheim, *Monson's Tracts,* I and II).

Gilbert Yorke. Appointed vice-admiral after Hawkins' death. Superseded as captain of the *Hope,* after his death on 7 December 1595, by Thomas Drake. Commanded the *Michael* in Frobisher's voyage of 1577 and was vice-admiral in Frobisher's 1578 expedition. Captain of the queen's pinnace *Scout,* 1584 (Corbett, *Spanish War,* p. 298). Document 14 implies that Thomas Drake was in turn superseded by Samuel Thomas. The latter had sailed with Drake in 1587, when he signed several of the articles drawn for Drake against William Borough (*ibid.* pp. 159, 163–4). Samuel Thomas, gent., of Tower Wharf, London, owned and set forth in 1591 and 1592 the 60-ton

---

[1] Document 14 mentions nine costing £40 each; if the others mentioned in that context cost about the same there would have been about 21 altogether. Seven were set up in the Virgins, four at San Germán Bay and three at Escudo I. (Bodleian Journal; Troughton, document 19; Adams Journal).

privateer *Pretence* of London (Andrews, 'Economic Aspects of Elizabethan Privateering', p. 263).

John Troughton. See p. 81 below and documents 19 and 42.

Thomas Drake. Drake's youngest brother and heir. Served with Drake in the voyage round the world; as captain of the *Thomas Drake* in 1585–6; and as captain of the *Revenge* in 1589 (Corbett, *Spanish War,* p. 299; Oppenheim, *Monson's Tracts,* I, 182). Succeeded Yorke as captain of the *Hope* and was then succeeded in the *Adventure* by Jonas Bodenham. Bodenham, on becoming captain of the *Defiance,* was succeeded in the *Adventure* by Henry Savile. Savile had possibly been captain of the *Amity* until this time. He had commanded queen's ships in 1589 (under Drake) and 1594 (Oppenheim, *Monson's Tracts,* I, 183, 204, 304). See also document 40.

William Wynter. Son of Sir William Wynter of the navy board. Commanded the *Foresight* in 1587, 1589, 1590 and the *Minion* in 1588 (Corbett, *Spanish War,* pp. 100, 298; Oppenheim, *Monson's Tracts,* I, 184, 242). Owned the *Exchange* in this expedition. A certain William Wynter was employed as a master in Cumberland's Puerto Rico expedition (G. C. Williamson, *George, Third Earl of Cumberland* (1920), pp. 178–179). See also Baskerville (document 20) and Maynarde (document 18).

David Serrocold. The Serrocolds (Sarocoulds, etc.) were London merchants, one of whom, John, had sailed with Drake in 1577 and with Lister and Withrington in 1586 and had commanded the *Bark Burr* in 1588 (Z. Nuttall (ed.), *New Light on Drake* (1914), p. 390; *Principal Navigations,* III (1600), 769–78 (XI (1904), 202–27); Laughton, *Defeat,* II, 327).

Henry Savile. See note on Thomas Drake above and document 40 below. Whoever was captain was succeeded by Charles Caesar at Río de la Hacha. Charles, perhaps a relative, but not the son, of Sir Julius, had been captain of the *Bark Bonner* in 1588 (Laughton, *Defeat,* II, 326). It is not improbable that Sir Julius and his father-in-law, Sir Richard Martin, invested in this voyage. Martin had adventured heavily in Drake's voyages of 1577 and 1585 (Alexander Brown, *The Genesis of the United*

States (1890), II, 944) and Caesar had put money into similar ventures (T. K. Rabb, *Enterprise and Empire* (1967), p. 258).

William Myddelton. A cousin of Sir Thomas Myddelton, whose ships he had commanded in 1589, 1590 and 1591 (A. H. Dodd, 'Mr Myddelton the Merchant of Tower Street', in *Elizabethan Government and Society, Essays Presented to Sir John Neale* (eds. S. T. Bindoff, J. Hurstfield and C. Williams, 1961), p. 258, and references there cited).

Alexander Vaughan. Captain of the privateer *Swallow* in 1598 (Andrews, *Elizabethan Privateering,* p. 272).

Edward Goodwin. Operating for Watts in the West Indies, 1597 (P.R.O., H.C.A. 13/32, 30 December 1597) and captain of Watts' *Pegasus* in Cumberland's expedition, 1598 (Oppenheim, *Monson's Tracts,* II, 217). Reported to Watts after return in 1596 (document 19).

Timothy Shotten. Purser of Watts' *Alcedo* 1594 (P.R.O., H.C.A. 13/31, 17 March 1594/5). In a context referring to a rutter of the China coast and the East Indies it is stated that 'Timothy Shotton towardes Master Wattes hath also one. Now he is at sea. 1596.' (B.M., Sloane MSS, 2292, last page.)

Henry Austen. Of Plymouth, gent., captain of the *Hazard* of Plymouth, 1591–2, of the *Bark Austen,* 1594 (Andrews, 'Economic Aspects of Elizabethan Privateering', p. 314; P.R.O., H.C.A. 13/30, 5 July 1592).

Bernard Drake. Another cousin of Drake's, one of the Drakes of Ashe (but not Sir Bernard, who died in 1586). Again captain of this ship in 1598 (Andrews, 'Economic Aspects of Elizabethan Privateering', p. 361).

Richard Gifford. When the *John Trelawney* was destroyed Gifford was transferred to the *Help* and so became a Spanish prisoner. He returned to England, having escaped from Spain, in 1600 and resumed his career as a sea-captain, now in the service of Sir Robert Cecil. An account of their association and of Gifford's successive privateering voyages to the Mediterranean from 1600 will shortly be published in the *English Historical Review.*

Henry Duffield. Cal. Hatfield MSS, x, 36.

Robert Wignall. Pilot of Drake's flagship, the *Elizabeth Bonaventure,* in 1587 (Corbett, *Spanish War,* p. 188). Master of the queen's *Nonpareil* in Drake's 1589 voyage (Oppenheim, *Monson's Tracts,* I, 183, 204).

Josias Ravenscrofte. Witness to codicil to Hawkins' will, 16 June 1595 (Somerset House, P.C.C., 26 Drake). Died within two hours of Drake's death (Bodleian Journal).

William Morrice. Gent., of Plymouth. Adventurer in the *Elizabeth Fishbourne* in 1591 and commanded Fishbourne's *Gift* in 1591 or 1592 (P.R.O., H.C.A. 25/3 (9), 25 May 1591; 24/59, no. 64).

THE MASTERS

Michael Meryall. Part-owner of the *Elizabeth Constant* (P.R.O., E. 351/2233).

Edward Tyllesley. See P.R.O., E. 351/2233.

Olaf Maister or Olive (Olave, Oliver) Masters. Master's mate of the *Bark Burr* in 1586 (P.R.O., H.C.A. 13/26, 3 May 1586); master (1589, 1590) and captain (1592) of the Colthurst-owned *Passport* (Andrews, 'Economic Aspects of Elizabethan Privateering', p. 261); captain of the *Concord* 1594 (P.R.O., H.C.A., 24/62, no. 68). See also above, p. 36.

Benjamin Gonson. Probably a relative of Sir John Hawkins' brother-in-law, Benjamin Gonson. Again master of the *Amity,* 1598, when described as 'sailor, of Ratcliffe' (Andrews, 'Economic Aspects of Elizabethan Privateering', p. 352).

Rowland Coytmore or Quoitmore. Captain of this ship in 1598 (Andrews, *Elizabethan Privateering,* p. 268). Of the family of Coytmor of Coetmor, Caernarvonshire (cp. A. H. Dodd, *Studies in Stuart Wales* (1592), p. 135). Master of the *Harry* of London in two voyages to Leghorn, 1592–4, and of the *Susan and Parnell* (or *Susan Bonaventure*) in similar voyages, 1597–1600 (D. Fischer, 'The Development and Organization of English Trade to Asia, 1553–1605' (unpublished London Ph.D. thesis, 1970), pp. 450–6.

Piers Lemon. Captain of the *Makeshift,* 1588 (Laughton, *Defeat,* II, 326). Although reported captured off Cartagena, he or a man of the same name was privateering in 1598 (P.R.O., H.C.A. 13/33, 13 October 1598). See also below, p. 180, n. 4.

OTHER PERSONNEL

The personnel totalled about 2,500 (including somewhat over 1,500 sailors and somewhat under 1,000 soldiers), which in relation to approximately 6,000 tons of shipping meant economical manning by contemporary English standards.[1] The various references to prest money and conduct money suggest that Drake and Hawkins pressed a considerable proportion of their mariners,[2] but whether pressed or not the great majority would have been drawn from that stock of seamen who more or less regularly sailed the southward-going merchantmen, the privateers and the queen's ships. As for the soldiers, several hundred of them claimed to have been pressed and a large number apparently received prest money.[3] Of their recruitment it is known only that some came from Gloucestershire and Herefordshire.[4] The captains and masters of the ships were seasoned campaigners; some were no strangers to the Caribbean; some were eminent mariners of the day – Yorke, Wignall and Abraham Kendall, for example, not to mention the generals. The two Portuguese pilots[5] who sailed from England with the fleet were presumably taken not so much for their nautical skill as for their specialized knowledge of particular coasts.

It will be clear from the above notes on the fleet that Drake and Hawkins each commanded a personal following among the ship-owners and seamen. The composition of their respective squadrons

[1] The twelve undermanned companies of soldiers probably numbered rather less than 1,000 (Maynarde, document 18). J. A. Williamson, *Hawkins of Plymouth* (1949), p. 281: 'The Queen's ships which fought the Armada were manned at the rate of one man to two tons', which was an improvement on earlier standards.

[2] Commission to Drake and Hawkins, dated 29 January 1594/5 (P.R.O., C. 66/37 Eliz., pt. 14, m. 18; printed in Marsden, *Law and Custom of the Sea*, I, 284–7; document 14).

[3] Sir John Fortescue wrote to Cecil on 9 June 1596 that the soldiers waiting to be paid declared that they had been impressed and had sailed for wages, not for shares; he thought there were not more than 400 claimants (Hatfield MSS, 41, no. 64).

[4] P.R.O., E. 351/2233.

[5] VTD. One of these was Simón Moreno – see p. 191 below.

was doubtless largely determined by these ties. Drake, moreover, had a following of landsmen: Captain John Marchant, quarter-master of the expedition; Captains Anthony Platt and Richard Stanton, both company commanders; and various gentlemen such as Thomas Maynarde, Brute Browne and William Whitelocke, who formed a personal entourage. Hawkins may have gathered about him a similar group. The army was clearly dominated by the adherents of the earl of Essex. Sir Thomas Baskerville (colonel-general), Sir Nicholas Clifford (lieutenant-general), Arnold (sergeant-major) and Nicholas Baskerville, and Captains Grimston, Boswell, Poore and Garrett were Essex men already. Captain Salusbury probably and Captain Arthur Chichester certainly became Essex men at this juncture. Of the other captains mentioned, Barkley was possibly a relative of the Baskervilles; Bowster, Bridge, Fenton, Rush and Stratford, like Worrell the trench-master, cannot be placed.

John Marchant and Anthony Platt. Had served with Drake as land captains in the 1585 voyage (*Principal Navigations,* III (1600), 534 (X (1904), 98)) and had been lieutenant-general and sergeant-major respectively in the Cadiz voyage, when they appeared as Drake's main supporters in his quarrel with Borough (Corbett, *Spanish War,* pp. 150, 183–4, 187).

Richard Stanton. Had served in Drake's 1585 voyage (*Principal Navigations,* III (1600), 534 (X (1904), 98)).

Thomas Maynarde. For Maynarde's personal connection with Drake, see pp. 80–1 below.

Brute Browne. Esquire, of Langtree, Devon. Related to Maynarde (document 18). Volunteer on the queen's *Rainbow,* 1588 (Laughton, *Defeat,* II, 324).

William Whitelocke. Third son of Richard Whitelocke, merchant of London. The eldest son, Edmund, was suspected of complicity in Essex's conspiracy, but was soon discharged. The fourth son, James, wrote an account of his family: John Bruce (ed.), *Liber Famelicus of Sir James Whitelocke, a Judge of the Court of King's Bench in the Reigns of James I and Charles I* (Camden Society, 1858). Of his brother William he relates that he 'was broughte up withe the rest in lerning, but had no minde to it, and therfore was bound apprentice to a marchant in London, but when the Portugall voyage was undertaken, he left maister and thrift and all, and put himself into the action, and so fell from that civill course to a martiall life. He was brought up from shipbord, at his return, in a sheet, he was so extream weak, and did hardly recover again by my mother's great tendernesse of him, and, when he was well againe, followed the warrs alto-geather. He served Sir Frauncis Drake in his chamber, and followed him to the Groin, and his other sea voyages, and behaved himself verye valiantly, to the goodliking of his maister, and so continued in his service untill sir Frauncis dyed at sea, at whiche time he was neerest about him, and put his armor upon him a little before his deathe, whiche he wolde have doon, that he might dy like a soldiour. Sir Frauncis gave him divers ritche legacies of plate and jewells at his deathe, but he was ransaked of all by the brother of sir Frauncis, and by meer wrong barred from his maister's bountye. He followed that course of life, untill at the last, going forthe in a ship of war from London to the Indian seas, he lost his life in a conflict withe the Spanyards. He was a verye tall young man, strong of bodye, flaxen hear, fair of complexion, exceeding wastfull in expence, and carelesse of all worldly matters that tended to thrift. He was about the age of 27 yeares olde when he dyed.'

Sir Thomas Baskerville. See pp. 82–4 below.

Sir Nicholas Clifford. In a letter to Essex (document 13) signed himself 'your lordships pore kynseman and servant'. Was Essex's personal lieutenant in the Normandy campaign (*Cal. Hatfield MSS*, IV, 169–70). Knighted 1591. M.P. for Haverfordwest, as Essex's nominee, 1593 (W. R. Williams, *The Parliamentary History of Wales* (Brecon, 1895), p. 167). His elder brother, Sir Conyers, was also an Essex man.

Nicholas Baskerville. Younger brother of Sir Thomas, with whom he served as a captain of foot from 1591 (see pp. 253–4 below).

Captain Grimston. Served with Essex in Normandy in 1591–2 (*Cal. Hatfield MSS*, V, 169–70).

Captain Boswell. Went out to join Essex in Normandy with certain gentlemen of Essex's *entourage,* in October 1591 (*Cal. Hatfield MSS,* IV, 154–5). See also P.R.O., S.P. 78/25/123).

Captain Poore. Probably either Edward or Henry Poore, who were both captains under Essex in Normandy in 1591–2 (*Cal. Hatfield MSS,* IV, 169–70). Henry Poore was to take a company of 150 men overseas in July 1593 (*A.P.C., N.S.,* XXIV, 414–15).

Captain Garrett. Probably the Lieutenant Garrett who acted as Essex's messenger to Sir Francis Vere in March 1595 (*Cal. Hatfield MSS,* V, 155–6).

Captain Salusbury. John, younger son of John Salusbury of Rug and Bachymbyd, M.P. for Merioneth. Had served with his kinsman Owen in the Netherlands and in 1586–7 was involved in Stanley's plots. Accompanied Essex to Cadiz in 1596 and to Ireland in 1599 and was imprisoned briefly for complicity in Essex's rebellion, in which Owen was killed (*The Dictionary of Welsh Biography down to 1940,* 1959). His elder brother, Robert, borrowed money from his kinsman Sir Thomas Myddelton from 1590 (Dodd, 'Mr. Myddelton the Merchant of Tower Street').

Captain Arthur Chichester. Had sailed, probably as a captain of soldiers, in 1588 in one of the queen's ships. Served in Essex's Cadiz expedition as a volunteer. 1597 was sergeant-major of the army under Baskerville in France. Served under Essex and Mountjoy in Ireland. Was created Lord Chichester of Belfast in 1613, became Lord Deputy of Ireland and a member of the Privy Council (*The Dictionary of National Biography* (63 vols., 1885–1900)).

Captain Barkley. Maynarde mentions a captain 'Bartlett', who was probably the same man. Barkley is listed as one of the land captains in 'Full Relation'.

Captain Bowster. Mentioned in P.R.O., E. 351/2233. A Captain Bowyer or Boyser was captured by Avellaneda (*Cal. S.P.D., 1595–7,* pp. 346–7, 375–6).

Captain Bridge. Mentioned in P.R.O., E. 351/2233. Captured by Avellaneda (*Cal. S.P.D., 1595–7,* pp. 346–7, 375–6).

Captain Fenton. Listed as a land captain in 'Full Relation' and mentioned in P.R.O., E. 351/2233.

Captain Rush. Listed in 'Full Relation' and mentioned by Maynarde, as well as by Clifford in a letter to Essex (*Cal. Hatfield MSS*, v, 290). Was perhaps the Captain Francis Rushe who was to take a company overseas in July 1593 (*A.P.C., N.S.,* XXIV, 414–15).

Captain Stratford. Replaced Grimston. Wounded off Puerto Rico. Mentioned in Maynarde and Adams Journal.

Captain Worrell. Mentioned only in Maynarde.

The original 12 land captains were probably Nicholas Baskerville, Barkley, Grimston, Rush, Boswell, Platt, Chichester, Stanton, Fenton, Poore, Salusbury and Garrett. Sir Thomas and Arnold Baskerville, Clifford, Marchant and Worrell were officers without companies. P.R.O., E. 351/2233 mentions a company commander called 'Bushe', but this is presumably a mistake for 'Rushe'. The Captain Christopher Crofts also there mentioned in connection with the preparation of the army is not known to have sailed. The Lieutenant Huntley mentioned in 'The briefe of our voyage' (B.M., Sloane MSS, 2177, f. 19) was possibly a relative of Baskerville's.

FINANCES

Financially the expedition was organized as a terminable joint stock venture. Initially it was arranged that the queen should contribute six ships and two-thirds of the other costs, which should include the hire (tonnage) of twelve merchantmen and wages for 2,500 men,[1] while the remaining one-third of the fitting out costs, including tonnage and wages, should be met by Drake, Hawkins, and any others they could persuade to subscribe. In the event some economy was achieved by deciding to award the soldiers and the shipowners shares in the booty instead of wages and tonnage respectively. Thus the returns of the voyage were (so far as can be

---

[1] P.R.O., S.P. 12/250, no. 16 (f. 111), estimate of the charges, dated 24 October 1594. The same estimates are used in document 14. At this stage the queen's ships to be employed were the *Garland*, the *Mary Rose*, the *Bonaventure*, the *Hope*, the *Foresight* and the *Crane*.

FINANCES

deduced from various allusions) to be divided into eighteen parts, of which three were allotted to the army, three to the private ship-owners, four to the other private adventurers and eight to the queen.[1] The cost of fitting out appears to have amounted to about £31,000, to which the queen contributed £20,000. After the voyage about £12,000 was laid out on wages and other expenses, to which the queen contributed £8,000.[2] The real cost of the expedition, however, rose well above £43,000, for the royal ships were supplied free of charge, and the private vessels for bills of adventure which proved to be almost worthless, since the returns

---

[1] This conclusion does not quite agree with Baskerville's assertion that there was to be an equal division between the shipowners, adventurers and men of war (document 16), but it seems to be the only solution that makes sense of the various references to shares in the documents herein.

[2] Particulars of the amounts spent by Drake and Hawkins were submitted after the voyage by Thomas Drake and Lady Margaret Hawkins respectively. Drake's account amounted to £12,842 9s 10d; Hawkins' to £18,661 18s 7d. It therefore appeared that they had spent £1,504 8s 5d more than their third in the fitting out costs (P.R.O., S.P. 12/259, no. 61 (f. 171). This document, dated 9 July 1596, puts the total post-voyage expenses at £8,000, the amount disbursed by the queen, but document 14 suggests that the post-voyage expenses were nearly £12,000. It should be emphasized that the exchequer account does not necessarily, nor even probably, give an accurate statement of the actual expenses. It seems extraordinary that Drake and Hawkins, having spent £22,000 by 1 March 1594/5, should have disbursed less than £10,000 in the following six months. Thomas Myddelton's journal shows that in 1595 he borrowed £1,000 from Hawkins to use towards the purchase of Chirk Castle from Lord St John of Bletsoe, and a further £1,000 which he lent to the earl of Shrewsbury. In the same year he made further large payments for Chirk Castle (National Library of Wales, 'A jurnal of all owtlandishe accomptes', pp. 195, 199, 313). It may be suspected that the queen's money was being used for a variety of purposes and that the long duration of the preparations was not entirely inconvenient for Hawkins and Myddelton. The use of public money for private purposes was quite normal at the time. Detailed information about private investment in this expedition is meagre. Hawkins' financial resources and contacts were probably superior to Drake's. We know that in 1593 Drake sold his house, called the Herbar, in the parish of St Mary Bothaw in London, to the City magnate Alderman Paul Bayning for £1,300; and on 27 August 1595 his manor of Pensengnance in Cornwall to Richard Carew of Antony for £250 (Sotheby & Co., *Catalogue of Valuable Americana* for sale on 5–6 November 1962, pp. 78–9 and H. P. Kraus, *Sir Francis Drake, A Pictorial Biography* (Amsterdam, 1970)).

49

amounted to a mere £5,000 in gold, silver, pearl and coin.[1] Their shares in the plunder could hardly have recompensed the owners for the deterioration (and in some cases, loss) of their ships. As for the surviving soldiers – probably little more than 400 in number – they received £880 13s 4d, of which the captains doubtless took the lions' shares.[2]

Although the official accounts (documents 14 and 15) afford many insights into the equipment of an expedition which was in certain respects abnormal, the picture they present is incomplete. They tell us little about the armament of the private vessels and they naturally omit to mention whatever goods (if any) were subscribed by way of adventure in the joint stock. Nor do they throw much light on the problem of the adequacy of the victualling and supplies. It is unlikely that all the goods listed as bought by Drake and Hawkins were of the desired quality or delivered aboard intact. According to the exchequer account, no less than 2,074 pairs of shoes were purchased at an average price of 1s 5d a pair, but Baskerville's army reached Capirilla barefoot and on this march, it was said, a pair of shoes was sold for thirty shillings.[3] The fact that Hawkins apparently spent a great deal more than Drake on fitting out does not necessarily imply that the latter skimped more than the former. What is known of the personal allegiance of the shipowners, captains and masters suggests that Hawkins' squadron was considerably the larger of the two in terms of tonnage. Drake's squadron was clearly overmanned to judge from the English narratives, but this was perhaps because he tried to achieve manpower comparable to Hawkins' without having comparable shipping.

[1] Document 14. Some supplies may have been subscribed upon bills of adventure, in which case they would not appear in the statement of account. It is particularly likely that the shipowners would have contributed materials (apart from their ships) on this basis, thus raising the real costs still further above the nominal.

[2] According to document 14, the £8,000 laid out by the queen after the voyage was for wages of mariners and soldiers, so that it is possible the soldiers received some wages as well as shares. See also document 16 and Ch. 8.

[3] Documents 14 and 20; 'Full Relation'.

14. *The exchequer accounts for the voyage*[1]

Thaccompte of Thomas Midleton Esquier,[2] *whom oure Soveraigne Ladie the Quenes most excellent Majestie hathe appoynted and aucthorised togeather with Richard Carmarthen Esquire*[3] and William Boroughe Esquier deceased[4] late comptroller of her *Majesties* Navye for the keepinge Bookes of Accompte & Payementes of diverse greate som*m*es of money concerninge the victuallinge and furnishinge to the Seas as well six of her highnes owne shippes, as sondrie other marchaunt Shippes in warrlike manner under the Conduc*t*ion of S*ir* Frauncis Drake & S*ir* John Hawkins knigh*te*s by vertue of her *Majesties* warrauntes under her hande & Signett to them directed, The tenor whereof is here verbatim recited viz. *Trusty* and welbeloved wee greete you well. Whereas wee have com*m*itted to S*ir* Frauncis Drake & S*ir* John Hawkins knigh*te*s a speciall Service to be by them done on the Sea, for which purpose wee have graunted to them thuse of certen of our owne shippes of warre, and have alsoe caused an Imprest to be made of some nomber of other shippes belonginge to our Subiec*te*s. And for the charges of this service for wages, victualles, munitions, Tonnage of Shippes hier and other necessaryes wee have lymitted a portion of Threasure to be yssued and at tymes requisitte to be paide for the same, wee have therefore made choise of you three as men of knowledge in theis kindes of services and doe aucthorise you or at leaste twoe of you to conferre from tyme to tyme with the saide S*ir* Francis Drake & S*ir* John Hawkyns, and to enforme your selves of the particuler som*m*es of money & charges by them demaunded, And as you shall finde the same necessarye to be allowed soe to keepe Accompte thereof.

---

[1] P.R.O., E. 351/2233. This document is too long to be presented in full. It has been shortened by modernizing the presentation and numerical usage and by contracting the detail on particular items throughout. For example, under the heading 'Wheat' nine purchases itemized in the original are here reduced to one entry, though not represented as one purchase. This is one of the more extreme instances of contraction; the most extreme is under the heading 'Wages and Entertainment'.

[2] A London merchant: see Dodd, 'Mr. Myddelton the Merchant of Tower Street'; Andrews, *Elizabethan Privateering*, pp. 113–18.

[3] Surveyor of the custom house in London.   [4] Died 1599.

And you Thomas Midleton shall have the payement thereof oute of such portions as our Threasurer of England shall cause to be paide to your handes, of which payementes by you to be made upon the bookes of Accompte perfected & subscribed by you three with the acquittaunce of the saide Sir Frauncis Drake & Sir John hawkins, wee shall discharge you from all further Accompte. And where the said Drake and Hawkyns have taken upon them to be at the Charge above our Charge of as muche as shall make a thirde parte of our portion to be imployed in this service,[1] wee will that alsoe you shalbe enformed thereof and have good regarde that they shall contribute in this service a thirde parte, And thereof also you shall keepe an Accompte aparte from the Accomptes of our disbursements. [Borough to keep the books. Dated 4 December 1594. Two warrants of privy seal are then recited. The first, dated 4 December 1594, estimates the cost of furnishing the fleet at £31,650 and orders the treasurer and chamberlains of the exchequer to make over to Borough, Carmarthen and Myddelton in instalments as required the sum of £20,000. Wages and tonnage are estimated at £19,900, and to meet the queen's share of this the exchequer is to make over £13,266 13s 4d on the return of the fleet. The second warrant, dated 29 May 1596, orders the exchequer to pay to Thomas Myddelton, for wages of mariners and soldiers, £8,000. The accountant (Myddelton) now yields up his account of all moneys received by him from the exchequer; it is stated that by 1 March 1595 £10,000 had been made over and that Drake and Hawkins, having already spent altogether £22,000, thought that the charge would exceed their first estimates. On that date, therefore, Burghley allowed a further £5,000 immediately, the remaining £5,000 to be paid later. The executors of Drake and Hawkins having acknowledged receipt of these sums, totalling £28,000, Myddelton is declared quit – signed Lord Buckhurst[2] and Sir John Fortescue,[3] 9 March 1603. The account of Lady Margaret Hawkins and Thomas Drake esquire now follows, which is not

---

[1] Literally means that Drake and Hawkins would bear a quarter of the charges, but the rest of the sentence and much other evidence show that this was never intended.

[2] Lord Treasurer.

[3] Chancellor of the exchequer.

only for the abovementioned sums, but also for goods received from the queen's storehouses, defalcations for prests upon apparel, moneys received on the return of the fleet for goods sold, to all which is added their one third share. Details of these receipts are given, including the sum of £4,085 16s 11d for silver, gold and Spanish coin and £831 8s 4d for pearls. The total charged to these accountants is £48,039 11s 2d. The full statement of expenses then follows:

EMPTIONS AND PROVISIONS

The accountants are allowed for moneys paid by Drake and Hawkins for victualling and furnishing the fleet as follows:

GRAINS OF SUNDRY SORTS[1]

Wheat: various quantities listed at prices from 32/- to 100/- a qr., totalling 1,887½ qrs. 1 peck, £3,899 14s 5d

Malt: at prices from 18/- to 48/- a qr., 503 qrs. 4 bushels, £441 18s 0d

Rye: 16 qrs. 6 bls. at 48/- a qr., £40 4s 0d

Barley: 6 bls. at 6/- a bl., £1 16s 0d

Pease: at prices from 20/- to 60/- a qr., 244 qrs. 7 bls., £266 9s 6d

Total grains: 2,653 qrs. 3 bls. 1 peck	4,650	1	11

BAKING OF WHEAT AND RYE

61 bls. for 36/-; 447 bls. for £14 18s 0d	16	14	0

BISCUIT

At prices from 12/9d to 21/- a cwt., total 131 cwt. 19 lbs.	114	14	5

BREAD

For a certain proportion of loaf bread for the ships' companies	5	10	2

BEER[2]

At prices from 40/- to 60/- a tun, total 1,339 tuns, 1 puncheon, 1 kilderkin	2,985	9	9

[1] The price of corn was very high in 1595, the country being in the middle of a run of bad harvests. A note on the prices of sea victuals, dated 18 September 1595 (*Cal. S.P. D., 1595-7*, p. 101) shows that between 1585 and 1595 victual prices in general roughly doubled, while wheat rose from 20/- to 40/- a quarter and malt from 15/- to 26/-. Thus the provisioners of this fleet appear to have made reasonable bargains for their wheat and malt, though in all respects the victualling was bound to be expensive.

[2] The price of beer is said to have risen from 24/- to 36/- a tun, 1585-95 (*ibid.*), in view of which the price here appears excessive.

Brewing of 194 tuns beer (the brewers finding hops) at 9/– a
tun   87 6 0

WINES

Canary wines, 2 pipes, £27
Muscatel, 1 hogshead, £7 10s 0d
Gascony wines, the greater part in bottles at 4/6d each, and a
small quantity in cask at £20 to £23 a tun, total £575
Spanish wines at £8 and £9 a tun, £332 13s 4d
Total for wines   942 3 4

BEEF[1]

At 18/– a cwt.   131 17 10

CIDER

10 hogsheads at £4 a tun   10 0 0

FISH

Stockfish[2] at £18, £20 and £22 a last, £230
350 lbs. Iceland ling and 200 lbs. ling haberdine,[3] including
freight, £46 3s 10d
1,042 Holland ling, £55 5s 2d
Dry Newland fish[4] at 10/6d to 12/– a cwt., approx. 1,800 cwt.,
£1,046 18s 10d
Buckhorn[5] at 3/4d a cwt., £3 16s 8d
Corfish[6] at 21/– a cwt., £117 12s 0d
Tunny at 3/4d a small barrel and 6/8d a great barrel, £15 6s 8d
North Sea cod at 100/– a cwt., £62 10s 0d
Sturgeon, 6 firkins at 26/8d each, £8
Skatefish, at 3/– a cwt., £3
Herring, 2 barrels at 13/4d each and 10 barrels of red herring for
£10 9s 6d
Total for fish   1,600 9 4

OATMEAL

At prices from 4/9d to 8/– a bl., 53 qrs. 3 bls.   122 17 0

---

[1] Rose from 12/6d to 20/– a cwt., 1585–95 (*ibid.*).
[2] Dried fish. Rose from £12 to £18 and £20 a last, 1585–95 (*ibid.*).
[3] Aberdeen ling. Most of the ling was bought for between £5 and £6 a cwt., a
reasonable price, since ling rose from £3 to £5 5s 0d a cwt. 1585–95 (*ibid.*). Of
the Iceland ling here mentioned, however, one cwt. cost £20.
[4] Newfoundland cod in the broader sense of the term.
[5] Whiting or other fish dried hard as a buck's horn.
[6] Salt cod.

BUTTER
At prices from 2/- to 4/- the gallon, 232½ gallons; 160 firkins
at 18/- each; 1,966 lbs. at 3¾d a lb.; 22 pots at 3/- each and 20
pots for £3 14s 0d

Total for butter   219 17 4

CHEESE[1]
At 50/- a wey; 30/- and 41/- a cwt.; 2/- and 4/- a piece; and
1¼d and 2½d a lb. Total for cheese   104 5 11

PORKS
250 provided in the country, with £20 12s 4d for the charges of
driving them and salt to pack them up with. Total   338 10 0

LEAD
2,000 lbs. at £6 0s 9d a thousandweight   12 1 6

SACKS
100 quarter sacks at 2/5½d each   12 5 10

WESTCOUNTRY WOODS[2]
270 at 6d the talle and 180 at 5d the talle[3]   10 17 11

CALICOES
52 pieces for 200 suits of apparel at 10/- each   26 0 0

TREGAR[4]
20 pieces at 105/- a piece   105 0 0

DOWLAS[5]
4½ pieces at £6 10s 0d a piece   29 5 0

GRAPERS AND ANCHORS
11 grapers and 3 small anchors   11 12 0

HASPS, ETC.
3 doz. hasps, 11 doz. staples, 10 doz. grommets[6]   1 12 0

LARD
154 lbs. at 5d a lb.   3 4 2

MATCH
At 13/4d and 20/- a cwt.   5 13 4

INSTRUMENTS OF MUSIC[7]
Sundry instruments of music for 8 musicians and nine trumpeters   14 11 0

---

[1] Rose from 28/- to 55/- a wey, 1585–95 (*ibid.*). The greater part of the cheese here
was bought at 50/- a wey.

[2] Rods.   [3] Tally.   [4] Linen from Tréguier, Brittany.

[5] Linen from Daoulas, Brittany.   [6] Or grummets: small metal rings.

[7] After Drake's death 'a chest of instrum*entes* of musicke' was removed from the
Defiance, comprising a lute, 'hobboyes sagbutes Cornettes & orpharions bandora
& suche like' (P.R.O., C. 2/33/96, Richard Drake *v.* Jonas Bodenham, 1598).

FLAGS
4 at 60/–, gilt with her majesty's arms upon silk; 30 of St George
at 16/8*d* each   37 0 0
STREAMERS
3 at £8, with her majesty's badges in silver and gold; and 80
at 25/–   124 0 0
ENSIGNS
26 of 11 and 12 breadths at 46/– each   60 0 0
BUDGE BARRELS[1]
2 doz. great, at 2/6*d*, 6 doz. small at 20*d*   9 0 0
PLATE LAMPS[2]
5 doz. at 12*d* each   3 0 0
SUCKETS[3]
3 barrels   15 0 0
MUSKETS
25 at 18/–, white with their furniture; 100 at 23/–, furnished;
21 at 13/4*d*, white; and one fair gilt musket, 40/–   153 10 0
NEEDLES
70 doz.   1 13 0
BOOKS
One Bible, 30/–; 25 psalters at 2/6*d*; and 2 service books at 3/–   4 18 6
PETTERAS[4]
One of iron weighing 200 lbs.   3 0 0
SILK AND THREAD
Silk buttons and perry buttons;[5] silk and thread for button
holes; and thread, buttons, lace and tape for 200 suits of apparel   21 14 0
CUSHIONS
Of bed leather used in both barges   1 19 10
RICE
At prices from 23/– to 28/– a cwt.   207 1 7
POWDER
At 12*d* a lb., £100 a last and £4 a barrel   313 14 6
CUSQUS[6]
5 tons at £8 a ton and 1,100 qrs. 17 lbs. at 10/– a cwt.   45 14 0

[1] A small cask designed for carrying powder in safety from sparks.
[2] Metal lamps.   [3] Succades: sugared fruits or sweetmeats.
[4] Or *pedrero,* a small gun firing stones, broken iron, etc.
[5] Not known, but 'perry' meant jewellery.
[6] *Sic.* Possibly cuskins (drinking pots) or *couscous,* known at the time as 'cuskoes,
or negroes meat' (e.g. B.M., Harleian MSS, 598, f. 22).

OIL

1 hogshead, £8; 2 great barrels, £8 10s 0d; 1,029 roves,[1]
£218 14s 3d; 152 half-roves, £35 9s 0d; 1 hogshead train oil,
£3 10s 0d; scouring oil for armour, £2   266 2 3

VINEGAR

5 tuns at £8 a tun; one barrel of white vinegar at 10/–; 95 jars
at 5/– a jar   64 15 0

MUSTARDSEED

At prices from 2/8d to 10/6d a bushel   28 19 3

GARLIC

140 double trace at 10d a trace   5 16 8

RAISINS

11 barrels weighing 12 cwt. 2 qrs. 21 lbs.   13 19 1

SHIPS

One ship called the *Richard* bought to carry victuals to the
Indies, without hope to return, with 6 pipes of wine and 2
barrels of powder   220 0 0

PINNACES

Elm planks with carriage, £25 9s 10d; ironwork, £31 4s 8d;
deals and spars, £14 0s 10d; marking stones, lines and other
necessities, £5 2s 10d; carpenters' work, £217 13s 8d; timber
and plank, £179 16s 8d; for watching the yard by night when
the pinnaces were set up, 71/6d. In all, £477. Nine other
pinnaces at £40 each, £360. Total   837 0 0

KETCHES

One with her furniture called the *Blessing* of Ramsgate, £61;
another, the *Nannycocke* of Ramsgate, furnished, £41; for
sheathing and putting them into serviceable order, £51 15s 9d   153 15 9

MASTS

15 small masts for pinnaces   13 15 4

BARGECLOTHS

Two   14 12 4

IRON SHOT

At prices from £5 to £10 a ton   128 13 1

STONE SHOT

144 at 16d each   9 12 0

ALMONDS

2 cwt.   5 0 0

[1] From Spanish *arroba*, about 4 gallons.

SALT
At prices from 2/2*d* to 2/6*d* a bushel   89 10 8
BALSAM
At 40/– a lb.   18 12 6
CASK
Approx. 1,900 tuns at prices from 8/– to 20/– a tun; also 5
Canary wine pipes, 3 dryfats, 1,129 Humber barrels, 364
herring barrels, 22 hogsheads, 450 barrels, 16 rundlets, 48
firkins for nails, 74 kilderkins and 2 lasts of barrel. Total   1,757 14 7
IRON HOOPS
2,476 at 8¼*d* a hoop; 1,140 tuns at 12/– a tun with smiths'
charges for binding and rivetting   839 14 9
BRASS ORDINANCE
Falcons: 4 of 33 cwt., £110
Bases: 7 with chambers, £50; 1 with 2 chambers, 61/6*d*; and
5 for £40 3*s* 0*d*. Total   203 4 6
CARRIAGES
For minion and falcon   5 0 0
IRON ORDINANCE
2 minions and 5 falcons weighing 55 cwt., £22; 15 base
chambers and 5 forelocks[1] of iron, £9 17*s* 0*d*   31 17 0
CANVAS
Various quantities of Normandy, Vitry, Rouen and un-
specified origin   247 7 3
SPARS
167 to lie in the cellars under the beer, 60/6*d* and 20 great spars
at 3/– each   6 0 6
BARRICOES[2]
12 at 4/–; 252 at 16*d*   19 4 0
DEAL BOARDS
At 100/– to 112/– a hundred   40 15 4
OARS
324, at 1½*d* and 1¾*d* a foot   43 19 10
HARPING IRONS[3]
29 at 2/–; 8 at 18*d*   3 10 0
FISGEES[4]
40 at 2/6*d*; 18 at 2/3*d*   7 0 3

[1] Bolts or pins.   [2] Small casks.
[3] Harpoons.   [4] Fish spears.

14. THE EXCHEQUER ACCOUNTS FOR THE VOYAGE

IRON AND IRONWORK
3 tons Spanish iron, £40 10s 0d; bolts, spikes, etc., £28 14s 3d;
a bar of iron, scuttle and ring-bolt, 17/–   70 1 3
NAILS OF SUNDRY SORTS
340,600, at prices from 1/3d a thousand to 23/4d a hundred   126 11 8
SCYTHES
80 Spanish scythes at 18d each   6 0 0
PIKE HEADS
18 at 12d each   18 0
CRESSETS
4 at 4/– each   16 0
ROSIN
216 cwt. 3 qrs. 24 lbs. of rosin and 17 doz. beech oars,
£96 6s 9d; and 136 chests for £51   147 6 9
OAKUM AND OAKUM BAGS
White oakum at 6/– and 10/– a cwt., £5 15s 0d; black oakum
at 6/8d a cwt., £14 13s 4d; 70 oakum bags, £6 12s 4d   27 0 8
NEATS TONGUES
100 at 12d each   5 0 0
FLAT BOATS
2 for carrying timber   4 3 4
CORDAGE
Ratlyns and marlyns at 26/8d a cwt., £35; Cable: 8 ton of old
cable, £40 and one cable for the *Exchange,* £10; coils of rope at
prices from 16/– to 24/– a cwt., £710 12s 5d; scantlings[1] for
the *Nannycocke* and *Blessing,* £15 12s 9d.   Total   841 5 2
SAILS AND MAKING OF SAILS
100 pieces of Ipswich Midreneux canvas, £160; 150 bolts of
French Midreneux canvas, £187 10s 0d; 308 yards of old
sails, £7 14s 0d; twine, £14 7s 3d   369 7 3
SUNDRY NECESSITIES
Pens, paper, ink-dust, wax, etc., £8 11s 0d; platters, cans,
dishes, etc., £17 18s 5d   26 9 5
SACKCLOTH
100 ells at 12d each   5 0 0
SEINES OR GREAT NETS
4 at £4 each and 12/– for their tanning; 1 at £2 5s 0d; 1 trawl
net, £2 10s 0d   21 7 0

[1] Small pieces of wood used in shipbuilding.

FISHING LINES
36 doz. at 12/– a doz.; and 62 lines and 700 hooks for
£4 15s 10d   26 7 10
SOUNDING LEADS
At 15/– a cwt.   3 13 11
DRUMS
2 at 30/– and 11 for £14   17 0 0
PIPES
25 doz. of match pipes[1] at 4/– a doz.; 13 smoke pipes at 8/–
each   10 4 0
TIMBER
Spent in the ship the *Amity*   1 1 6
TAR
15 barrels at 20/–   15 0 0
BRASERS[2]
10 doz. at 3/– a doz.   1 10 0
SLIPS[3]
12 doz. at 20d a doz.   1 0 0
COOPERS' TOOLS
A provision of sundry sorts for sea service   13 5 4
FAGGOTS
At 6/8d a load and 7/– or 8/– a cwt.   2 16 8
DIVERS PROVISIONS
and other charges not entered in the ledger but referred to sundry
bills   269 17 1
BILLETS
At prices from 14/– to 20/– a thousandweight   224 4 6
KETTLES
17 at £6 10s 0d and divers others   11 15 7
BACON
197 cwt. 3 qrs. for £257 1s 4d and other lesser quantities   273 2 2
LASTING VICTUALS[4]
A kind of victuals for sea service devised by Mr Hugh Platt,
4 Barrels at £4 10s 0d a barrel   18 0 0

[1] Used to contain lighted match.   [2] Braziers ?
[3] Possibly cylindrical iron cases used for charring wood.
[4] These were supplied by the inventor Hugh Platt and consisted of 'a certaine victuall in the form of hollow pipes', which was 'called by the name of *Macaroni* among the Italians' (J. J. Keevil, *Medicine and the Navy*, 1 (1957), 108–9; Hugh Platt, *Sundrie new and Artificiall remedies against Famine* (1596)). Count Maurice of

PISTOLS
40 for £30 2s 2d; 4 damasked at 60/- each; 8 at 66/8d each   68 15 6
FOWLING PIECES
18 at prices from 25/4d to 30/8d each   23 18 0
DAGGS
12 at 20/- each   12 0 0
PETRONELS
One   1 10 0
HALBERDS AND PARTIZANS
92 at prices from 6/7d to 12/- each   47 17 0
ARMING SWORDS
133 at 6/- each   39 18 0
TARGETS OF PROOF
120 at 24/- each and 17 others   157 0 0
RAPIERS
200 at 5/6d each and 14 others   62 0 0
SHIRTS OF MAIL
20 at 30/- each   30 0 0
BONE SPEARS
3 at 2/6d each   7 6
COMMISSIONS FOR THE GENERALS
2 with 2 duplicates under the great seal, at 66/6d each   14 10 0
BLACK BILLS
19 at 2/6d each   2 7 6
BARGES
2 with their oars   36 3 0
PIKES
4 doz. at 3/4d each; 400 at 2/6d   58 0 0
PHYSIC AND CHIRURGERY[1]
Electuarium contra scorbutum:[2] 60 lbs. at 5/- a lb., £15
Electuarium prunellorum:[3] 6 lbs. at 2/8d a lb., 16/-

Nassau had written to the earl of Essex recommending Platt on 25 March/ 4 April 1595 (*Cal. Hatfield MSS*, v, 154).

[1] I am much indebted to Mr E. Gaskell, librarian of the Wellcome Institute of the History of Medicine, for helping me to locate contemporary recipes of these electuaries.

[2] Probably the *Aqua Doctoris Stephani*, 'a compound distilled water with twenty-one ingredients, which found a place in the *London Pharmacopoeia* of 1618' and which Richard Hawkins took on his South Sea voyage in 1593 (Keevil, *Medicine and the Navy*, I, 101–2).

[3] *Prunellum*= sloe (R. E. Latham, *Revised Medieval Latin Word-list*, 1965). I have found no reference to this electuary elsewhere.

Diaphenicon:[1] 18 lbs. at 5/- a lb., £4 10s 0d

Electuarium Justinum:[2] 3 lbs. at 5/- a lb., 15/-

Electuarium de sucro rosarum:[3] 12 lbs. at 5/- a lb., £3

Diacatholicon:[4] 10 lbs. at 6/8d a lb., £3 6s 8d

Carecostina:[5] 10 lbs. at 5/- a lb., £2 10s 0d

Electuarium Indum:[6] 8 lbs. at 5/- a lb., £2

Electuarium vitae:[7] 6 lbs. at 6/8d a lb., £2

Confectio hamech:[8] 6 lbs. at 6/8d a lb., £2

Mithridate:[9] 5 lbs. at 40/- a lb., £10.

Divers other provisions for physic and chirurgery for the furnishing of two chests more, £67 12s 4d. Sundry other drugs made up in two other chests, £35 11s 3d. Money paid to divers surgeons[10] above their wages for the supplying of their chests, £42 4s 4d. Two spare chests for the relief of the whole fleet, £55

Total for physic and chirurgery   246 5 7

LANTHORNS

22 doz. at prices from 13/- to 40/- a doz.   25 6 0

[1] See Nicholas Culpeper, *Physicall Directory or a Translation of the London Dispensatory* (1649), p. 118. He describes it as 'a very violent purge' recommended for fevers; 'mixed in Clysters, it may do good in chollicks and infirmities of the bowels coming of Raw humours'.

[2] See Valerius Cordus, *Pharmacorum Omnium* (Nuremberg, 1592), p. 20. In a footnote to the recipe he describes it as useful for kidney pains and for breaking up calculi.

[3] Culpeper, p. 193: 'It purgeth choller and is good in tertian agues and diseases of the joynts, it purgeth violently, therefore let it be warily given.'

[4] Culpeper, p. 119: 'It is a fine cooling purge for any part of the body, and very gentle. . . . It is usually given in Clysters.'

[5] Culpeper, p. 185, gives 'carycostimum': 'Authors say it purgeth hot Rewms, and takes away inflamations in wounds . . . may safest be given in Clisters.'

[6] Culpeper, p. 192: 'It purgeth the bowels as also the joynts of putrified flegm, it breaks wind, is therefore profitable for the Chollick.'

[7] J. Wittich, *Arcula Itineraria* (Leipzig, 1590), pp. 38–9, 199. It appears to have been used for stomach upsets, plague, and as a general tonic.

[8] Culpeper, p. 191: 'a purge for melancholly, and salt flegm, & diseases thence rising, as Scabs, Itch Leprosies, Cancers' etc.

[9] Culpeper, pp. 179–80. The recipe contains a very large number of ingredients, which accounts for the relatively high cost. Culpeper recommends it for a great variety of illnesses, concluding: 'it would fill a whol sheet of paper to reckon them all up particularly'.

[10] James Wood, chief surgeon of the fleet, died off Porto Belo (VTD). The surgeon of the *Salomon* was captured at Grand Canary (p. 135 below).

CAVEARA
32 cwt. 5 lbs. at 26/8d a cwt. and 2 cwt. at 26/3d   45 14 8
TANNED HIDES
4 at 20/–   4 0 0
DANSK PLATTERS
60 doz. at 3/4d a doz.   10 0 0
WOODEN SPOONS
100 doz. at 2½d a doz.   1 0 0
BUTTER PLATTERS
20 doz. at 18d a doz.   1 10 0
TRAYS OF WOOD
4 doz. at 14/– a doz.; 4 doz. at 17/–   6 4 0
MUSTARD DISHES
40 doz. at 6d a doz.   1 0 0
SCALES
2 doz. great scales at 12/– a doz.; 2 doz. of smaller sort at 8/– a doz.   2 0 0
WOODEN DISHES
20 doz. at 12d a doz.   1 0 0
FLANNELS
600 ells at 10d an ell   25 0 0
SIEVES
2 doz. at 9/– a doz.   18 0
MATTOCKS
19 at 20d each   1 11 8
AXES
20 for shipwrights at 18d each; 20 cutting axes at 14d each   2 13 4
HATCHETS
41 at 10d each   1 14 2
BOWLS
12 doz. at 4/– a doz.   2 8 0
SHOVELS AND SPADES
10 doz. at 7/– a doz.; 20 doz. at 13/4d   16 16 8
BUCKETS
120 bound with iron at 2/2d each; 60 at 3/–; 6 hooped with
wood at 10d   22 5 0
FUNNELS
6 great at 12d each; 3 doz. of double plate at 4/– a doz.; 3 doz.
at 2/– a doz.   1 4 0
SCOOPS
10 doz. at 6/– a doz.   3 0 0

PICKAXES
82 at 3*d* a lb.   5 4 0

SMITHS TOOLS
Sundry sorts delivered amongst the fleet with 34/– for providing
them   19 8 2

CANS
200 hooped with brass at 3/4*d* each; 57½ doz. Hamborow cans
at 3/– at a doz.; 50 with white hoops at 18*d* each; 51½ doz. at
prices from 4/6*d* to 16/– a doz.   71 10 5

JUGS
12 four-gallon jugs at 10/– each   6 0 0

BASKETS
112 doz. at 2/– and 2/6*d* a doz.; 6 at 8*d* each, 12 at 12*d* each,
2 at 2/6*d*   13 11 0

FLASKETS
3 doz. at 12/– a doz.   1 16 0

SUGAR
5 chests at £8 each   40 0 0

CANDLESTICKS
10 doz. at 2/– a doz.   1 0 0

BEDS
927 Brazil beds[1] at 4/6*d* each   208 11 6

FAT SHEEP
100 at 12/– each; 30 at 14/–   81 0 0

BRASSCOCKS
2 doz. at 40/– a doz.   4 0 0

TERRIERS[2]
2 pairs at 2/8*d* a pair   5 4

TAPBORES[2]
48 at 12*d* each   2 8 0

VICES
2 doz. at 8/3*d* a doz.   16 6

GIMLETS
2 at 8/– each   16 0

FUNNEL PIPES
2 doz. at 12*d* each; 4 at 10*d*   1 7 4

WAISTCOATS[3]
100 at 3/– each   15 0 0

[1] Hammocks.   [2] Boring tools.
[3] Perhaps waist cloths, or canvas covering for hammocks.

14. THE EXCHEQUER ACCOUNTS FOR THE VOYAGE

LOCKS

14 doz. at 12/– a doz.; 24 at 6/– each   15 12 0

DRYFATS

234 at 5/– each, with 3/8d for staving of 6 fats   58 13 8

RHENISH WINE FATS

39 at 7/– each   13 13 0

WADMOLES[1]

629 yards at 10d a yard   26 4 2

SHIRTS

400 at prices from 20d to 2/10d each   49 3 4

CURRANT BUTTS[2]

83 at 2/8d and 2/9d each   11 6 8

LINEN BREECHES

100 pairs at 18d a pair   7 10 0

LINEN NETHERSTOCKS

100 pairs at 12d a pair   5 0 0

CANDLES

Of wax: 3 cwt. at 100/– a cwt., £15; of tallow: 1,660 lbs. at
4d a lb.; 300 lbs. at 4½d a lb.; and 2,673 lbs. of wick at 1d a lb.
for candles and making thereof, the tallow being her majesty's
own; total for tallow candles, £44 19s 0d;   59 19 0

BISCUIT BAGS

1,212 at 12d each   60 12 0

SEACOLES

3 chaldrons at 15/–; 12 at 16/–   11 17 0

PUMPS

7 at 3/4d each; one of iron at 7/–   1 10 4

TRUNKS

8 of leather at 2/– each   16 0

LEATHER JACKS[3]

100 at 2/6d each   12 10 0

CASES OF KNIVES

2 at 9/6d each   19 0

CHESTS

For bacon, with charges for packing the same   3 19 8

BOTTLES OF WOOD

12 at 20d; 6 at 16d; 200 quarter bottles at 12d   11 8 0

SHOES

172 doz. and 10 pairs at 15d to 19d a pair   149 11 4

---

[1] Musket rods.   [2] MS 'Curran buttes'.   [3] Pitchers.

STOCKINGS

15 doz. pairs worsted at 5/- and 5/6d a pair; 70 doz. pairs
woollen at 2/6d and 4/- a pair 171 12 0

OXEN

At prices from £6 11s 6d to £9 each 811 5 4

MONMOUTH CAPS

16 doz. at 26/- a doz.; 20 doz. at 20/- a doz. 40 16 0

CAPBANDS

40 doz. at 12d a doz. 2 0 0

BOWS

100 at 3/4d each 16 13 4

BOWSTRINGS

5 gross and 2 firkins to put them in 2 1 0

ARROWS

150 sheafs at 4/- a sheaf; 100 sheafs at 3/4d a sheaf, with cases
and girdles 51 13 4

MUSKET ARROWS

117 doz. at 3/- and 3/4d a doz. 19 2 4

GRAPNEL

One for a barge 1 0 3

STEEP TUBS

3 at 8/- 1 4 0

ARMOURS

1 white armour, 24/-; 1 of proof, £6; 4 at 40/- each; 2 complete at 70/- each; light armours at 20/- each and 30 graven
morions, £60. Total for armours 82 4 0

BALLAST

For sundry ships 5 1 0

CALIVERS

3 at 12/- each 1 16 0

Total for emptions and provisions _____ £24,233 1 9

CARRIAGE

BY WATER

Rouen wheat, malt, fish, beer, etc. 266 11 0

BY LAND

Cask, timber, plank, wood, etc. 53 3 8

Total for carriage _____ £279 14 8

14. THE EXCHEQUER ACCOUNTS FOR THE VOYAGE

WAGES AND ENTERTAINMENT

Allowance is made for payments to sundry ministers, artificers, sailors and others, names and the nature of the service being in many cases specified.[1] 32 payments are itemized, the largest of which are:

DAVID GEORGE			
For baking of biscuit	264	15	0
SUNDRY SAILORS			
Serving aboard her majesty's ships and others, after the rate of 10/- the man *per mensem*	1,029	0	8
COOPERS			
For work done	95	13	5
Total for wages and entertainment	£2,090	12	1

BILLETING AND BOARDWAGES

HARBOUR VICTUALS			
For companies at Plymouth and other places, at the rate of 6d the man *per diem,* serving in various merchantmen; also 28 days' victuals for 1,060 men delivered to the whole fleet (£637 8s 3d)	1,229	8	7
HARBOUR WAGES AND BOARDWAGES			
To sundry other merchantmen from 1.2.1595 to 26.5.95 at the rate of 6d the man *per diem*	330	7	10
BOARDWAGES OF SOLDIERS[2]			
At Plymouth, Tavistock and Saltash during July and August for numbers varying from time to time at 4/- the man by the week	799	0	8

[1] Those named are: William Hawkins, James Newall, William Stallenge, Richard Packe (master gunner of the *Defiance*), John Awdley, Captain Fishbourne, Edward Tyllesley (master of the *Hope*), Eustace Abbot, John Fuller, John Molton, Anthony Kitley (sailors), Thomas Clarke (drummer), Simon Wood, James White (master's mate of the *Defiance*), William Folde, Captain Stanton, one Ames (cook of the *Defiance*), Captain Arthur Chichester, Captain Marchant, Lieutenant Jacques, Edward Major, Walter Venables, John Roe, Richard Twide (sailor, released out of prison), Thomas Drake, David George (master workman in baking of biscuit), Robert Read (tailor), Humphrey Fones, Thomas Norris, Anthony Lewes, Captain Troughton, Michael Meryall (master of the *Garland*). All or nearly all of these were paid for services connected with the provisioning and equipment of the fleet.

[2] Payments to John Awdley, William Webb, Captain Anthony Platt and Captain Christopher Crofts.

BOARDWAGES AND LODGING

For 11 musicians and 7 trumpeters at London and Plymouth,
at 7/– a man by the week, with £11 10s 0d for apparel   83 14 0

BILLETTING OF SOLDIERS[1]

At Plympton, Plymouth, Milbrook, Stonehouse, Saltash and
Tavistock during July and August for numbers varying from
time to time at the rate of 4/– the man by the week or thereabouts   627 18 3

BOARDWAGES

For 8 musicians and 9 trumpeters at London and Plymouth for
Hawkins' squadron, at 7/– a man by the week for 11 weeks   65 9 0

Total for billetting and boardwages   £3,135 18 4

MISCELLANEOUS CHARGES

POSTAGE   196 11 0

TRANSPORTATION

Of the *Delight* and the *Exchange* with provisions to Plymouth   129 0 0

CASK WORK, ETC.

To bricklayers, painters, a coppersmith and a carpenter for
various jobs   24 10 2

PILOTAGE

To various masters   16 10 0

DRAWAGE AND CRANAGE

Of provisions at Plymouth   38 10 11

CELLARAGE

With hire of lofts and other rooms to bestow sundry of the
provisions at Plymouth   113 12 10

DIETS AND PHYSIC

Of sundry sick persons, with the burial of divers of them,
£14 9s 0d; 20 boatswains' dinners at the launching of the
Defiance, with wine for the generals' dinner, 44/3d; fresh victuals
and wine for the generals against their coming aboard from
16 April to 20 June, 57/–; fresh victuals for the master and
officers on the same ship, 30/10d   21 1 1

NECESSARY ALLOWANCES

To divers persons for expenses   148 6 0

PREST MONEY

1d a man a mile, with presters' charges (30/–)   235 13 4

[1] Payments to Captains Humphrey Reynolds, John Marchant, Christopher Crofts
and Anthony Platt, and to Thomas Norris.

CONDUCT MONEY
For sundry men discharged   5 6 0
PORTAGE OF MONEY
To Thomas Myddelton and Martin Sherryff 12 15 8
PROVISIONS DELIVERED
Various munitions delivered to her majesty's store by Hawkins
in lieu of like quantities lent out to him[1]   369 0 0
                 ————————
Total of miscellaneous charges   £1,310 17 0

DIETS, WAGES AND ENTERTAINMENT
AFTER RETURN

The accountants are also allowed for moneys paid by Thomas Myddelton and his ministers to the captains, soldiers and sailors by order of Sir Robert Cecil and Sir John Fortescue after the return of the fleet. In particular to the following:

HUMPHREY REYNOLDS, CAPTAIN OF THE 'GARLAND'
For his diets from 22 July 1595 to 2 June 1596, £30; to his
crew for the same period, £1,448 12s 6d; to 3 mariners for
conduct on discharge, 27/6d   1,480 0 0
JONAS BODENHAM, CAPTAIN OF THE 'DEFIANCE'
His diets, £40; crew, £1,443 15s 2d; 1 conduct, 15/- 1,484 10 2
GILBERT YORKE, THOMAS DRAKE, AND SAMUEL THOMAS
Severally captains of the *Hope*. Their diets, £30; crew,
£937 2s 10d; 11 conducts, £4 12s 6d   971 15 4
JOHN TROUGHTON, CAPTAIN OF THE 'BONAVENTURE'
His diets, £30; crew, £1,014 16s 8d; 21 conducts, £10 2s 6d 1,054 19 2
THOMAS DRAKE AND HENRY SAVILE
Captains of the *Adventure*. Their diets, £30; crew, £650 13s 11d 680 13 11
WILLIAM WYNTER, CAPTAIN OF THE 'FORESIGHT'
His diets, £30; crew, £794 5s 7d; 6 conducts, £3   827 5 7
DAVID SERROCOLD, CAPTAIN OF THE 'CONCORD'
His diets, £20; crew, £355 12s 6d; 6 conducts, 45/-   377 17 6
RICHARD BARNARD, CAPTAIN OF THE 'SUSAN
BONAVENTURE'
His diets, £20; crew, £446 5s 9d; 8 conducts, 40/-   468 5 9
CHARLES CAESAR, CAPTAIN OF THE 'AMITY'
His diets, £20; crew, £339 1s 8d   359 1 8

[1] Cp. document 15.

WILLIAM MYDDELTON, CAPTAIN OF THE 'SALOMON BONAVENTURE'
His diets, £20; crew, £360 13s 3d; 5 conducts, 25/-   381 18 3

WILLIAM MORRICE, CAPTAIN OF THE 'ELIZABETH CONSTANT'
His diets, £20; crew, £384 19s 6d   404 19 6

ALEXANDER VAUGHAN, CAPTAIN OF THE 'SAKER'
His diets, £20; crew, £443 2s 1d   463 2 1

JAMES FENTON, CAPTAIN OF THE 'JOHN BONAVENTURE'
His diets, £10; crew, £316 18s 2d   326 18 2

EDWARD GOODWIN, CAPTAIN OF THE 'JEWEL'
His diets, £10; crew, £313 3s 10d   323 3 10

TIMOTHY SHOTTEN, CAPTAIN OF THE 'PEGASUS'
His diets, £10; crew, £259 9s 9d   269 9 9

BERNARD DRAKE, CAPTAIN OF THE 'FELIX'
His diets, £20; crew, £300 17s 6d; 3 conducts, 15/-   321 12 6

HENRY AUSTEN, CAPTAIN OF THE 'DESIRE'
His diets, £10; crew, £166 15s 3d   176 15 3

ANTHONY LISTER, MASTER OF THE 'HELP'
and to divers mariners with him   83 0 10

PIERS LEMON, MASTER OF THE 'JOHN TRELAWNEY'
and to sundry of the said ship's company that returned in divers ships   58 7 4

GEORGE LARRYMAN
For conduct money paid to all mariners of her majesty's 6 ships from Chatham to Deptford to receive their wages   40 0 0

STEPHEN ENGLESBY AND JOHN AUSTEN
For bringing the *Foresight,* the *Defiance* and the *Garland* from the Downs to Chatham   12 16 10

SUNDRY CAPTAINS, MASTERS, PURSERS AND OTHERS
For victuals provided for bringing about the queen's and sundry merchant ships from Plymouth and other places into the Thames   1,419 9 7

Total of diets, wages, etc. after return   £11,986 3 0

SOLDIERS' PAY

Also the accountants are allowed for money paid to Nicholas Baskerville and Arthur Chichester for a third part due to the soldiers upon their return, the same being parcel of

£4,917 5s 3d due to her majesty and these accountants upon
gold, silver, plate, pearl, etc. By agreement

Total paid to the soldiers for thirds   £666 13 4

THE ACCOUNTANTS' THIRDS

They are also allowed for one third part of the returns after
deduction of the soldiers' share,

That is   £1,416 17 4

PRICE OF SUNDRY PEARLS

They are also allowed for the price of sundry pearls before
charged in this account which were on her majesty's command
delivered to Mistress Mary Radcliffe

Total   £831 8 4

REWARD TO CERTAIN SOLDIERS

They are also allowed for money given by her highness by way
of gracious reward to certain soldiers upon their return (sums
given to the companies of various captains specified)

Total   £214 0 0

SUM TOTAL OF THE ALLOWANCES AND PAYMENTS
AFORESAID:

                                                         £46,164 5 10

And so the said accountants stand in debt, £1,875 5s 4d, against
which further small sums are set off, reducing the debt to
£1,485 1s 8d, which sum is paid into her majesty's receipt at
Westminster, 14 March 1603. And so the said accountants do here
remain clearly discharged and quit. T. Buckhurst. J. Fortescue.]

15. *The account of the ordinance*[1]

[The declaration of the account of Lady Margaret Hawkins and
Thomas Drake esquire for the receipt of ordinance and munitions

[1] P.R.O., A.O./1/1688/30. As the last part of this document implies, it relates
directly to document 14, being signed by the same officers and presumably
produced about the same time (March 1603). The text is here modernized and
slightly contracted in the same way as document 14.

for six of her majesty's ships and for the amounts returned to the ordinance office after the voyage:[1]

	Issued	Returned
BRASS ORDINANCE		
Cannon periers	4	4
Demi-cannons	6	6
Culverins	54	53
Demi-culverins	72	72
Sakers	30	30
Minions	6	6
Falcons	2	2
Fowlers	13	13
Chambers to fowlers	26	25
Portpieces	10	10
Chambers to portpieces	20	20
CAST IRON ORDINANCE		
Demi-culverins	6	6
Sakers	2	2
IRON ROUNDSHOT		
Demi-cannon	160	88
Culverin	1,720	490
Demi-culverin	2,970	993
Saker	1,647	319
Minion	300	115
Falcon	500	130
IRON CROSSBAR SHOT		
Demi-cannon	50	27
Culverin	340	135
Demi-culverin	480	191
Saker	260	110
Minion	60	43
Falcon	30	12
CHAIN SHOT	17	1
JOINTED SHOT	8	4
HAIL SHOT	6,800	1,185

[1] This prefatory passage rehearses a warrant, dated 19 May 1595, issued to Sir George Carew, lieutenant of the ordinance, authorizing him to deliver the guns and munitions; also an indenture between Drake and Hawkins and the lieutenant and other officers of the ordinance for the 'reanswering' of the same.

15. THE ACCOUNT OF THE ORDINANCE

	Issued	Returned
STONE SHOT		
Canon perier	60	36
Portpiece	150	80
Fowler	220	135
CORNPOWDER	16 lasts, 350 lbs.	4,000 lbs.
MATCH	55 cwt.	840 lbs.
LEAD		
For shot	54 cwt.	2 cwt.
Sheet lead	520 lbs.	nil
Covers of lead	84	41
SMALL GUNS AND THEIR FURNITURE		
Muskets	520	270
Bandeliers	520	220
Rests	520	127
Moulds	520	173
Calivers	220	112
Bandeliers, flasks and touchboxes to them	220	70
Moulds	220	70
ARTILLERY		
Longbows	174	107
Longbow arrows	340 sheafs	179
Bowstrings	37 doz.	5 doz.
Longbow arrows for fireworks	144	92
Arrows with fireworks	64	70[1]
Crossbows for fireballs	2	2
Balls with receipts to them	77	20
Slurbows	10	7
Slurbow arrows for fireworks	130	12
Slurbow arrows with fireworks	36	34
Balls with fireworks	54	36
Musket arrows	42 doz.	20 doz.
Tampions to them	35 doz.	nil
MUNITIONS		
Long pikes	454	179
Short pikes	160	27
Pikes with fireworks	28	8
Black bills	350	166
Trunks with fireworks	27	26

[1] Sic.

73

	Issued	Returned
HABILIMENTS OF WAR		
Crows of iron	95	50
Sledges of iron	14	5
Pickhammers	12	2
Spikes of iron	90	2
Nails	11,000	nil
Copper nails	245	nil
Linchpins	148 pr.	12 pr.
Talling hooks spare	228 pr.	24 pr.
Ladle hooks	267 pr.	66 pr.
Wadhooks	21	14
Melting ladles	36	11
Forelock keys	126	3 pr.
Ladles[1]	189	123
Cases of plate[1]	209	98
Funnels of plate	25	11
CORDAGE		
Britchings ready cut	.151	202[2]
Bowsing tackles	138 pr.	145 pr.[2]
Rope of sundry sorts	15,314 lbs.	314 lbs.
Lashers	55	121[2]
CARPENTERS AND TURNERS WORK		
Trucks spare	39 pr.	10 pr.
Axle-trees[3]	48	13
Formers for cartouches	33	14
Forelocks of wood	40	6
Chests for bows and arrows	41	10
Commanders	21	5
Tampions of wood	1,600	nil
Pulleys, double and single	254 pr.	36 pr.
Heads and rammers	144 pr.	18 pr.
Coigns	126	48
Scallops	41	4
Ladlestaves	18 doz., 4	2 doz., 7
Ladlestaves for trunks	60	9
OTHER NECESSARIES		
Grand barrels	12	1

[1] The numbers for various types of gun are specified.
[2] Made of new rope.   [3] MS 'Extrees'.

74

	Issued	Returned
Budgebarrels	38	12
Leather bags	39	1
Sheepskins	16½ doz.	nil
Small baskets	10 doz.	6
Lanthorns	12	nil
Tanned hides	34	14
Canvas for cartouches	420 ells	nil
Paper royal	24 quire	nil
Oil	6 gallons	nil
Tallow	½ cwt.	nil
Thread	3 lbs.	nil
Glue	3 lbs.	nil
Needles	6 doz.	nil

STUFF FOR FIREWORKS

	Issued	Returned
Saltpetre	5 cwt.	
Sulphur	5 cwt.	
Camphor	5 lbs.	
Rosin[1]	10 lbs.	
Asafetida	15 lbs.	
Salamoniac	10 lbs.	
Linseed oil	5 gallons	
Turpentine	120 lbs.	
Verdigris	10 lbs.	nil
Rosin	420 lbs.	
Marlin	2 cwt.	
Twine	40 lbs.	
Pitch	2 barrels	
Tallow	30 lbs.	
Canvas	50 ells	
Trunks for fireworks	50	

Sum total of the deficiencies, £2,846 17s 5½d, whereof deducted for powder and shot received by the master of the ordinance for the Cadiz voyage £245 5s 0d. The remainder is wholly allowed the accountants (a) because her majesty was to furnish these ships at her proper costs and charges for her adventure in the voyage and (b) because the wastage of the queen's ships and the merchantmen,

[1] MS 'Rosoing'.

if ratably charged according to the queen's responsibility for two thirds of all charges, would have been to her highness' loss by the sum of £800. Therefore the accountants are declared quit. T. Buckhurst. J. Fortescue.]

16. *Baskerville's conditions of acceptance of the office of colonel-general*[1]

First to have them sett downe whatt entertaynment I shall have for this office of collonell generall, which if they refuse tournyng me of to the venter of the Jorney, then to sett me downe under their handes and sealles whatt parte I shall have owtt of the sayd venter. *he is to have 500ᶫⁱ adventure. he shall have iij partes of any foure shares yᵗ any of yᵉ Generalls shall have.*

Secondly seing the comande of the menn of warr is delyverid to me by her maiesties comysion as Collonell generall, I callenge as of due the makinge of all Inferyer officers under me, as hathe bin ever in all warrs permyttid to everye particuler collonell by the Lawe of Armes. *for this they are both sides content to be overruled by my Lords.*

Thirdly that all monnyes I shall lay owtt for the better furnyshing of my self in this viage uppon due prooffes made to the generalls (if I am tournid to the fortune of the vyage) may be alowid me owtt of the venture, and Likewise such reasonable other chargis as I shalbe forcid to spend att plymouth and ells wher in atending the sayd vyage after their departure from hence. *this article is answered before in the first.*

Fourthely since the menn of warr must go upon the thirds only, and nott in her maiesties pay I desire that this agreement may be signed indenture wiss between the generalls and the Colonell and other Cheffe officers of the menn of warr and thatt wee may have an officer payd by us to be permittid to Loke into the treasure and other comodities thatt shalbe gotten and to take Inventory of Itt and thatt devision may be made ther of owr partes befor our

---

[1] Hatfield MSS, 34, no. 21. A draft which does not differ in substance is in B.M., Harleian MSS, 4762, ff. 8–9. The notes (here italicized) are marginal and in a different hand. Two such notes on the last two items are illegible.

retourne. *they are content to lett him be acquainted with all or any other principall men of quality.*

Fyftly I desire thatt the captains and other Cheffe officers may have some Imprest for their better furnyshing of ensignes dromes armes for themselves and for their officers and that every one of them may hear be apoyntid by the generalls In whatt shipe he is to goe and thatt the benyfitt of the best placis In the ships may be devided betwene the sea and Land Captains Indifferently and thatt they and their officers *with* the rest of other gallant menn of warr may be permytid to goe by sea to plymouthe and nott forcid upon their owne charge to goe by Land *which* they ar in noe Cass able to doe having attendid this Jorney past all exspectacion. *this shall not be stood upon for the Captaynes shall be helped by them thatt named them.*

Sixtly thatt If devision shall nott be made befor our retourne and thatt ther be by her m*ajesties* apoyntment comysioners sentt downe bothe to vewe the thinges gotten both from her m*ajesties* and from the other venturers my request is thatt I Lykwise be apoyntid one of them in the behalf of the menn of warre, who are to have 3 part*es* owt of the sayd bottye.

Lastly I desire (thatt since ther is an equall division betwene the owners of the ships adventurers and menn of warr In thatt shalbe gotten In this viage) thatt the Lyke Course may be taken *with* us for the securyty of our parte, as is taken *with* them in all thing*es* and In as full and ample manner.

17. *Baskerville's bill of adventure*[1]

1595 xxiiij° die Julij Anno R*egine* Elizabeth xxxvij°
The same daie and yeare, Wee S*ir* Francis drake, and S*ir* John hawkyns knight*es* do acknowledge by theis pr*esentes*, That S*ir* thomas Baskervile knight shall have the adventure of Five hundred

---

[1] B.M., Harleian MSS, 4762, f. 132. Signed and sealed by Drake and Hawkins. Baskerville sent this document to his father-in-law, Sir Thomas Throckmorton, before he sailed, and on his arrival home asked for its return. Baskerville did not invest this sum, but was granted this share in lieu of pay. He probably did, however, adventure some money in the voyage (see document 47).

poundes of current English money, in this vioadge, To be (by
Gods permission) perfourmed into forrayne partes, with six of her
majesties shippes and soundrie other marchantes shipps Latelie
commytted to our chardge: And according to the somme, The said
Sir Thomas Baskervile, his executors or assignes shall receave the
proffytte of such Commodities as shalbe retourned in the same
vioadge, ratablie, and as farre fourth as her Majestie or any other
Adventurer shall have in the like case. Geiven under our handes,
the daie & yeare first above wrytten.

      fra: Drake   John Hawkyns

III. *The English Narratives*

The following are the contemporary English narratives known to be extant.

1: *The Bodleian Journal*[1]   2: *'The briefe of our voyage'*[2]

These two journals, typical of the most elementary kind of Elizabethan sea-journal, are of about 1,000 words each. Though of unknown authorship, they are clearly connected, since their texts are nearly identical, except for the omission from 2 of all the events between 12 November 1595 and 1 March 1595/6 and from 1 of the list of lost ships and officers, which appears as an appendix to 2. They add little to other available information.

3: *The Adams Journal*[3]

A journal of about 2,000 words, apparently collated from two copies available to Adams, this contains a useful list of the fleet and some other detail not otherwise known. Like the two above mentioned, it is crude in form and rather inaccurate in content. The author remains unknown.

4: *The 'Full Relation'*[4]

Another sea-journal, of a more ambitious kind, about 5,000 words in length, containing a list of the land officers, substantial descriptive

[1] Bodleian Library, Tanner MSS, 77, f. 95. Headed 'Anno dominie 1596'. Herein referred to as Bodleian Journal.

[2] B.M., Sloane MSS, 2177, ff. 18–19. Headed 'The briefe of our voyage with Sir Frauncis Drake and Sir John Hawkins into the West Indies'. Herein referred to as 'The briefe of our voyage'.

[3] William Adams, 'Chronicle of Bristol', ff. 212–19 (Bristol Record Office, which also holds another copy of the MS with only slight variations of text in respect of this voyage). Published: Francis F. Fox (ed.), *Adams's Chronicle of Bristol* (Bristol, 1910), pp. 143–9. A text of this part of the chronicle, based on the two MSS, is to be published by the Bristol Record Society. Herein referred to as Adams Journal.

[4] 'A Full Relation of Another Voyage made by Sir Francis Drake and others to the West Indies; who set forth from *Plimouth* the 28. of *August*, 1595.' Published together with Walter Bigges, *A Summarie and True Discourse of Sir Francis Drake's*

passages and a considerable amount of detail otherwise unrecorded. Although what he adds to the major narratives (nos. 6–9 below) is not of much significance, the author has an innocent curiosity and a memory for detail which lend his story a special charm.

5: Monson[1]

William Monson was already an active sea-captain by this time and was acquainted, both then and later, with some of the adventurers, including notably the earl of Essex. On the other hand he did not, so far as is known, play any part in the proceedings himself. His very brief account contains obvious inaccuracies (for instance, that Hawkins' death was hastened by grief at the repulse at Puerto Rico) and considerably more comment than factual substance. It has already been remarked that Monson probably had good grounds, by virtue of his association with Essex, for his comment on the aims of the venture, but in other respects his account, whatever its interest as an expression of opinion by an admiral of the navy, is of limited value as a source.

6: 'The voyage truely discoursed'[2]

This account, printed by Hakluyt in 1600, is easily the best of the sea-journals relating to the voyage, being considerably more informative and accurate than the others. As a detached record of the voyage by a professional seaman, it lacks the strong personal flavour of the three accounts printed below, but is generally more reliable and contains much detail not to be found elsewhere.

7: Maynarde[3]

Thomas Maynarde belonged to the Devonshire family of May-nardes, who were kinsmen of the Drakes. He was probably the

West-Indian Voyage (1652). Authorship unknown; no manuscript or earlier printing has been traced. Herein referred to as 'Full Relation'.

[1] M. Oppenheim (ed.), *The Naval Tracts of Sir William Monson,* I (1902), 312–15 prints a modernized text based on several MSS versions, adding his own valuable notes. Herein referred to as Monson.

[2] *Principal Navigations,* III (1600), 583–90 (X (1904), 226–45). Author unknown, but from internal evidence appears to have sailed aboard the *Phoenix.* Extract, document 41 below. Herein referred to as VTD.

[3] Document 18. Herein referred to as Maynarde.

second son of John Maynarde, who held the manor of Sherford from Sir Francis.[1] On this assumption the writer of our narrative was a protégé of Drake's and one of his personal *entourage,* a young man. His close attachment to the general lends his story, admirably written as it is, a certain pathos, especially because Maynarde himself displays an arrogance and impatience which recall Drake's younger days. But Maynarde was an observant and thoughtful critic of strategy and tactics; it may be doubted whether his judgement of situations at the time was as keen and sound as he was eager to claim after the event, but his comments on the conception and conduct of the campaign are generally restrained, reasonable and articulate. They are indeed, frequently borne out by other evidence, as are his perceptive character sketches of Drake and Hawkins.

8: Troughton[2]

John Troughton, captain of the *Elizabeth Bonaventure,* was as near to being a professional naval officer as it was possible to be in Elizabeth's day, and was closely associated with Sir John Hawkins.[3] His comparatively short account (about 1,800 words) is, however, marked less by professionalism than by partisanship for Hawkins against Drake and personal rancour directed at Baskerville, whose assumption of the general command at Porto Belo he clearly resented. Troughton's patent bitterness vitiates all his criticism, but is itself a vivid illustration of the factional rivalry which divided the force. Drake, Hawkins and Baskerville each commanded the special loyalty of certain men bound to them by ties of kinship, interest and patronage, and this (if we understand

---

[1] J. L. Vivian (ed.), *The Visitations of the County of Devon* (Exeter, 1895), p. 561; B.M., Harleian MSS, 1162, f. 117; Somerset House, P.C.C., 50 Barrington; Eliott-Drake, *Family and Heirs,* 1, 59. Thomas Maynarde died in 1626. He refers in the narrative to Brute Browne (of Langtree, Devon) as his 'brother', which might mean half-brother or brother-in-law.

[2] Document 19.

[3] He continued to hold naval commands until at least 1600 (Oppenheim, *Monson's Tracts,* 11 (1902), 38, 87, 90, 114). On 16 June 1595 he witnessed a codicil to Hawkins' will (Somerset House, P.C.C., 26 Drake). After the voyage he wrote to the queen on Hawkins' behalf, mentioning a further codicil and defending his own conduct in the return voyage (document 42).

Elizabethan society and Elizabethan fighting men aright) must have been at least as powerful a source of friction as jealousy between soldiers and seamen.

9: Baskerville[1]

Sir Thomas Baskerville's 'discourse' is of particular interest as the statement of the man who bore the chief responsibility for the land forces and, after Drake's death, for the entire fleet.

The author appears to have been a base-son of Thomas Baskerville, esquire, servant to Walter Devereux, first earl of Essex. After the earl's death the younger Thomas became servant in livery to the earl of Leicester and later (without Leicester's consent) servant in livery to Robert, the second earl of Essex.[2] Sir Thomas is described as of Goodrest, Warwickshire, and married Mary, daughter of Sir Thomas Throckmorton of Tortworth, Gloucestershire, whose first wife was the daughter of Sir Richard Berkeley. Baskerville's brother Nicholas married Constance, daughter of George Huntley of Boxwell, Gloucestershire, with which family the Throckmortons of Tortworth were already connected.[3]

In 1585 Thomas Baskerville went out to the Low Countries as a captain in Leicester's expeditionary force and distinguished himself by his bravery in the defence of Sluys in 1587, being knighted the following year by Peregrine Bertie, Lord Willoughby, whom he accompanied to France in 1589. In 1591–2 he served under

[1] Document 20.

[2] Longleat MSS, Devereux Papers, Vol. v, ff. 24–24v. I am indebted for this and other information about Baskerville to Dr H. A. Lloyd. Sir Thomas is described in the 1665 visitation of Berkshire (B.M. Additional MSS, 14284, f. 38) as son of Henry Baskerville of the City of Hereford. The latter was closely related to Sir James Baskerville, reported in 1538 to be steward of Pembrokeshire and to have married the daughter of Walter Devereux, Lord Ferrers of Chartley (Williams, *Parliamentary History of Wales*, p. 52; J. R. Gairdner (ed.), *Letters and Papers, Foreign and Domestic, of the Reign of Henry VIII*, XIII, pt. i (1892), no. 320). The second earl of Essex wrote in 1589 thanking Burghley 'for the bestowing of the ward of my cosin Baskervile' (B.M., Lansdowne MSS, 60, f. 203). Whatever doubts may linger about Sir Thomas' parentage, his connection with the Devereux is scarcely questionable.

[3] J. Maclean and W. C. Heane (eds.), *The Visitation of Gloucestershire, 1623* (1885).

Essex as sergeant-major of the English army in Normandy and it was Essex who gained him a seat in Parliament for Caermarthen boroughs in 1593. In 1594 he was sergeant-major of the expeditionary force sent to Brest and at this time had dealings with Sir John Hawkins in connection with the transport of the troops. After a successful campaign he returned to England in February 1595. Baskerville was therefore an experienced and trusted soldier when he was appointed, by Essex's agency, colonel-general of the army bound for Panama. He had even demonstrated his devotion to duty and to the art of war by writing a considerable treatise on the office of sergeant-major, a work well grounded in continental theory and practice. This remained unpublished, but the ambition which inspired it may be read in Baskerville's hand on the flyleaf: 'Celuy est assez malheureux que de son travayle n'espere aucune guerdon.'[1]

As to his character, Essex's recommendation of him (to Cecil) as 'a very worthy gentleman and as honest as any man that lives'[2] cannot be given much weight, while his own vehement assertion of his honesty in a letter to his wife[3] is even less admissible as evidence. Sir Nicholas Clifford, who had known him for some years, summed him up as 'a true lover of himself'[4] and his hard bargaining over his position and interest in the voyage suggests that he was no less careful of his personal advantage than most of Elizabeth's men of war.[5] He represented the enterprise to his wife as a treasure hunt, 'the fortune of which being a matter so well digested, I hope shall settell our fortune'.[6] 'I leave then to thy Judgmennt,' he wrote, 'whyther Itt be nott six mounthes well spent to gett such a botye'.[7] There was nothing abnormal in this attitude, however, nor does anything in the record of the voyage necessarily affect Baskerville's reputation as a brave soldier.

[1] *Dictionary of National Biography; Cal. Hatfield MSS,* iv, 169, 293, 563; v, 240; P.R.O., E. 351/243; document 8; B.M., Harleian MSS, 5260.
[2] *Cal. Hatfield MSS,* vi, 195–6 (24 May 1596).
[3] Document 47.
[4] Document 13.
[5] Document 16.
[6] B.M., Harleian MSS, 4762, f. 109 (24 July 1595).
[7] B.M., Harleian MSS, 4762, f. 14 (21 August 1595).

At first reading, perhaps, the qualities the 'discourse' may suggest are naïvety and a certain myopic self-centredness. Hawkins is not mentioned at all and there is very little about Drake. The Canaries episode is omitted altogether and nothing is said about the strategic issues, nor even about the shipping for which Baskerville was responsible. His own meaningless skirmishings around Río de la Hacha receive exorbitant attention. Was he unaware, even months later, of the significance of this wasted time? Did he simply fail to imagine what the queen and the Cecils would demand to know? Was he so lacking in sympathy and perception, so preoccupied with his own doings, that the conduct, the leadership and even the deaths of Drake and Hawkins left him indifferent? In considering such questions, however, it must be borne in mind that this was essentially an exercise in self-exculpation. Perhaps it seemed advisable to keep silence for the time being on large and disputable issues, rather than to anticipate awkward questions. It must be allowed, too, that Baskerville did himself less than justice. Although much might be said in criticism of his conduct of the army, he deserves credit for the retreat from Capirilla after that gruelling march and combat, where his troops, by all accounts, fought well; and for re-organizing and keeping the fleet sufficiently together to repulse Avellaneda.[1] What his contemporaries thought of his performance is not clear, for his rapid promotion to the colonel-generalcy of the army in Picardy indicates merely that he retained Essex's favour. He died in Picardy on 4 June 1597, leaving his estate to his wife, 'with the bringing uppe of my childe, and after her decease to come unto my young sonne. And I doubt not but my lord of Essex wyll have a care of him'.[2]

Of these nine narratives Maynarde, Troughton and Baskerville have been chosen for presentation here not only for their intrinsic interest but also because the first two have been inadequately, and the last not at all published before. The only other account of

[1] The inference from Troughton's account that there was some dispute over Baskerville's assumption of the command is supported by the statement attributed to Andrés de Yegros, a Spaniard who escaped from the English fleet at Porto Belo (document 37).

[2] Somerset House, P.C.C., 59 Kidd.

comparable importance, Hakluyt's 'The voyage truely dis-coursed', is easily accessible in its only known version. Maynarde, Troughton and Baskerville, moreover, appropriately represent the three component factions in the expedition.

Two other documents of narrative significance, the anonymous log and the profiles of the coast, from both of which extracts have been selected to illustrate this book, are the subject of a special note by Commander Waters (see Appendix).

18. Thomas Maynarde's narrative[1]

Sir Francis Drake his voyage 1595

It appears by ye attempts and knowen purposes of the Spaniarde, as by his greedy desire to bee our neighboure in Bretaine, his fortifienge upon the river of Brest, to gaine so neare us a quiet and safe rode for his fleet, his carelesnes in losinge the stronge houldes and townes which he posessed in the lowe countries not followinge those warres in that heate which he wonted. the rebellious rysinge of the Earle of Tyrone (wrought or drawen thereto undoubtedly by his wicked practises) that hee leaveth no means unatempted which hee judged might bee a furtherance to turne our tranquilitie into accursed thraldom: so robbinge us of that quiet peace which

[1] B.M., Additional MSS, 5209. The MS, written and signed in the same Elizabethan hand, takes up the greater part of a small volume. This contains only one other item, following directly after the narrative – a draft of a letter addressed to Sir Ralph Winwood, unfinished and undated, which reports briefly a voyage for the West Indies by way of the Cape Verdes, where great misfortunes of storm and sickness apparently beset the expedition. Maynarde's own words – 'Your loves I thinke can pardon these faltes & secret them from the vew of others' – leave room for doubt as to whether he intended his narrative for publication. The marked literary flavour of his style, however, suggests that he was writing with a general public in mind and was merely signifying, in the passage quoted, his readiness to accept some editing of his text. In any case it is hardly surprising that such a critical account of such a story of failure should not have reached print until the nineteenth century. It was first published in W. D. Cooley (ed.), *Sir Francis Drake his Voyage, 1595, by Thomas Maynarde, together with the Spanish Account of Drake's attack on Puerto Rico* (Hakluyt Society, 1st series, IV, 1849), but with many errors of transcription, a few of which are seriously misleading.

wee from the hands of Her Majestie next under God aboundantly enjoye. This his blood-thirstie desire foreseene by the wisedome of our Queene and counsayle they helde no better meanes to curbe his unjust pretenses then by sendinge forces to invade him in that kingdome from whence hee hath feathers to flye to the toppe of his high desires, they knowenge that if for two or three yeeres a blowe were given him there that might hinder the cominge into Spaine of his treasure, his povertie by reason of his dayly huge payements woulde be so greate and his men of warre most of them mercenaries y^t assuredly would fall from him, so woulde he have more neede of meanes to keepe his owne territories then he nowe hath of super-fluitie to thruste into others rights.

This invasion was spoken of in June 1594. a longe time before it was put in execution[1] and it beinge partly resolved on Sir Francis Drake was named generall in November folowinge. A man of greate spirit and fitt to undertake matters, In my poore oppinion better able to conduct forces and discreetly to governe in con-ductinge them to places where service was to be done, then to comande in the execution therof. But assuredly his very name was a greate terror to the enemie in all those partes havinge hearetofore done many thinges in those countries to his honorable fame and profitt. But entringe into them as the childe of fortune it maye be his selfewilled and peremptorie comand was doubted. And that caused her majestie (as should seeme) to joyne Sir John Hawkins in equall commission.[2] A man oulde and warie entringe into matters with so laden a foote, that the others meate woulde be eaten before his spit could come to the fire. men of so different natures and dispositions that what the one desireth the other would commonly oppose against. And though theyr warye cariages sequestred it from meaner wittes yet it was apparently seene to better judgments before our goenge from Plymouth. that whom the one loved the other smaly esteemed. Agreeinge best (for what I could conjecture) in

---

[1] It had been mooted earlier still, according to Sir Richard Hawkins. See p. 12 above.

[2] Since Hawkins' name had been associated with Drake's in this project from the first, Maynarde's surmise may be mistaken. The assumption that Drake would have disliked dividing the command is reasonable, but he may have needed his kinsman's direct involvement to get the project accepted.

givinge out a glorious title to theyr intended jorneye, and in not so well victualinge yᵉ navie as (I deeme) was her majesties pleasure it shoulde bee, both of them served them to goode purpose, for from this havinge the distributinge of so greate sommes theyr miserable providinge for us would free them from incurringe any greate losse whatsoever befell of the jorney.[1] And the former drewe unto them so greate repaire of voluntaries that they had choice to discharge suche fewe as they had pressed and to enforce the staye of others which gladly would be pertakers of theyr voyage. But notwithstandinge matters were forward and that they had drawen together nere 3000 men and had ready furnished 27 shippes, wherof 6 were her majesties yet many times was it very doubtfull whether the jorney should proceed. and had not the newes of a gallion of the kinge of Spaine which was driven into St. John de Portrico with 2 millions and a halfe of tresure come unto them by the reporte of certaine prisoners wherof they advertised her majestie it is very likely it had beene broken. But her majestie persuaded by them of the easie takinge therof comanded them to hast theyr departure.

So on Thursday beinge the 28 of August in the yeare 1595 havinge stayed two moneth in Plymouth we went thence 27 sayle and were 2500 men of all sortes. This fleet was devided into 2 squadrons not that it was so appointed by her Majestie for from her was granted as powerfull authoritie unto eyther of them over the whole, as any parte But Sir Francis victualinge yᵉ tone halfe and Sir John the other, it made them as men afectinge what they had done to chalenge a greater prerogative over them then the whole, wherin they wronged themselves and the action: for wee had not runne 60 or 70 leagues in our course before a flagge of councell was put out in the garlande unto which all comanders with the cheife masters & gentlemen repayred. Sir Francis complayned that he had a 300 men more in his squadron then were in the other, and that hee was much pestered in his owne shipp wherof hee would gladly be eased. Sir John gave no other hearinge to this motion, but seemed to dislike that hee should bringe more then was concluded betwixt them. & this drewe them to some cholericke speeches. But Sir

[1] See Ch. 2 for details of the victualling. It is impossible to prove or disprove this charge.

John would not receave any unles he were entreated: to this Sir Francis stoute hearte could never be driven. This was on the 2cond of September, and after they were somwhat qualified they acquainted us that Sir Thomas Baskervile our coronell generall was of theyr counsayle by vertue of the broade seale and that they would take unto them Sir Nicholas Clifforde and the other Captaines appointed by her Majestie, which were 11 for the Land and 4 for the shippes in which they themselves went not. They gave us instructions for directinge our course if by foule weather or mischange any should bee severed & orders what alowances we should put our men unto for preservation of victualls with other necessary instructions. In the end Sir John revealed the places whether wee were bound, in hearinge of the basest mariner. observinge therin no warlicke or provident advice, nor was it ever amended to the time of theyr deaths, but so he named St. John de Porterico where the treasure before spoken of was to be taken even withoute blowes, from whence we should go directly to Numbre de dios and so over land to Panama what other things should fall out by the way he esteemed them not worth the naminge. This beinge sufficient to make a farre greater armie rich to theyr content. some 7 or 8 dayes after this, we were called aboarde the Defiance where Sir Francis Drake propoundinge unto us whether we should give upon the Canaries or Maderas for hee was resolved to put for one of them by the way. We seeinge his bent and the earnestnes of the coronel generall together with the apparant likelihood of profit, might soone have bin drawen therto, but consideringe the weightie matters we had undertaken & how needfull it was to hasten us thether but generall haukins utterly mislikinge this motion it beinge a matter as hee saide never before thought of and knewe no cause why the fleete should staye in any place till they came to the Indies unles it should be by his takinge in of so great numbers to consume his waters and other provision the which if Sir Francis would acknowledge, hee would ridde him and releive him the best hee could. Now the fyer which laye hid in theyr stommackes began to breake forth. and had not the coronell pacified them it would have growen farther, but theyr heate somwhat abated, they concluded to dine next day aboarde the garlande with Sir John when it was resolved[1] that we should put for the Grand Canaries though in my conscience whatsoever his tonge said Sir Johns harte was against, these matters were well qualified and for that place we shaped our course. In which we met with a smale flemminge bounde for the streights and a small manne of Warre of Waymouth who kept us companie to the canaries.[2] On Wensday the 24 day we had sight of Lancerotta and Forteventura the 25 all night we descried the Canaries it beinge a monethe after our departure from Plymmothe on Fryday beinge the 26 we came to anchor. some saker shott from a forte which stands to the West.Norwest of the harboure. Sir Francis spent much time in seekinge out the fittest place to land, ye enimie therby gaininge time to drawe theyr forces in redines to impeach our approch, at length we puttinge for the shore in our boates and pinnaces found a great seege & such power of men to encounter us that it was then thought it would hazarde the whole action if wee should give further upon it, wherupon we returned without receivinge or doinge any harme worthy the writinge, but undoubtedly had we lanced under the forte at our first cominge to anchor we had put fayre to bee possessors of the towne for the delayes gave the enimie greate stomackes[3] & daunted our owne and it beinge the first service our new men were brought into it was to be doubted they would prove the worse ye whole jorney folowinge. We presently wayed hence and came to anchor ye 27 at the West SouthWest parte of this Iland, where wee watered. Heere Captaine Grimstone. one of the 12 captaines for Lande was slaine by the mountanors with his boy & a surgeon.[4] hence wee departed the 28

---

[1] Troughton (document 19): 'uppon the confessinge of need', but it may be doubted whether this was more than an excuse for attacking Las Palmas, since water could be (and was) obtained without fighting, while the victuals, though not supplemented in the Canaries, appear to have remained sufficient, at least until the fleet reached the Caribbean.

[2] The Weymouth man joined on 9 September and ten days later 'we met with a Frigate of the Earle of *Cumberlands* who brought us word that the Kings men of Warre were going homewards' ('Full Relation').

[3] See Ch. 4. The best English account of the episode is VTD.

[4] VTD: 'the Salomons Chirurgian taken prisoner, who disclosed our pretended voyage as much as in him lay: so as the Viceroy sent a caravel of adviso into the Indies'. But see Ch. 4 below.

houldinge our course southWest 3 weekes then wee ran West SouthWest & West and by South till the 27 of October on which day we had sight of Maten[1] an Ilande lyenge southest from Dominica, our generalls ment to water at Gadalupe for Dominica beinge inhabited by Indians our men straglinge som would have theyr throates cutte. Generall Drake lyenge a heade the fleete ran in by the mouth of Dominica. Sir John by south, Ye 29 we anchored under Gadalupe Sir Francis beinge there a daye before us,[2] on the 30 Josias cap. of the delight brought newes to the generalls that the Francis a smale[3] of companie was taken by 5 frigotts, Wherupon Sir Francis would presently have folowed them either with the whole fleete or some parte for that he knew our intentions were discovered by reason they were so openly made knowne as I afore have set downe by Sir John Haukins. Sir John would in no wise agree to eyther of these motions & he was asisted in his opinion by Sir Nicholas Clifforde, all others furtheringe his desires, which might be a meanes to staye them for goinge into Porterico before us, but Sir John prevayled for that hee was sickly, Sir Francis beinge loth to breed his further disquiet Ye reason of his stay was to trimme his shippes, mounte his ordinance take in Water, set up som new pinnaces: and to make thinges in that readines that he cared not to meete with the kinges whole fleete. Heere we stayed doinge these necessaries 3 dayes. this is a desarte and was without inhabitants. on the 4th of November we departed & beinge becalmed under the lee of the land. Sir Francis caused the Richarde one of the victualers to be unladen and suncke the 8th wee anchored amonge the virginees other West Ilandes. Heere wee drewe our companie on shore that every man might knowe his coulours & we founde our companie shorte of the 1200 promised for Lande Service fewe of the Captaines havinge above 90 most not 80, som not 50.[4] which fell out partly for that the generalls had

[1] Martinino, later Martinique.
[2] On the night of 26–27 October in a storm Drake 'with foure or five other ships bearing on head of the fleete was separated' (VTD).
[3] A word apparently omitted. See VTD, Troughton (document 19) and Ch. 5 for further detail on this event.
[4] 'wee devided our men into 12 companye' (Bodleian Journal).

selected to them: a companie for theyr guarde of many of the gallantest men of the armie. Sir John his sicknes incresed: Sir Francis apointed Capitaines to the marchants shippes. this consumed time till the 11. when we passed a sounde though by our mariners never passed by fleete afore[1] & we came to anchor before Porterico on the 12 about 3 of the clocke in the afternoone at what time Sir John Haukins died. I made my men ready presently to have lanced knowinge that our sodaine resolution would greatly have danted the enemie & have held our [men] in opinion of assured victory. but I was countermanded by authoritie & duringe the time of our deliberation the enimie labored by all meanes to cause us to disankar, so workinge that within an hower hee had planted 3 or 4 peeces of artillery upon the shore next unto us, and playenge upon the defiance knowinge her to bee the admirall whilest our generalls sate at souper with Sir Nicholas Clifford and diverse other, a shotte came amongst them wherwith Sir Nicholas Brute

[1] The Munich Log, the Paris Profiles, VTD and Adams Journal are the most useful sources on the fleet's course from Martinino to San Juan de Puerto Rico. Guadalupe was approached via Martinino, Dominica, Marigalante and Los Santos. From 29 October to 4 November the ships remained at Guadalupe and then steered roughly northwest to leeward of Montserrat, Redonda, Nevis, St Kitts, St Eustatius and Saba. Thence the course was again northwest (VTD's 'Southwest' is obviously an error) to 'a sounde in the Virgines northe northeaste from Santa Cruse' (Munich Log) or 'the Iland called the *Virginies* [where they rode] in a great bay betweene 2 Ilandes' (Adams Journal). This 'very good rode, had it bene for a 1000 sails' (VTD) must have been Gorda Sound, at Virgin Gorda, which was reached on 8 November. The sequence of events from the 8th until the arrival off Puerto Rico on the 12th is obscure because the best sources (VTD and Munich Log) both contain errors of dating. The impression left by the sources generally is one of confusion, as if the ships were reduced to seeking their way to Puerto Rico by a process of trial and error. The VTD account, however, is credible if read as a retrospective summary of the course: 'we weied and set sayle into the sea due South through a small streit but without danger, and then stode West and by North for San Juan de Puerto rico, and in the after noone left the 3 small Islands called The passages to the Southward of us, and that night came up to the Eastermost end of St John'. This suggests a course southwest from the northern side of Virgin Gorda through what is still called the Sir Francis Drake channel, then west through the narrows between Tortola and St John, and finally west and by north passing north of St John, St Thomas and Culebra in succession.

Browne Captain Strafford who had Greenstones companie and some standers by were hurte,[1] Sir Nicholas died that night, so secondinge Sir John Hawkins in his death as he did in his oppinion at Guadalupe. my brother Browne lived 5. or 6. days after & died much bewayled. this shotte made our generall to way and fall further to the westward where wee rode safely. The 5 frigotts before spoken of rode within our forts, wee had no place nowe to lande our men but within them in the face of the towne which was dangerous for that both shippes and forts were to playe on us, it was therfore concluded that boates should fire them where they rode Captain Poore and my sealfe had the comande of this service, for the regiments Captain Salisburie comandinge the grand Captain companie was sent by the generalls, diverse sea comanders were also sent[2] and on the 13th at night passing in harde under the forte, we set 3 of them on fire, only one of which, it was my chance to undertake was burnt, on the others the fire helde not by reason that beinge once out they were not mainteined with newe, the burnte shippe gave a greate light, the enimie therby playenge upon us with theyr ordinance and smale shotte as if it had beene fayre daye, and sinkinge some of our boates a man could hardly comande his marriners to rowe they foolishly thinkinge every place more dangerous then where they were when in deede none was sure. Thus doinge no harme wee returned with 2 or 3 prisoners when indeed in my poore oppinion it had binne an easier matter to bringe them out of the harborowe then fire them as wee did, for our men aboard the shippes numbred. 5160 peeces of artyllerie[3] that played on us duringe this service; and it had binne lesse dangerous to have abidden them close in the frigotts & in the darcke then as wee did, but great comanders many tymes fayle in theyr judgment beinge crost by a compartner, but I had cause of more greife then the Indies could yeilde mee of joye losinge my Alfierus, Davis

[1] Bodleian Journal: the great shot broke Clifford's thigh-bone. VTD: it struck the stool from under Drake, who was at supper in the steerage. 'Full Relation': 'was struke from under him, as he was drinking of a cup of Beare.'

[2] 'Full Relation': 'five hundred Men which went within the harbour'.

[3] An error for 160, the figure given in 'Full Relation', Bodleian Journal and Adams Journal, and based on Spanish prisoners' statements. The official Spanish report lists 70.

Pursell master Vaughan a brother in lawe of Sir John Haukins with 3 others, Thomas Powton with 5 or 6 more hurte and maimed,[1] & was somwhat discomfited for the generall protested heere to set up his rest, but examininge the Prisoners by whom hee understoode that these frigotts were sent for his treasure and that they would have fallen amonge us at Guadalupe had they not taken the Francis, his minde altered callinge to counsaile comanded us to give our oppinions what we thought of the strength of the place, most thought it would hazard the whole action. But one Rush a captaine more to mee aleadged that without better puttinge for it, the bare lookinge upon the out side of the forts wee could hardly give such judgment, & I set it playnely under my hande that if we resolutely attempted yt, all was ours & that I perswaded my sealfe no towne in the Indies could yeilde us more honnor or profitte. The generall presently saide I will bringe thee to 20 places farre more wealthye and easier to bee gotten, such like speeches I thinke had bewitched the Coronell for he most desired him to hasten him hence, the enimie the day after wee had fired the frygotts suncke together 4 to save us labour, but cheifly to strengthen theyr fortes. 2 other greate shippes they suncke and fyred in the mouth of the harborowe to give them light to play on us from theyr fortes as we entred the first night. And hence we went the 15th, heere I left all hope of good sucesse. on the 19 we came to anchor in a faire baye (the baye of Sta. Jermana) at the westermost parte of the Ilande where we stayed till the 24 settinge up more newe pinnaces, & unlodinge the other newe victualer,[2] the generall takinge the most parte into his owne shippe as hee did of the former. Captaine Yorke in the hope was made viceadmirall. This is a very pleasant and fertile Iland havinge upon it goode store of cattell fruites and fish with all thinges necessary to man sustenance and were it well manured no place could yeilde it greater aboundance or better, departing hence, we had our course for Corasaw ye 2cond daye after our

15
19
ye baye
of Sta
Jermana

[1] VTD: 'wee lost some forty or fifty men, and so many were hurt'. Adams Journal: 'they killed and hurt of us together 140 men'. Baskerville (document 20): '200 hurte and slayn men'.
[2] The John Trelawney, or Pulpit. Adams Journal and Bodleian Journal: four pinnaces were built here.

puttinge of the exchange a smale shippe spronge her mast, and was suncke the men and parte of the victualls were saved by other shippes

Upon Corasaw there is greate store of cattell & goates, and wee fell with it upon Saterday ye 29. but our generall deceaved by the currante & westerly course made it for Arabir, an Iland lyenge 10. or 12. leagues to the westwarde & so made no staye,[1] when next morninge descryenge whether hee founde his error wee bore with Cape De la Vela & from thence our coronell with all the companies in the pinnaces & boates were sent to the cittie of Rio de la Hacha and with smale resistance wee tooke it the 1 of December at night. The generall came unto us the next morning with the fleete. This towne was left bare of goodes, the inhabitants havinge intelligence of our cominge had caried all in the woodes and hid theyr treasure in casshes, but stayenge heere 17 days wee made so goode search y^t little remained unfounde within 4 leages of the towne, we tooke many prisoners Spaniards & negroes, some slaves repairinge to us voluntarily. The generall with 200 men went in boates to Lancheria.[2] which is a place where they fish for pearle standinge 10 leagues to the Estwarde of theyr towne from whence they brought goode store of pearle & tooke a carvell in which was some monie, wine, and myre.

Duringe our stay heere the governour once, diverse others often, repayred unto us to redeeme theyr towne, Lancheria, boates and slaves. They did this to gaine time to convey away the kinges treasure & to advertize theyr neighbour townes to convey theyr treasure in more safetye then themselves had done. for the whole (except the slaves which voluntarily repayred unto us) was yeilded unto them for 24000 peases, 5.^s 6.^d a peece y^t to bee payde in pearles bringinge these to theyr towne at the daye and valuinge in double the price theyr were worth, our generall delivered the hostages & set theyr, Lancheria and boates on fire carryinge theyr slaves with us.[3] The wealth we had heare was given to countervayle the charge of the jorney, but I feare it will not so prove in the end. Our vice-

---

[1] 'Full Relation' confirms that Drake mistook Curaçao for Aruba.
[2] La Ranchería.
[3] For use as porters at the Isthmus? Cp. Diego Mendes' statement (p. 217 below) about 12 negroes 'for the road' brought from Río de la Hacha.

admirall Cap*taine* Yorcke died heere of sicknes. This is an exceed-
inge goode countrye champion and well inhabited, great store of
cattayle horses sheepe goates fish and fowle wheron wee fedde, but
smale store of graine or fruite neere the towne, rich only in pearle
and cattell.[1]

The 20th, beinge Saterday, we came to St. Tomarta, we suncke
to catches before we came to Rio de la Hacha w*hich* wee brought
out of England. Presently upon our cominge to anchors we landed
and gave upon the town, we founde smale resistance more then a
fewe shotte playenge out of the woods as wee marched towards the
towne Companies were presently sent abroade to discover and
search the countrye, The inhabitants had to longe forewarninge to
cary theyr goods out of our possibilitie to finde them in so shorte
time, little or nothinge of valew was gotten only the Leiftenant
governor and some others were taken prisoners and firyinge the
Towne the 21, we departed.

Captain Worrell, our trenchmaster, died at this towne of
sicknes, this was a very prettie towne & 6 leagues of there was a
gould mine. if part of our companie had bin sent thither upon our
first arrivall at Rio de la Hacha doubtles we had done much goode,
but now they had scrube it very bare. In this place was great store
of fruite and much fernandobouke for that the winde blewe so
extreamly and the rode wilde we could not shippe it. before we
departed hence it was concluded that wee should passe Cartagena[2]

[1] Bodleian Journal describes Río de la Hacha as 'a place of good relief'; VTD:
'In the houses we refreshed our selves.' There is no word yet of serious disease in
the fleet, but one or two deaths from sickness are mentioned and there were
probably some fifty or more wounded from Puerto Rico. No extensive re-
victualling had so far been possible. These considerations may help to explain the
decision to take Río de la Hacha and the lengthy stay there, but they were not
offered in explanation by any of the English narrators.

[2] VTD: 'We lost that night the company of the Phenix, captaine Austin, Peter
Lemond, and the Garlands pinnesse, which stood along the shore, and being
chased off by gallies out of Carthagena Peter Lemond with nine of our men was
taken, the rest came safe to our fleete.' This was construed by the Spaniards as an
attempt to reconnoitre Cartagena (B.M., Additional MSS, 36317, f. 78). The
prisoners' statements formed part of the material for the general account of the
voyage in A. de I., Santa Fe, 17. On the failure of the English to attack Cartagena
see Ch. 6 below.

and go directly for Numbre de Dios. we anchored in the rode on Sundaye folowinge beinge the 27 & landinge presently receavinge some smale shotte from the towne, we founde smale resistance more than a little forte at the east side of theyr towne in which they had left one peece of ordinance, which brake at the first shotte, they gave upon us as we gave upon them: certaine prisoners were taken in the flyinge who made it knowne that havinge intelligence longe before of our cominge theyr treasure was conveyed to places of more safetie, eyther to panama or secretly hidden and it might very well bee for the towne was left very bare, wherfore it was resolved that we should hasten with speede for Panama. Nombre de Dios standeth on the north-side sea, Panama upon the south distant some 18 or 19 leagues. There were only two wayes to get thither one by the river Chagree which lyeth to the westward 20 leages upon this it is passable within 5 leagues of Panama: the other through deserts and over mountaines voide of inhabitants, this was troublesom and harde as well for want of meanes to cary our provision of meate and munition as for the ill passage with an armie through these deserts and unknowne places y^t by the river our generall held more dangerous fayninge there was no place for our fleete to wade safely.[1] This made our coronell to yeelde to the waye by the mountaines though he and others foresawe the danger before our settinge hence, but he resolved to make tryall of what coulde be done, so on Monday the 29 we began our jorney, takinge with us the strongest and lustiest of our armie to the number of 50 men[2] and 7 coulours. before our settinge hence we buried Captaine Arnold Baskervile serjant major generall a gallant gentleman, ye first daye wee marched 3 leagues the next 6 leagues where we came to a greate house which the enimie had sett on fire, it beinge a place where the

---

[1] 'Wade' means to pass through – in this case, presumably, to pass up the river. Since it was obvious that the fleet itself could not go up the Chagre, Maynarde perhaps meant that Drake thought the pinnaces and boats could not make it. Yet clearly Drake did not think so, for he planned to use the river approach to join Baskerville in Panama. 'Ride' would make no better sense.

[2] Obviously a slip. VTD gives 750; Baskerville (document 20, the best authority on this) 600; 'Full Relation' 600; Adams Journal '700 or 800'. The Spaniards usually 900, say but Conabut, the best Spanish authority, gives 600 (document 35).

kinges mules do use to lodge cominge from Panama to Numbre
de dios with his treasure, it is the midway betwixt both places the
house would receave 500 horses, we had not martched fully a
league on wendensday morninge we came to a place fortified upon
the toppe of an hill which the enemie defended, we had noe other
way to passe nor no meanes to make our approach but a very deepe
lane where but one could passe at once unles it were by clammeringe
upon the bancks and creepinge up the hill through the brakes which
som of our men did and came to the trees which they had plasshed
to make theyr palizadoe over which they could not passe, the many
bowes so hindered them. It was my chance clammeringe up the
bancks to repaire to 3 musketters which I had holpen up to fall
directly betwixt 2 of theyr places fortified cominge upon 2 paths by
which they fetched theyr water and givinge presently upon them,
ye place beinge open, my smale number found to goode resistance,
and I driven to retire with the losse of these fewe, heere was the only
place to beate them from y^er houlde wherof I sent the coronell
worde, Captaine Poore & Bartlett and others repayringe to mee I
shewed them the path, we hearde the enemie plasshinge and fellinge
of trees farre before us, the coronell sent for us to come unto him, he
debated with us what he foresawe before our cominge from Numbre
de dios and though hee thought in his oppinion we should feare
the enimie hence, yet havinge retreits upon retreites they would kill
our best men without takinge little or any hurte themselves, and our
men began to droppe apace, our powder and match were spilde by
much raine and waters which we had passed, unles it were such as
som of our souldiers had with more care preserved. The provision
for our meate at our cominge from Numbre de dios was 7 or 8 cakes
of bisked or ruske for a man which was eyther by wette spoyled or
theyr greedines had devoured so there remained to fewe one dayes
bread to most none at all. Our hurte men as Captaine Nicholas
Baskervile[1] and some other of accounte we should be driven to
leave to the mercie of the enimie unles they could houlde companie.
before our cominge to Panama, had we beaten them from all these
houlds (which I thinke would have bin to dangerous for us to
have attempted consideringe the estate we were in) we must have

---

[1] Shot in the thigh (Bodleian Journal), but survived.

fought with them at a bridge where they had intrenched themselves in a far greater number then we were, and it is manifest if we had not within 3 days gotten some releife we had bin overthrowen though no enimie had fought against us. but our stomacks callinge these with other dangers to his carefull consideration, he resolved to retire, and so comanded us to cause the slaine to be throwne out of sight ye hurte to be sent to the quarter from whence we came that morninge, & the rest to be drawen away. Heere were slaine Captaine Marchant, our quarter master with som other officers gentlemen and souldiers[1] Upon our cominge to the quarter, the coronell tooke vew of the hurte, and for such as coulde ride he procured all the horses of the armie,[2] for the other he intreated the ennemie to entreate them kindly as they expected the like from us towards theyrs of which we had a farre greater number.

Jan. 2. On the seconde of January we returned to Numbre de dios our men so weryed with the ilnes of the waye surbaited for want of shoes and weake with theyr diet,[3] y^t it would have bin a poore dayes service that we should have done upon an ennimie had they beene there to resist us. I am perswaded that never armie great or small undertooke a march through to unknown places so weakly provided and with so smale meanes to helpe themselves unles it might bee som few goinge covertly to do som sodaine exploite before it were thought of by the enimie and so returne unespied, for undoubtedly 200 men foreknowinge theyr intentions and provided with all thinges necessarie are able to breake or weaken ye greatest force that any prince in Christendome can bringe thither, if hee had place to frinde more than wee had. This marche hath made many swere that hee will never venture to buy gould at such a price againe. I confesse noble spirritts desirous to do service to theyr Prince and country may be soone perswaded to all hardnes and

---

[1] VTD: 20 or more killed. Baskerville: 60 or 70 soldiers slain and hurt apart from officers.

[2] See Baskerville's note to Drake requesting horses (document 36 below).

[3] 'Full Relation': 'In this March a paire of Shoos was sold for thirty shillings, and a Bisket Cake for ten Shillings.' One of Sotomayor's prisoners said the rations were 'a little biscuit and cheese in the sleeves of their doublets and nothing else' (document 33). Baskerville describes his men as barefoot.

danger, but havinge once made tryall therof would be very loth (as I suppose) to cary any force that way againe for behouldinge it in many places, a man would judge it dangerous for one man to passe alone almost inpossible for horses and an armie. The daye that our Generall had newes of our returne hee ment to way and fall nearer to the river Chagree with the fleete, leavinge some few to bringe us, if we were enforced to retire, wherof hee little doubted, but beinge beaten from the place where it appeered all his hopes rested for gayninge to himselfe and others this masse of treasure which he so confidently promised before, it was high time for him to device of some other course. Wherfore on the 4 of Jannuary, he called us to Jan. 4 counsayle and debated with us what was nowe to be done. All these partes had notice longe before of all our intentions as it appeered by letters written from the governor of Lima to the governor of Panama & Numbre de dios givinge them advice to be carefull and to looke well to themselves for y* Drake and Hawkins were makinge readie in Englande to come upon them. Lima is distant from these places more then 300 leagues all overlayde with snakes. It appeereth that they had good intelligence. This made them to convey theyr treasure to places which they resolved to defend with better force then we were able to attempt. Like as upon the cominge of the sun, dewes and mistes begin to vanish, so our blinded eyes began now to open & wee founde that the glorious speeches of an 100 places that they knew in the Indies to make us rich was but a baite to drawe her majestie to give them honorable imployments and us to adventure our lives for theyr glory, for now cards and mappes muste bee our cheefest directors, he beinge in these partes at the furthest limit of his knowledge. There hee founde out a place called Laguna de Nichoragua upon which standeth certaine townes as Granada Leon and others. Also the bay of Hanboros[1] a place knowne to be of smale wealth of it sealfe unles it be brought thither to be imbarqued for Spaine, he demanded which of those we would attempt our coronell saide both one after another and all to little to content us if wee tooke them. It was then resolved y* wee should first for the river and as matters fell out for the other. Nombre de Dios together with theyr negroe towne were fyred & we suncke and

[1] Honduras.

fyred 14 smale frigotts which we founde in the rode. we gott heere
20 barres of silver with som gould and certaine plate more would
have benne founde had it bene well sought, but our generall
thought it folly for us to gather our harvest graine by graine beinge
so likely at Panama to thrust our handes into the whole in heapes
and after our returne beinge troubled in minde hee seemed little
to regarde any consayle y[t] should be given him to that purpose, but
to hasten thence as fast as he might. This is a most wealthy place
beinge setled upon a grounde full of camphyre environed with
hilly woodes & mountaines the bottom a dampish fenne. hence
wee departed the 5. and held our course for Nichragua on the 9 we
founde a very deepe and dangerous baye playenge it heere up and
downe all men weary of the place y[e] 10. we descryed a smale Ilande
called Escudes where we came to anchor, and heere we tooke a
frygotte which was an advice of the kinges[1] by this we learned y[t] the
townes standinge upon this lake were of smale wealth and very
dangerous by reason of many shoals & greate roughes our marriners
should have it, beinge an 100 leagues. yet if the winde would have
permitted, we had assuredly put for them and never returned tone
halfe againe, heere we stayed at a wast Ilande where there was no
releife but a few tortoyses, for such as could catch them twelve
dayes. This is counted the sickliest place of the Indies, and heere
died many of our men[2] victualls begininge to growe scarse with us.
In the end findinge the winde to continew contrary, he resolved to
departe and to take the winde as god sent it, so on the 22. we went
hence, havinge there buried Captaine Plott, Egerton and divers
others. I questioned with our generall beinge often private with him
whilest wee stayed heere to see whether hee would reveale unto mee
any of his purposes, & I demanded of him why hee so often con-
jured mee beinge in England, to staye with him in these partes as
longe as himselfe: and where the place was. hee answered mee with
greife protestinge y[t] hee was as ignorant of the Indies as my sealfe

---

[1] VTD: 'an Advisor sent from Nombre de Dios to all the ports along the coast
Westward'. 'Full Relation': 'a spye comming from Nombre de dios, and going
to the townes there to give intelligence of us'.

[2] VTD: on the return to Porto Belo 'we had sicke and whole 2000' and the *Delight*
and Captain Eden's frigate were scuttled because 'the Queenes ships wanted saylers'.

and that hee never thought any place could bee so changed, as it were from a delitious and pleasant arbour, into a wast and desarte wildernesse, besides the variablenes of the winde & weather so stormie and blusterous as hee never saw it before, but hee most wondred that since his cominge out of England hee never sawe sayle worthye the givinge chace unto, yet in the greatnes of his minde hee would in the end conclude with these wordes. It matters not man God hath many thinges in store for us, and I knowe many meanes to doe her majestie goode service & to make us ritch, for wee must have gould before wee see Englande. when, goode gentleman, (in my conceite) it fared with him as with som careles livinge man who prodigally consumes his time fondly perswadinge himsealfe y^t the nurse that fedde him in his childhood will likewise nourishe him in his ould age and findinge the dugge dried & withered enforced then to behould his folly tormented in minde dieth with a starved bodie, hee had beside his own adventure gaged his owne reputation greatly in promisinge her majestie to do her honorable service and to returne her a very profitable adventure and havinge sufficiently experienced for 7 or 8 yeares together, how hard it was to regaine favor once ill thought of the mistresse of his fortune now leavinge him to yeilde to a discontented minde. And since our returne from Panama he never caried mirth nor joy in his face, yet no man hee loved must conjecture that hee tooke thought thereof. But heere hee began to grow sickly. At this Iland we sancke a Carvell which we brought out of England puttinge & victualls into a last taken frigatt. from hence a great currante setts towards the Estward by reason wherof with the scant of winde we had on wedensday beinge the 28 we came to Portabella[1] which is within 8 or 9 leagues of Numbre de dios. it was the best harborough we came unto sence we left Plymoth. This morninge about 7 of the clocke Sir Francis died, the next day Sir Thomas Baskervile caried him a league of and buried him in the sea.[2] In this place the

s^{r}Fr. Drake dieth

---

[1] Baskerville (document 20) represents the decision to move to Porto Belo as his own. It was the obvious base for an attack by the river, a project the Spaniards thought was not abandoned until Drake's death (see Ch. 6).

[2] VTD: 'The 28 at 4 of the clocke in the morning our Generall sir Francis Drake departed this life, having bene extremely sicke of a fluxe, which began the night

Inhabitants of Numbre de dios meant to build a towne it beinge far more healthye then where they dwell heere they began a forte which alreadie cost yᵉ kinge 7000 poorses & a fewe houses towards there towne which they called civitas Sti. Philippi, them we fired rasinge the fortification to the grounde heere we found as in the other places all abandoned theyr ordinance cast into the sea, some of which wee founde and caried aboard the garland. Our generalls beinge dead most mens hartes were bent to hasten for England, as soone as they might. But Sir Thomas Baskervile havinge the comand of the Armie by vertue of her majesties broade seale endevored to prevent the disseveringe of the fleete & to that end talked with such as hee hearde intended to quite companie before they were disembogued & drew all companies to subscribe to certaine articles signifyenge our purposes. vz. yᵗ puttinge hence wee should turne it backe to St. Tomarto[1] if the winde would suffer

before to stop on him. He used some speeches at or a little before his death, rising and apparelling himselfe, but being brought to bed againe within one houre died. He made his brother Thomas Drake and captaine Jonas Bodenham executors, and M. Thomas Drakes sonne his heire to all his lands, except one manor which he gave to captaine Bodenham.' 'Full Relation': 'his interment was after this manner; His Corps being laid in a Cophin of Lead, he was let downe into the Sea, the Trumpets in dolefull manner echoing out this lamentation for so great a losse, and all the Cannons in the Fleet were discharged according to the custome of all Sea Funerall obsequies.' See also the account by Sir James Whitelocke (pp. 45–6 above). Baskerville's statement that 'sir frauncis fell sike as I thinke throughe greffe' and Maynarde's impressions of his state of mind suggest that mental depression played a part in Drake's death. On 27 January, the day before his death, he signed an indenture declaring Thomas Drake his heir. This was witnessed by Charles Manners, Thomas Webbes, Roger Langifforde, George Watkins, Jonas Bodenham and W. Maynarde. In the margin is a note to the effect that it was later produced in connection with a lawsuit, Thomas Maynarde being one of the signatories of this note. The document is now deposited in the Central Public Library of the City of Plymouth. Drake also signed a codicil to his will (Somerset House, P.C.C., 1 Drake) granting his cousin Francis, son of Richard Drake of Surrey, the manor of Yarcombe, upon payment of £2,000 to Thomas Drake; and granting Jonas Bodenham the manor of Sampford Speney. For the will and subsequent litigation see Eliott-Drake, *Family and Heirs*.

[1] Santa Marta. Adams Journal: 'towardes *St Marta* according unto the minde of the lieutenant generall of St Marta, he promised to ransome himselfe, and give us some victualls'.

us otherwise to run over Jamica where it was thought we should bee refreshed with som victualls, matters thus concluded ye delight ye Elizabeth & our late taken frigotts were suncke. many of the Negro men & base prisoners were heere put on shore[1] & heere we wayed on Sunday the 8. of February our victualls began to shorten apace yet we had lyen a longe time at very harde alowance. 4. men each morninge one quarte of beere & one cake of bisket for diner and for supper one quarte of beere and 2 cakes of bisket & two cans of water with a pinte of pease or halfe a pinte of rise or somwhat more of oatemeale this was our allowance beinge at Portabella & 6 weekes before, but that we had som time stockfish. from thence there is a currant y^t sets to the Eastward by the helpe of which on the 14 wee had sight of an Iland shorte of Carthagena 15. or 16. leagues,[2] further then this we could not go to thestward for that the current had left us, ye 15 at night it beinge faire weather[3] we lost sight of our fleete. heere as I grew discontented knowinge it touched my poore reputation so to leave the armie & I had many thinges to perswade mee that it was done of purpose by the Captaine[4] & master therby gaininge an excuse to departe I shewed the Captaine of the danger he should run into by leavinge so honorable forces when they had neede of our companie & God knoweth that had I had but judgment which way to have cast for them I would rather have lost my life then so forsake ye like he deposed on the bible & Christianitie made me beleive him, but playenge it up and downe about 12 of the clocke & discoveringe none of them the wind blew so contrary that the seamen affirmed by houldinge this course we should be cast backe in the bay & they perswaded that our fleete could not attaine St. Tomarto but were gone over for Jamica whether they would follow them. I plainly forsawe that if we missed them there it was like we should no more meete till wee came to Englande which would have made me to perswade a

Feb. 8.

---

[1] But after the voyage the privy council gave authority 'to this bearer Edwarde Banes to take of those blackmoores that in this last voyage under Sir Thomas Baskervile were brought into this realme the nomber of tenn, to be transported by him out of the realme' (*A.P.C., N.S.*, XXVI (1902), 16).

[2] The islands of Baru (VTD).

[3] VTD, Baskerville and Troughton say the weather was bad.

[4] William Wynter – see document 20.

longer search upon the maine, but my hope of there beinge there together with the weaknes of our men and the smale meanes we had to reteine them fearinge lest my delay might endanger her majesties shippes & the whole companie I yeilded to theyr perswasions we were in 10. degrees & a halfe when we put from hence & we came till the 22 when we had sight of a very dangerous shoale which our seamen thought they had passed neere 2 dayes before. if we had fallen with it in the night we had bin all lost, the shoale is named Secrana. on Shrove Wensday beinge 24, we fell with Jamica & by meanes of a Malatow & an Indian we had this night 40 bundles of dried beife which served our whole companie so many dayes we came to anchor at the westermost parte of the Iland in a faire sandie bay where we watered and stayed in hope to have som newes of our fleete 7 dayes this our stay brought no intelligence wherfore our seamen thought that our fleete not able to recover this place were fallen eyther with Cape Locantes[1] or Cap St. Anthonie these places we ment to touch in our course & hence we went the 1 of March on the 6 we saw a shippe on the Leaward of us & the next morninge we made her to be the Pegasine one of our fleete who as they sayde lost the admirall neere the time wee did beinge by the Coronell sent to the Susan Bonaventure whom they left in great distresse by reason of a Lake they had taken & I greatly feared by theyr reporte they are perished.[2] There were in her 130 or 140 persons many gallant gentlemen and good men. if they perish this shippe shall repent it. houldinge our course for these places we descried 5. sayles asterne of us we stayed for them and soone made them to be none of our fleete & we had good reason to perswade us they were enimies they had the winde of us but we soone regained it which made them upon a peece of ordinance shott of by the greatest shippe tacke about we tackt with them then when the captaine of this shippe faythfully protested unto mee not to shoote a peece of ordinance till we came boord and boorde & then I promised him with our smale shot to win the greatest or lose our persons. This wee might have done without endangeringe her majesties shippes but our enimie playenge upon us with theyr ordinance made our

---

[1] Corrientes.

[2] The ship apparently survived (see p. 43 above).

gunnors fall to it ere we were at musket shott & no nerer could I bringe them though I had no hope to take any of them but by boordinge, heere wee popt away powder and shot away to no purpose for most of our gunnors would hardly have stricken Paules steeple had it stoode there I am a younge seaman yet my smale judgment & knowledge makes me avowe that never shippe of her majesties went so vilely made¹ out of her kingdom not twenty of them worthy to come into her shippes and it I know not what had possessed the Captaine but his mind was cleane altered tellinge me he had no authoritie to lay any shippe aboorde wherby he might endanger this her majesties & they beinge as he sayde yᵉ kinges men of warre they would rather fire with us than be taken. had I beene a marchant of her burden (god favoringe me) they would have bin mine as many as stoode to the tryall of theyr fortune. But the paltrie Pegosie we lately met withall never came neere us by a league which was som colour to our men to give them over. so after I had endevored by my sealfe my leivetenant and other gentlemen by perswasion to worke the captaine resolutely to attempt them & findinge no disposition in him but to consume powder and shott to no purpose but firinge it in the ayer I yelded to give them over perswadinge my sealfe that God had even ordained that we should not with any valure attempt where we wer resisted with never so weake forces. Thus away we went and the winde choppinge us southerly our seamen held that our fleete coulde neyther ride at Corants nor at St. Anthony which made me condescend to leave the Indies with all her treasure & to plye the next course to disimbogue for little hope was left mee that we should do her majestie any service or good to our selves when upon the faigned excuses of endangeringe her shippes which she sent forth to fight if occasion were offered: And I perswade my sealfe that her majestie priseth not her ships deerer then the lives of so many faythful subjects who gladly would have adventured theyr lives, and upon no brain-sicke humor but from a trew desire to do her highness som service for the charge and adventure she had bin at in this glorious spoken of jorney, fortunes childe was dead thinges would not fall into our mouthes nor riches be our portions howe dearly soever we

¹ Probably means 'manned'.

adventured for them. Thus avoydinge Silla (after the proverbe) we felle into Charibdis & indeed we were not now farre from it. our master a carefull ould man but not experienced upon these coastes rather folowinge the advice of others then relienge on his owne judgment brought us on the 12. 3 howers before daye into a very shallow water upon a dangerous bancke w*hich* som held to be the Meltilettes others for the Torgugas eyther like inough to have swallowed us, had not God blest us w*ith* fayre weather, freinge our selves of this danger upon Monday the 15 of March we entered the Gulfe & by 10. of the clocke we brought the cape of Florida west of us. on the 17. (the Lorde be thanked) we were disimbogued after this we ran w*ith* most fowle weather & contrary windes till the 1. of May when we had soundinge in 90 fathoms beinge in the Channell & on the 3ᵈ we had sight of Sylly the w*hich* day ere night we came to Anchor, yᵉ Lord be therfor praysed. 1596.

To give mine oppinion of the Indies I verily thinke that filtchinge men of warre shall do more goode then such a fleete if they have any forewarninge of theyr cominge and unles her ma*jes*tie will undertake so royally as to dispossesse him of the Landes of Porterico Hispaniola & Cuba her charge will be greater in sendinge thither then the profitt such a fleete can returne, for havinge but a few dayes warninge it is easie for them to convey theyr goods into assured safetie, as experience hath taught us. Theyr townes they dare not redeeme beinge enjoyned the contrary by the kinges comandement, these places will be taken & possessed till new supply come by 20,000 men & by this her majestie might debarre the kinge of Spaine of his whole profitt of the Indies & the first gaininge them will returne her a sufficient requitall for her adventure God grant I may live to see such an enterprise put in practise & the kinge of Spaine will speedily flye to what conditions of peace her majestie will require. Thus I have truly set downe the whole discourse of our voyage usinge therin many Idle wordes and ill compared sentences, It was done on the sea w*hich* I thinke can alter any disposition. Your loves I thinke can pardon these faltes & secret them from the vew of others.

The first of March yᵉ fleete fell w*ith* the pinnas on the lande of Cuba w*hich* day they had sight of the Spanish fleete by 11. of the

clocke where Sir Thomas Baskervile gave directions for the fleete
as thus: The Garland beinge admirall with one halfe of the fleete
to have the vanguard. the hope, (beinge viceadmirall) with the
other halfe the rereward. The fight continued feircely 3. howers
within muskett shott, that night they saw the Spanish viceadmirall, (a ship of 700 tonne) burned with other 6 lost and suncke
by the next morninge when they departed. The hope[1] receved a
Leake and was faine to go from the fleete to an Iland called Sta
Crusado inhabited by canniballs, where they had store of hens &
Indian wheate for 9 weekes. March 8, the fleete shott the Gulfe &
came for England leavinge Florida on the starboord side & when
they came to the inchanted Islands they were dispersed & came
home one by one.

                    Tho: Maynarde

19. John Troughton's journal[2]

[Covering letter]
Right honourable, my dutie moste humblie remembred, Althoughe I ame verie sorrie, to write suche newes as I knowe wilbe
verie unpleasing; yet I have thought it my dutie to advertice; On

---

[1] The *Hope* shot the gulf with Baskerville and reached England before him.
Maynarde may be thinking of the *Help*, which was captured by Avellaneda on
12/22 March ten leagues from Havana, some of her crew being put into the
galleys and others sent to Seville. The *Little Exchange*, under Captain John
Crosse, owned by Sir Robert Crosse and Sir Walter Raleigh, was captured at
about the same time and place. She was not a member of Drake's fleet, for she
left Plymouth in January 1596, possibly with instructions to warn Drake about
Avellaneda's armada (*Cal. Hatfield MSS*, VII, 232; *Cal. S.P.D., 1595-7*,
pp. 196, 346-7, 375-6; document 39). This evidence does not support Maynarde's
account, but the exchequer accounts for the voyage (document 14) contain an
entry for payment of wages after the voyage to Anthony Lister, master of the *Help*,
and divers mariners with him. It looks as if some of the *Help*'s crew got away,
either before or at the time of the capture, and reached England after the adventures
Maynarde speaks of.
[2] P.R.O., S.P. 12/257, no. 48. Published in Samuel Purchas, *Hakluytus Posthumus, or Purchas his Pilgrimes*, IV (1625), 1184-5 (XVI (1906), 126-31), but
without the covering letter and with the errors noted below.

Fridaie laste there arived certen ships of Sir Frauncis Drakes Fleete at Famouth; but himselff and Sir John haukines with many other men of worth I understand are dead; herewith I do send a packett of lettres for Alderman Wattes wherin his Servaunt Capitaine Goodwine doth send a particuler relacion of the whole voiage; which I have made bould to enclose within your honours lettre, the rather for that by the said Alderman Wattes, you may be enfourmed at large of all thinges in more ample sorte, then I can any waie declare;[1] I perceave their companies are retourned in great distresse for want of victualles, and therfore there muste be present order taken, that they maie be supplied therwith. Some things they have brought but as it is reported nothing neare to countervaile the charge of the journey;

On Fridaie and Saterdaie laste here arived divers ships both englishe and dutche, belonging to her Majesties Fleete nowe bound Fourthe, and there are also come heither by lande divers companies of souldiers wherof Sir Fardinando Gorge hath alreadie written more particulerlie;

As I shall come to the knowledge of any farther matter that maie importe, your honour shalbe adverticed therof, And so beseeching thalmightie for the long continuaunce of your honours prosperous healthe, I moste humblie take my leave, Plimouth the xxv^th of Aprill anno 1596

Your honours moste humble to comaunde
William Stallenge

[Endorsed] To the right honourable Sir Robert Cecill knight, one of her Majesties moste honourable privie counsaile; Yeeve theise at coorte

25. Apr. 1596
Mr Stallenge to my mr.
From Plymmoth

---

[1] Edward Goodwin, captain of the *Jewel* (see p. 42 above). The particular relation was presumably Troughton's journal. The fact that Stallenge refers Cecil to Watts for further information is consonant with the latter's importance as a promoter of the expedition.

[Enclosed]

Our Jurnall in anno domini 1595.

The xxvij[th] of Auguste havinge our dispatche from her majestie Brought all our Fleet into the sound of Plymouthe, and the 28th daie, we set saile for our pretended viadge. In our Course alongest the coeste of Spaine, was divers metinges with our generalls, wher passed many unkind speches, and suche as Sir John hawkins never put of till deathe. In this tracte was put on a resolution, with Sir Francis Drake and Sir Thomas Baskervile, to take the grand Canaria, whereuppon a Councell was held, and therin propounded by Sir Francis how nowe a greet Benyfyte, muche honour and good refreshinge was ofreed us, and therfore wold stand on most voyses,[1] as father fatharinge, hard speches on suche as was of a contrary opynion. Sir John hawkinges to whom he spake This utterly refused, with thes resonns followinge. First their could be no need consitheringe our small tyme out, Secondly not posible to cary yt without hazerdinge all, and Therdly not good to loose tyme, which wold never be recovered, To this last resonn, Sir Thomas Baskervile answered, First for Tyme, he wold require but fower daies in this manner, In fower howrs he wold take yt, and in the rest wold he burne yt downe except they wold compound. Thus the fowrth daie wold he be shipped redy for our viadge. In Thes contraversies, Sir Francis wold goo for the Canarya with suche as wold follow him, and Sir John hawkins with the rest for the Ingies. Yet after this hard debatinge, at the eeernest requeste of som frendes, Sir John hawkins, uppon the confessinge of need, was content to asiste them yet in his judgment labore lost with much hazard of all. Thus alltogether standinge alongest. The xxvj[th] of September, we cam to ancre afore the forte that gwardes the landinge place at grand Canaria, wher was put into our bottes and pynases, all our land men under the conduct of Sir Thomas Baskervile Collonell generall, who drew heed nere the mydest of the Beatche, Betwixt the fort and the Towne, as most safeste for our landinge. To this place, even than did the Spanyardes drawe 2. or 3. very small peces of ordynance, with which, and with som

---

[1] Purchas omits the rest of the sentence.

Companies of soldyars, made some show of resistance, wheruppon notwithstandinge most of our smaller Shippinge, who accompaned our bottes with their Artillery, Sir Thomas made his retreet without puttinge foot aland, and than to knowe as yt was reported, yf the Generalls wold put there viadge theron or no. with this better consitheration, was all our men shipped againe, & so Stood alongest to the westermost end therof. Here went many ashore som for water, and som for pleasure, amongeste whom, The 28 daie was Captaine Grimston with 2 more in his company slaine, and by pessantes as was thought. with this evill beginninge, this night we waed and stood alongest for yᵉ Ingies. The xxviijth of October we came faire by the Southermost end of Dominica, and the 30th daie we came all to safe ancringe at Gwardalupa. Only the Delight and the Franses, two of our smalest pinases, who beinge to Lewardes out of sight, was there chased by five Spanishe shipps, in which chaise, the Franses was tooke, Thother escaped with this newes. The Laste of this moneth, Sir John Hawkins not hable to bear his grifes out longer, Sickned. Here was built vij pynases, The iiijth of November waire they Lanshed, and we stood of for Portarico. The viijth daie in the waie we ancred amonge the ylands, virgins, wher all our soldyardes was appointed to ther Land Capitaines. The xijth daie we came to ancre afore the harborow at Portorico, wher died Sir nicolas Clifford by a shott from a platforme, sittinge at Supper in the defyaunce, with this shott was likewise mʳ Brewt Browne hurt, who Lyved but fewe daies after and this daie also died, Sir John Hawkins, whose deathe of many was muche Lamented. In This harborow ridd those fyve Frigottes of the Kinges which came for the Treasure. This place beinge well vewed by our Generall, and Collonell generall, a concell was held, and therin agreed, That first and moste necessariest, these Frigottes should be Burnte, And for that service, was maned out the next night, 30^{ti} of our Bottes and pynases, with Fiar woorkes and other warlike weaponnes. These Frigottes, was so well defended aboorde, and with Thordynaunce ashore, That our men retorned with consuminge only one of them, out of which was saved som of the Spanyardes, who reported Certeynly That their the Treesure of Two myllions was, and so was our men tooke in the Franses.

Notwithstandinge all this Quickninge newes, after some few daies, we waied and stood alongest to the westermoste end of this yland, where we contented us with som refreshinge of water, Orenges and plantaines. Here was built iiij^{or} pynases more at this place sent he aboord me by his warrant 40^{ti} soldyars out of the defyance. The xxiiijth daie we waied and stood alongest for one yland called Kirawsaw,[1] with which we fell the 29th daie, but staied not. Thus standinge alongest. The Firste of December we ancred at Cape de la Vella. The second in the morninge was put in to our bottes and pynases, all our soldyars for Rio de la hatcha. This was tooke, The people beinge all fleed, yet here withe serche in the woodes, and intelligence of som negros, was fownd great store of pearle, plate, Jwells, rialls of plate, Boltes of silke, ritch apparell, with muche other Lugadge. The vjth of this moneth brought in Sir Francis from one other towne called Rangaria, great quantety of pearle, and Lugadge. The ninthe daie came in some Spanyardes with intent to Ransom their houses, negros, and som spanyardes prisoners and Concluded for 24000 pesos, every peso v^{s} vj^{d}. The xiiijth daie came in the same all in pearle. And the xiiijth daie Came in their Liftennant for the delivery. But in the valwinge, Ther quantety and quallyty wold not be tooke, wherfore departed they with fower houres respett for farther answer from there governore don Fansisco manso, his answer was him self wold come to confirance, which he did the xvjth daie. After dynner, our Generall & Co-generall with the Spanyardes had secret confirance about this ransom, wheruppon concludinge, They absolewtly broke of, and therfore in all haste was Fier put to some of the houses, and the governor Two hours tyme to clere him of our army. Thus havinge Burnt Ryo de la hatcha, Rangaria, and Tapia, The xviijth daie we waied and stood alongest for Sancta Marta. To which we came the xxth daie. here we only tooke some fyve prisoners, wherof one was the Liftennant there. The xxjth it was put to fier, and we sett saile for Nombre de Dios, to which we came the xxvijth daie, wher in like manner the people had acquitted the Towne, yet here was fownd by intelligence of som negros, as I hard xxij^{ti} Sowes of silver, golde in Bullion, some Jwells, great store of plate and ryalls of plate, with

[1] Curaçao: Purchas has 'Knaw-saw'.

much other Lugage. The xxixth daie Sir Thomas Baskervile Collonell generall with all his hableste Captaines & soldyars Tooke ther Jorney for Panama now the marke of our viadge who nere the midwaie beinge empeched by some Spanyardes & negros made there retreat to the Shipps at nombre de dios, at this encounter was some fewe of our men slaine, som hurt, Some of the which there lefte to the mersy of the Spanyardes. The vth daie of January all our men beinge shipped, The Towne and galliottes put to fier, we sett saile than by the advise of a Spanyard for the Ryver Nicorago in which waie wee fell with one yland called escudo, a place which afoordeth nothinge good, yet here we staid from the tenth daie untill the xxiijth whan we set saile and plyed to the eastward, which by gods spetiall favor The xxviijth daie we came in with Porta la Bella. This morninge died our generall Sir Francis Drake. This is the place where the people of Nombre de dios meneth to dwell at, Here found we a beginninge of a stronge platforme with 3 Brase peces unmounted. In myne opinionn This was our Beste remove, for if god had not prevented our generalls purpose for the River Nicorago, yt wold have hasarded all her majesties Shipps farr with the rest. Here tooke we in balast, water mendid oure sailes and Calked our Shipps suche as had need. The viijth of February Sir Thomas Baskervile Takin uppon him generall, we all sett saile for Sancta Marta homwardes, But not hable to recover hier than Cartagena, as we gesse in the Bonaventure with the Splyttinge of all our sailes, put over for Jamica, In this course loste we the foresight, The Susan Parnell, The help and the Pegozy. The xxvth daie came we faire by Camina granda,¹ which bore on us in the morninge east northest, and this daie was all our Fleshe and Fishe spent. The Second of Marche makin this our mesery like to be, knowne to Sir Thomas Baskevile who had given me his promise to relive me at my need, His answer was carlessly for us, and withall saide he wold go in with The yland Pynes to water, which I utterly misliked, The wynd than beinge good to stand alongest, very ill to loose, and more for that no englishe man in our Fleet ether knew or ever harde of eny wateringe or other good there. In this resonninge betwixt us, we discried Twenty saile of Shipps a heed us, who waire

¹ Grand Cayman: Purchas has 'Canaria Granda'.

the Kinges menn awarre, watinge our home comminge. yt was my
fortune in the Bonaventure to take too Taske The Visadmirall, one
of the Twelve apostells of the kinges, for so I thought by a great
golden saint mand her pupe, The manor of our feight and my
deservinge, I leave to the report even of myn enemyes.[1] yet Thus
much understand, Their admyrall with the rest all the next daie
beinge in the wind us, was content we shold pase in pease. Thus
beinge quietly and well all disimbogued some 200 Leages, I made
a second demaund of Sir Thomas his promise for vittells, which he
utterly refused, wherfor aswell in regarde of our generall lacke as
myn owne danger with a shott in our Feight, wherin it was indifferent
with me to Lyve or dye. Told him I muste make more haste home,
Than I persuned he wold, yet staied we with hym two daies longer,
whan in a storme I lost him, and this was the xiiij[th] daie of marche

[Endorsed] 1596

> Jornall of y[e] voyage of Sir Francis Drake, and Sir
> John Hawkyns, collected by Captain Troughton.[2]

[1] Troughton's valour was attested in several other accounts (see Ch. 7 below).

[2] Purchas omits the endorsement, and thus any mention of Troughton. He adds,
however, the following passage: 'Now for these two English Sea-worthies, as
wee have begunne their American Adventures, and ended them together, so I
have thought good to insert this following censure of a Gentleman in a Letter of
his, touching them both, as an Epitaph dedicated to their memory.

Sir, I have according to your request, and my owne plainnesse sent you here the
comparison betweene those two Commanders Sir Francis Drake and Sir John
Hawkins. They were both much given to travell in their youth and age, attempting many honourable Voyages alike; as that of Sir John Hawkins to Guiny, to
the Iles of America, to Saint John de Ulua. So likewise Sir Francis Drake after
many Discoveries of the West Indies, and other parts, was the first Englishman
that did ever compasse the World; wherein, as also in his deepe judgement in Sea
causes, he did farre exceed not Sir John Hawkins alone, but all others whomso-
ever. In their owne natures and disposition they did as much differ; as in the
managing matters of Warres, Sir Francis beeing of a lively spirit, resolute, quicke,
and sufficiently valiant: The other slow, jealous, and hardly brought to resolution.
In Councell Sir John Hawkins did often differ from the judgement of others,
seeming thereby to know more in doubtful things, then he would utter. Sir
Francis was a willing hearer of every mans opinion, but commonly a follower of
his owne: he never attempted any action, wherein he was an absolute Commander, but hee performed the same with great reputation, and did easily dispatch
great matters; Contrariwise Sir John Hawkins did only give the bare attempt of

20. *Sir Thomas Baskerville's 'discourse'*[1]

The Brute of this greatt treasure thatt was att port rica, *with* the Later direccions we receavid, mad us to strike thatt way wher undoughtidly we had nott faylid of a greatt fortune, If our hoppes had bin so favorid by god as to have taken the tyme, thatt offerid Itt self, butt having held a more southerly course then we nedid, foloing the opynyon of some thatt held for Guadalupe, we Lenthenid our way so much, thatt 5 frigattes of the kynges who wer

things, for the most part without any Fortune or good successe therein. Sir John Hawkins did naturally hate the Land-souldier, and though hee were very popular, yet he affected more the common sort, then his equals; Sir Francis contrarily did much love the Land-souldier, and greatly advanced good parts, wheresoever he found them. Hee was also affable to all men and of easie accesse. They were both of many vertues, and agreeing in some. As patience in enduring labours and hardnesse, Observation and Memory of things past, and great discretion in sudden dangers, in which, neither of them was much distempered, and in some other vertues they differed. Sir John Hawkins had in him mercie and aptnesse to forgive, and true of word; Sir Francis hard in reconciliation, and constancie in friendship; he was withall severe and courteous, magnanimous, and liberall. They were both faultie in ambition, but more the one then the other; For in Sir Francis was an insatiable desire of honor, indeed beyond reason. He was infinite in promises, and more temperate in adversity, then in better Fortune. He had also other imperfections, as aptnesse to anger, and bitternesse in disgracing, and too much pleased with open flattery: Sir John Hawkins had in him malice with dis-simulation, rudenesse in behaviour, and passing sparing, indeed miserable. They were both happy alike in being Great Commanders, but not of equall successe, and grew great and famous by one meanes, rising through their owne Vertues, and the Fortune of the Sea. Their was no comparison to bee made betweene their wel-deserving and good parts, for therein Sir Francis Drake did farre exceede. This is all I have observed in the Voyages, wherein I have served with them.

R. M.'

[1] B.M., Harleian MSS, 4762, ff. 70–4. The MS has no heading, endorsement or signature. It occurs in a volume of Sir Thomas Baskerville's papers and is written in his own hand, being evidently a draft of the 'discourse' to which he referred elsewhere (documents 44, 45 and 46) and of which he sent copies to Lord Burghley and Sir Thomas Throckmorton. The finished version has not been traced. The draft was composed on the voyage home, between the early days of March and 7 May 1596. It has not hitherto been published.

sent for the treasure recoverid the sayd porte befor us,[1] and falling
with the reargard of our flett, toke one of our smale barkes by
which the had knowledg of our wholl Intent nott only for thatt
place butt Lykwise for Number de dios and panama, which wer
therof presently advertisid, as aperithe by those Instructions I after
toke from their advisos. To be breffe after some 7 or 8 days stay att
guadalupe for the bilding of our pynacis, we sett sayle and upon
the 7 day after being the 11 of november we cam to anker befor
the porte,[2] which we fownd otherwise fortefied then we exspectid,
for upon the entrance of the harborow stod a castell of quarid stone
having 2 greatt Bolwarkes with Cavalliers towardes the Land and
3 plattformes on above the other towardes the sea upon which stod
mor then 30 pecis of cannon and collvering. without this castell
callid the moro standes another plattforme upon which is som 16
or 20 pecis of artelery and from thatt a Lytell standes the owld
castell which is a good strong place biltt much after the manner of
the castell of sluce and much abowght thatt greattnis. Just in
tryangle from the moro and this castell stands the abbye of St
domyngo upon a knape of a hill which Lykwise they had fortefyed
and under thatt a trench calid the callette wherin stod 3 pecis o
coulvering that comandid the rode upon the owttsid of the Iland.
one the other end of the sayd Iland being the easter parte stod an
other forte in the middest of the causey that went throwghe the
watter thatt partid the mayn from this Lytell Iland, and from thatt
forte to the callette I spake of before is 2 other placis fortefyed. Upon
all which places with the front of the towne they had mountid 175
peecis of ordenance,[3] besides those thatt remaynid In the 5 frigattes
which they had placid in this manner. The harborowe att the
entering is nott much broder then the ryver of Tames befor
London; upon the further shore is flattes so thatt of nesessyty yow
must come onder the moro within which ther is a sholl thatt comes
to the platform befor spoken of, ryght against which rode the

---

[1] This was the normal sailing route, which the frigates also followed. It was not the
fact that the English made for Guadalupe that enabled the frigates to catch them up,
but rather the waste of time in the Canaries, an episode Baskerville fails to mention.

[2] 12 November according to other accounts.

[3] The official Spanish report gives 70 (document 29).

frigattes as near the plattforme as the sholls would geve them Leave, the beter to be suckerid from the 2 castells and platforme. Just in the mydest of the cannell they sonke the 2 gallions the bygonia (thatt was Admyral of tera ferme) and the mylanes, and withoutt them towardes the further shole a ship callid the Inglishe and a carvell. In this order bothe the haven and Iland was fortefied the order of which wilbe better discribid by the plate.[1] which having vewid and fynding noe way to atempt itt butt by the moughe of the Harborow we putt althinges in redinis agaynst the nyght following with resolucion to burne the frigattes and so having Landid, to make passag for the enterance of our flett, the beginyng of the nyght we toke; butt we being forcid to way from the place we furst ankerid by reason of the continuall shot they bestowid amongst us (on of which unluckely gave Sir Nicolas Clyford) and to go to the westward could hardly recover the mouthe of the harborow by 12 of cloke; we enterid and In our passing wer excedingly Lardid from the fortes shipps and platforms and to the shipps we cam and 4 of them we fyrid, butt the Illnis of our firworkes with the exceding Labore and perill of the enymy quencid 3 and one was burnid, whose lyght discoverid us so playn, thatt we wer forcid to retire with Loss of 200 hurte and slayn men, and the most of our botes so beaten throughe with the cannon thatt with much adoe we kept them above water. som of the menn thatt quittid the burnid frigattes we savid who mad known unto us very pertycularly the forcis of thatt place which wer as followith. The towne on other was able to make 600, The king garison in the castelles wer 200, In the gallion calid the Bygonya which brought the Treasur, 200, In the mylaness the other galion 100, in the five frigates 500.[2] the morow after the day did no soner apear butt we saw the Admyral of the frygattes sinke and befor night all the rest[3] by which means all hope of entering the harborow with our flett was taken away from us and to atempt any thing our flett having no rode butt the open sea, and such a currant and so Ile grownd thatt we Lost

[1] See document 28.
[2] The total is considerably higher than any of the figures mentioned in the Spanish reports (see Ch. 5).
[3] The remaining three were not sunk.

many Ankers, the generall thought nott fitt, considering the strength of the placis we wer to atempt, the worst of which with thos forcis they had, was able to withhould a kinges powre for divers mounthes. so asking the advis of the captains of Land and sea and fynding their opynions to concur with his, we sett sayle for Terra ferm, and to Capo de velo we came and Ankerid wher we advisid to take the town of rio de La Hach in our way, and I with 400 menn enterid our pynacis Leving our shipps att rods under the cape, and by 12 acloke thatt nyght I landid befor the Towne and toke Itt, butt the governeur being advertisid from there days befor by advise from St domyngo and thatt day by his canoas thatt wer afishing for pearle who discoverid us, had caryed away the kynges chache and sent Itt to Zalu de pare 30 Leagues Into the cuntry. I in Landing having taken certain prisoners who servid for guides, followid after and som quantety of pearle we toke, but the cache escapid. The morow after we had som parley with the enymy about the ransom-yng of thir towne, butt fownd thatt nonn of them had powre to capytulatt throwghly for Itt and therfor we sent them away willing them to come no more withoutt absolut atoryty to conclud. to be shorte the oyador cam (which is an officer to hear and determyn all mater for the kyng) and we found hym to com Rather to entrate, then to make offer of any thing and so we would no further hear hym which he seing offerid 10,000 dukettes which we refusid and sent hym away willing hym to come no more withowtt resolusion to geve us our full demand, and so he departid; we having enterid again their Cuntry taken their a ranchery[1] with their Canoas and som quantetys of pearle and burnid their housis in the Cuntry brought them again to seke us and to composision we came; 25,000 duckettes they wer to geve us and pledgis they putt in, and within 4 days we wer to receav Itt in pearle; butt thatt day comyng we wer forcid to geve them 2 days more, att which tym ytt came butt so over ratid as we thought thatt we refusid Itt and brake of, and thatt nyght I enterid again into the Cuntry having notid by som thatt came from them thatt the most parte of their welth with their Ladies Lay som 8 Leagues Into the Cuntry. with much adoe passing many very Ill passagis att Length I came to the place and

[1] La Ranchería, a pearling settlement.

In my way falling upon certayn spanyardes in a wode of which on only escapid they wer advertisid and so with all they had retirid over a ryver and kept the passag against me. thatt Night I could nott atempt them by reason my men wer all tyrid with the greatt Jorney for they had travaylid 40 milles withowtt eating and drinking. the morow comyng I atemptid Itt and gott Itt with the Loss of 2 or 3 menn and followid them for som Leage or to in the wodes and forcid them all to quitt their horcis so thatt I gott som thre or fowr-score Jenattes from them all sadelled and bridelid with som prisoners butt seing no means to recover the rest, and thatt to go further was to Leaff my self In the wode I retournid; and thatt nyght I marcid som 3 or 4 Leagues fearing the enymy myght kepe another passag of a ryver against me by Burnyng a brig and keping the other sid, which I found to be true for the enymy had burnid the bridg butt I fownd nonn Lodgid one the other shore which mad me thinke their forcis wer nott fully assembelyd and so passing som menn over thatt could swim with their Arms I fownd means by the mornyng to mad a passig upon the ruins and so retornid to the flett and fownd sir frauncis to have burnid the towne with the aramchery and canoas. and so being bordid we sett sayle for st marta whyther we cam, Landid and toke the Towne, the enemy making some shew as If they meant to defend the passag of a ryver, butt after delyvering some harquebusades a bothe sides they retyrid having Left theyr Lyftenant governeur with us. In this place our shipping rode so Ille, by reason of the exceading wind thatt every smale of the monn comes from those myghty mountaynes coverid with snow, thatt the most of our shipps drove on abord the other so thatt the mornyng comyng, sir frauncis would no Lenger atend any fortune In thatt place, Notwithstanding we hard thatt nott far from thence wer the richest mynns thatt ever wer fownd In the Indies. being Bordid we sett sayle for Nombre de dios, and thither we came, and presently Landid; the enymy bestowing some cannonado there-upon retyrid to a forte they hade upon a Lytell hill upon the easter end of the Towne, butt seing our resolucion to asault Itt they quytid itt and retirid into the wodes, and we to the Towne, wher we found nott so much of any thinge as would supp us. Som of our Tropes we sent after the enemy who Lyttid upon som xx^{ty} barrs of sillver and on of gould with certayn other platte, and this was all this place yealdid us, for all their treasur with other goodes they had sent Long befor Into the southe sea to the province of Nicarague. Som prysoners we toke, amongst the which we found one the best guid of all the Indies for pannama. The next day we resting fytting our selves as well as our means would geve us Leave for thatt so tedious and so troblesom a Jorney, the myseris of which I protest was very greatt, for all of us nonn exceptid was forcid to cary nyn days bread with hym 40 bollettes his bandolyers of pouder his Armes and a pound and a half In his pockett. Thus Lodid we sett forward, and our way we fownd In this sorte. The first League upon the Tope of a mountayn coveryd with wode so narow, thatt the Breadthe was nott above xxty fote, throughe which passag was cutte. which being clay with the contynuall going of their reekos[1] and dayly falling of raine is so stary[2] and fowle thatt every steps is above the knee. The next 2 Leagues you take up the course of a ryver for the most part up to the girdell, att the entering of which the enymy Atendid us thinking to have defendid the passag butt seing we enterid the ryver having geven us 2 saulvos of Harquebusades retirid, and we held one our Jorney to the fote of the mountayn of Capyra wher we Lodgid and thus endid our first days Travayle. The next mornyng we marchid over the mountayn which is aboutt some Leagu and a half hyghe, the passag very Ill being all cley which by contynuall rayn thatt falls ther so foule thatt every stepe is to the mid Legg, the way thatt is cutt being so narrow thatt a horsman cann hardly pas without tuching his knees on eyther banke, and this is to be considerid thatt all the rest is so thick in wode thatt ther is no other passag to be thought one. over this mountayn we came, and fownd the enymy to be Lodgid att the fote of Itt att the entering of a ryver, who upon our comyng retyrid withoutt Ingaging hym self In any fyght, thoughe he had placis of such advantag thatt one hundereth menn would hav staggerid a greatt Army. This ryver we enterid, being somtymes to the middest somtyme deper and for the most part to the mid thighe, the course of which we followid for som 3 Leagues. 2 of which being passid the way grue very difficult, by reason the ryver faling from so hyghe mountayns mad greatt

---

[1] *Recuas* – mule-trains.　　　　[2] Dungy?

pittes som of 20 or 30 fadom, and the shalows full of greatt slypery rokes above the watter. over the depist of which holls we wer forcid to pas upon the sid of a rocke which slopid to thatt hole, which being coverid with som 3 fyngers watter mad Itt slippery thatt he thatt missid foting was drownid withoutt remedy. In this roke the moyles have mad with their contynuall travayle certayn Lytell holls with their fette which If they miss they ar Lost withoutt recovery. hear the kyng hath Lost and Loshithe dayly Infynitt treasure, which thoughe in thoss partes ther be excelent divers, yett by reason of the couldnis of the watter they could never gett any thing. over this place we passid having only Lost one mann, so folloing the course of this ryver som half Englyshe myle we stroke over the fote of a mountayn and enteryd an other ryver which we folloid for som League and a half, and then toke up a mountayn full of stayrs and as foule as the first, the top of which we followid for a League. which being defendid, we came to a greatt ynn callid the Venta of Cabrados[1] and in english of Broken watters, by reason of the asembly of many smal ryvers. This house we fownd fyrid by the enymys, and hard many droms and harquebuse shot rownd abowte us, which mad thinke the enymy nott to be far. In this place we Lodgid, being the only place we could make fire and se our selves together in and Ly dry in in all our Jorney,[2] the reason was the contynuall rayn thatt fell and the contynuall watter we went in, so thatt no wod would burne thoughe we had nothing butt wod and watter about us. hear we fownd our selfes in greatt misseris, for all the pouder we caryed in our pokettes was wholy Lost our mach greatly decayid our vytuall altogether spoylid and our selves barfote. yett the hopes of thatt rich place mad us to think of no exstremyty, and therfor assonn as the day aperid we putt forward; taking up the corse of thoss broken watters som Englyshe mile we asendid another mountaine very foul and stayry being all coverid with wode, as the rest is withoutt any shew of any playn, throughe which the passag is cutt. upon the tope of which mountaine being exeding narow the enymy had mad a forte being the strongist and

[1] La Venta de la Quebrada.
[2] The Spaniards (whether Amaya's men or Conabut's is not clear) had evidently set fire to the inn but not completely destroyed it.

fittist place to defend for the place was so asurid being upon the knape of a hill far hyer then the rest, the way to atempt itt nott being above 3 fote brode or 4 att the most, the desentes of the hills so stepe and so thike of Brambles thorns and wode thatt no way could be found to pas Itt, butt only throughe the forte, upon which we cam ere we knew of Itt and receavid assaulvo of harquebusades which slue som of our menn, thatt Itt stagerid our forlorne hope, till such tym as I came upe and causid them to geve upon Itt, and so being secondid by som new tropes we contynued the asaut for som 3 howrs wher I had my brother hurte[1] Captain marchant slayn with divers other Lyftenantes and officers and som 60 or 70 other soudiars slayn and hurte. In this asault captain powre and Captain Chichester did very bravly for they never Left the asaut to the end. seing our powder spent and the Impossibilyty of caryeng the place, I grewe to advise with the captains whatt course to hould, and having callid our guides, and fownd by them ther was no other way butt only throughe the forte and to gett thatt ther restid no hope, we resoulvid to retourne, nessesity calling us to use expedicion for all our powder vittualls and means to relive our selves wer wholy consumid, and many hurte men and those of our best Lay upon us, and how to cary them we knew nott, so taking upe our hurte and beryeing our dead we returnid into our quarter we Lay the nyght befor and ther dispacid on of our prysoners we had taken to don Alonso de sotto Mayor generall of thoss cuntris who was in thatt forte, to shew hym thatt Nessescity forcid us to Leave certain hurte soudiars behind us, which we Lokid shuld be well Intreatid att his handes, Considering the good wars we held with his nacion, which If In the Lest poynt he Infringid, we shewid the Law to be in our handes to reveng our selves and therfor willid hym nott to dowte the affect of Itt If with all curtesis he entertaynid nott our soudiars so taking up my Brother with 18 other hurte I retornid with marvelous troble and great difficultis, and cam to Nombre de dios the fyft day I cam from thence, wher I fownd the Town burnid, and the flett had bin departid, If my Letter[2] sent by a negro to the generall

---

[1] Nicholas Baskerville, who survived the voyage. Arnold had been buried in Nombre de Dios before the march began.

[2] Document 36.

had nott com. This Jorney brake wholy thoss tropes I caryed with me which wer 600 menn, for we never in this 5 days Lay dry by reason of the contynuall rayn and fogge nor found never place wher we myght Lodg together, wer itt nott att the Cabrados, nor never saw fyre butt only att thatt place nor ther had nott the benyfitt of thatt burnid house helpid us. having recoverid our flett we advisid of som other fortune and fowlowid the opynion of an ould gentill-man we tok who semid to be willing to follow our fortunes, his own having throwne hym Into great povertis.[1] he advisid us to go into the botom of the bay of Cameron and so to enter the Lagus of nycaragu within which som 70 Leagues, was a Cytye callid granada standing within 4 Leagues of the southe sea which towne was by his sayeing very rich. Towardes this place we went and rann Into the bay som 50 Leagues wher we fownd the windes and corantes so contrary thatt had we nott recoverid a Lytell Iland the wholl flett had bin Indangerid to hav ronn ashore. hear we Lay som 14 days att the end of which fownd the wether more favorable to go back and so sett sayle upon which day sir frauncis fell sike as I thinke throughe greffe and within 5 days after died, which I seing and the flett to want many things I thought Itt best to seke owtt porte bello the better to supply and Lykwise to make us redy for any other enterpris, and thither we cam wher after we had buryed the generall we taryed 12 days in rasing the forte thatt was ther abillding and putting of our flett in order, and so sett sayl If with resolucion Itt wer possyble to recover st marta hoping to have stroken more to our profittes this second tym then the first, butt being Inconterid with a storm which contynued upon us 7 days and sprong in the garland and divers other shipps greatt Leakes we wer forcid to Leave that course thinking to have recoverid the Ile of Iamayca, butt we wer so deceavid by the curraunt thatt we could nott recover no parte of Iland butt wer caryed upon the Cost of Cuba, so thatt then we sought for to fynd the Ill of pynas, and being redy, to have gon In with harborow, we descoverid twenty sayle of the kynges Armados making towardes us, which we seing mad with them butt allways kept the wind, and so about 2 acloke in the After nonn we came to fyght thir twenty against our xiii sayle and a carvell, for captain

[1] Probably Alberto Ojeda (see document 32).

winter with her majesties ship had befor ronn away from me with 2 or 3 other,[1] so this fyght contynued till Itt grew towardes nyght by which tym the vis admyrall with 5 or six other ships which mayntaynid the most parte of the fyght wer sorly beaten the Admyrall with the rest of the flett, fell asterne and so keping our wake sought to gett the wind which the visadmyrall and the rest of the shipps seing Lay so in the wind thatt we overslypid them, and so fell with his flett, which I seing and dowghting greater focis to be att Cap st antony willed my master to ster one his course directly and to geve them the wind I shuld have drawen my self so far into the bay of mexico the currant setting in thatt I shuld nott have recoverid the cap, which mad me of 2 evells chuse the Less. the Admyral with his sqadron haveng the wind came up on my brodsid butt the other 7 ships som of them Lay at hull som other in the wind and one whos stern was blowen up with her own powder bar rome with the Lande. nyght being com the vis Admyrall shott of a pece which mad us Judge her in som distress, butt presently we saw her in a Lyght fyr and so contyneid till she was burnid to the watter shoting of greatt store of ordenance and blowing up greatt quantety of powder, and sure I thinke nonn of her menn was savid for no ship durst com near her for fear of her ordenance and pouders and she had cast of her bote In the beginyng of the fyght, the admyrall kepyng the wind of us with his flett all nyght kep in our brod sid, In the mornyng asson as day Brake bar rome with me butt seing me to

---

[1] Cp. Maynarde's narrative. In Baskerville's papers (B.M., Harleian MSS, 4762, f. 80) occurs an unsigned, unheaded statement, in another hand than Baskerville's, accusing William Winter, captain of the *Foresight*, of cowardice and desertion: 'the 15. of februarie captaine winter did Dreame that we were nere the shore, when we were att the leaste 12. leagues of, and so caused the master for to caste abought the shipp at 3. of the cloke in the morninge whether the master woulde or no, onlie for to lose the fleete, not ceasinge untill he had gott all the companie for to do yt havinge the bonaventure the hoope the adventur and the susane under one lee ... on the 10. daye of marche we mett with 5 shipps the which we mough well have taken or the most of them for captaine Chichester and all the companie were all willinge to have fough lounger and gonne nere with them to as good intent as mough be, Butt captaine winter most cowerlie went into his cabine and wold not com nere and then captaine Chichester went downe to him to have him com up'.

strike my topsayls and to atend hym he agayn kept the wind, for he saw thatt he wantid 7 of his flett and thought itt better to Lett us alonn, seing ther was nothing to be gotten by us, and so keping still the wind kept company with us. one of our marchand shipps being gotten closs a bord the shor was forcid to tak about upon her other bourd and so to recover my wake the better to wether the Cape Corentes which the enymy seing sent 3 shipps thinking to have taken her or aforcid her to ronn her self ashor butt seing thatt I stroke my topsayles for her and thatt the defiance bar rom with me, they Left her and recoverid their flett which now was fallen Into our wake and so folloid us, which mad me to resoulve thatt If I saw the cape clere from other Armado to tary them and to fyght agayn, butt they having sid of the cape and seing a grett galle of wind att southe east which mad them to concestur ther flett could nott rid ther by Lytell and Lytle fell astern, and so mad In with the land, which mad me to thinke thatt they would knowing the cost have kepe closs abord Itt bothe to gett the wind of us and Lykwise to hav mad a shorter way to the havana to have Joynid with their flett, butt att the setting In of the Night those in tope tould Me thatt they bar into the sea which mad me thinke he Atendid to hear whatt was becom of the rest of his shipps thatt the day befor wer so beaten. [In this fyght the garland the bonadventur the defyance the Adventur and hope did very well and of the marchands the congard and Lytell Jhon][1]

---

[1] The passage in brackets is deleted.

IV. *The Canaries*

Whereas the English were reticent[1] about the episode at Grand Canary, the Spaniards produced a mountain of reports and literary works on the subject, but it is questionable whether this productivity owed as much to patriotic fervour as to factious spite.[2] In 1594 the

[1] The affair is dealt with briefly in most of the narratives and in the third-hand reports that reached the English government in late November and December (documents 24 and 25). Unfortunately the account written by Sir John Hawkins himself has never been found and may well no longer exist. It is mentioned in a letter from Lady Margaret Hawkins to Sir Robert Cecil dated 12 December 1595 (*Cal. Hatfield MSS*, v, 495–6). She writes that she has 'last night' received a letter from 'Master Hawkins' by one Captain Welshe, who came into their company by chance and went with them some 40 leagues beyond the Canaries. Hawkins, the captain said, had forborne to send any advertisement to her majesty, to Burghley, to the lord admiral or to any other of his friends at court only because nothing was done worth the writing. Nevertheless he thought it not amiss to set down himself what befell at the Canaries lest it should be mis-reported; wherewith he willed Lady Hawkins to make Burghley, the lord admiral and Cecil acquainted. She asks Cecil's advice as to whether she should acquaint the queen therewith or whether he would make it known to her, 'for although it be not as good as I wish and daily pray for, yet I thank God it is not very ill, and I would be loth that her Highness should understand by any other that I should hear directly from Master Hawkins and would not make it known to Her Majesty howsoever it were, for so I think it my duty. I send you a true copy of his own letter by my servant the bearer.'

[2] A masterly account of the whole episode is given in Antonio Rumeu de Armas, *Piraterías y Ataques Navales contra las Islas Canarias*, II, pt. ii (1948), 662–743 and III, pt. ii, 951–1022 (documents). The main Spanish materials are in Simancas, Guerra Antigua, *legajos* 432, 448, 459, 469. N. Alamo, 'Drake y Van der Doez en Gran Canaria', *Revista de Historia* (de las Islas Canarias), 35–6 (1932), 75–100; and 37–8 (1933), 153–7, 181–92, prints, from the MSS in the Museo Canario (Las Palmas), an *información* on behalf of Antonio Pamochamoso, Alvarado's lieutenant at the time of the attack. A short *relación* of unknown authorship and provenance, the content of which is of minor interest, is to be found in the Bibliothèque Publique et Universitaire, Geneva, Collection Edouard Favre, vol. 82, ff. 34–6 (printed in Rumeu de Armas, *Piraterías*, III, pt. ii, 951–3).

Canary islanders, after five years of unrest under the rule of Captain-General Luis de la Cueva y Benavides, had secured the latter's recall to Spain, the abolition of the captain-generalcy and the re-assertion of the authority of the *audiencia*, headed by Dr Antonio Arias, the regent. This created a difficult situation for the new governor, Alonso de Alvarado,[1] when he arrived in April 1595. As a non-islander and a military man he was regarded with suspicion by the civilians and must have found the influence of the ex-governor, Melchor de Morales, irritating. The Italian engineers Leonardo Torriani and Prospero Casola, who had come out with Benavides in 1589 to re-plan the fortification of the islands, had produced admirable maps and designs, but nothing had yet been done to realize their schemes.[2] In response to strong warnings of English and Moorish attacks that summer, the best Alvarado could do was to make some repairs and improvements to the existing forts and keep continuous guard at Santa Catalina bay (the most likely landing place) and elsewhere.

On the events of 26–8 September/6–8 October Alvarado's personal account and the lengthy *información* substantiating it[3] are more credible than the so-called 'relacion verdadera' compiled by the *audiencia*,[4] but neither of these openly partisan reports can compare in clarity, conciseness and liveliness with Casola's more

[1] Alvarado had served under Don John of Austria in Granada and at Lepanto and had played an active part in the repressive measures in Aragón. He died in 1599 of a wound received during the successful Dutch assault on Las Palmas.

[2] Torriani's MS 'Descrittione et historia del Regno del Isole Canarie gia dette le Fortunate con il Parere delle loro Fortificationi' was published in D. J. Wölfel, *Die Kanarischen Inseln und ihre Urbewohner* (Leipzig, 1940).

[3] Alvarado to the king, 12 October 1595 (Simancas, Guerra Antigua, *legajo* 448). The *información*, dated 28 October, is in the same *legajo*. Both are printed in Rumeu de Armas, *Piraterías*, III, pt. ii, 956–60, 963–81.

[4] Simancas, Guerra Antigua, *legajo* 432. This *relación*, avowedly written as a counterblast to unauthorized reports, attempted to show that the governor had advocated defending the city from its walls, while the *audiencia* had insisted upon and organized the manning of the beaches, a story which flatly contradicts not only Alvarado's case, but also the independent judgements of Casola (document 21), the anonymous letter-writer (document 23) and the island *cabildo* (14 October 1595: Simancas, Guerra Antigua, *legajo* 448, printed in Rumeu de Armas, *Piraterías,* III, pt. ii, 960–63).

objective description (document 21). What emerges from the Spanish material is that divided councils in the island camp produced confusion and delay that might have proved fatal had not Drake, for reasons which remain obscure, spent the greater part of the morning preparing to attack. The Spaniards, as landsmen, have nothing to say about the condition of the sea, which figures in one English account as the sole cause of withdrawal and in others as a contributory factor.[1] Nor could a Spaniard be expected to take into consideration the mental reservations and disagreements among the English, though an unknown Canarian wit did divine that Drake had reason not to risk serious loss for such refreshment as Las Palmas might afford.[2] Though he alone stints praise of the islanders' valour, the evidence taken together shows that neither side used its fire-power to much effect. The attackers suffered very few casualties, the defenders none at all.

Not the least interesting of the documents below is that which contains the depositions of the prisoners (document 22). However, the Spaniards probably gleaned more from their prisoners than the depositions suggest. Another account credits the prisoners collectively with the statement that the English 'resolved upon this course because Francis Drake assured them there would be no resistance . . . and they blamed Francis Drake much for having deceived them'.[3] It is a remarkable feature of the depositions that they mention neither Puerto Rico nor Panama. Several days after the statements were recorded, the *audiencia* reported that Drake was bound for the Indies, but that the prisoners did not know to which part, since the generals had kept this secret.[4] Nevertheless even before the date of the *audiencia*'s report the islanders appear somehow to have reached the conclusion that Puerto Rico was the main target. Accordingly a dispatch boat left La Palma, it is reported, on 29 September/9 October, and another left Tenerife on 3/13

[1] Documents 24 and 22; VTD.
[2] Document 23.
[3] Bibliothèque Publique et Universitaire, Geneva, Collection Edouard Favre, vol. 82, ff. 34–6.
[4] 'Relacion verdadera' (Simancas, Guerra Antigua, *legajo* 432).

October.[1] The first of these to reach Puerto Rico did so on 5/15 November, two days after Pedro Tello's arrival and thus too late to be of decisive moment.[2] Meanwhile a report that Drake had been repulsed with heavy loss reached Spain through private channels by 22 October/1 November,[3] and on 3/13 November the king in his instructions to Avellaneda specifically mentioned intelligence received from Tenerife (document 38).

The famous victory of October 1595 cannot be said to have had any great effect on the war. It inspired the Canarian poet, Bartolomé Cairasco de Figueroa, to write a 'canto heroico', as well as a lengthy 'romance',[4] and provided not a few other islanders with an

[1] On 14 October the *cabildo* of Tenerife wrote to the king that it had been learned from the prisoners 'that their design was to go to your majesty's Indies, whither we immediately dispatched in your majesty's service an advice boat, especially for Puerto Rico, which is their chief objective' (Simancas, Guerra Antigua, *legajo* 432). On the same day the *corregidor* of Tenerife reported that a light and weatherly caravel had departed on the 13th, and that the enemy's objectives were La Margarita, Santo Domingo, Puerto Rico and other places. An official record of proceedings at Tenerife gives the text of the first letter from the *audiencia* of Canaria, dated 8 October, requesting the dispatch of an advice boat to Puerto Rico and Santo Domingo, because, it states, these were the nearest places in the Indies. This record also, however, includes their second letter, of 10 October, ordering that the advice boat should make 'for Puerto Rico and Santo Domingo, whither it is understood this fleet is bound'. The *corregidor*'s letter and the official record are both in Simancas, Guerra Antigua, *legajo* 432. On 5 January 1596 the casa de la contratación reported to the crown the arrival of a ship which had left Puerto Rico on 10 November. The news she brought was that the dispatch boat from Tenerife had not arrived by that date; nor had a dispatch boat which, according to this report, had left La Palma on 9 October (A. de I., Contratación, 5170, lib. x, f. 1).
[2] Document 29.
[3] A. de I., Contratación, 5169, lib. ix, f. 427. The report was relayed by a merchant from his factor at Tenerife. The official channels of Spanish intelligence were blocked, according to the anonymous wit (document 23), because the Canarians could not agree who should have the honour (and presumably the reward) of carrying the news of victory to Spain.
[4] A copy of the 'canto', which is written in *esdrujulo* verse, is included in the volume 'Esdrujúlea', Museo Canario, Colección Millares Torres, t. 1. The 'romance' appeared in Cairasco's *Templo Militante, Triumphos de Virtudes, Festividades y Vidas de Santos* (Valladolid, 1603; Lisbon, 1615). Part of the former

occasion to indulge their taste for ballads and verses. On these our anonymous satirist (document 23) offers sufficient comment. His letter, for all its textual corruption and abstruseness of personal and literary allusion, presents a point of view so unusual in its detachment and cynicism that it stands in a class of its own in the documentation of this voyage. To the historian, familiar with the personalities and events from a variety of angles, its sympathetic appeal is almost irresistible.

21. *Prospero Casola's report, 8 October 1595*[1]

At dawn on Friday the sixth of this month, day of Santa Fe, the sentinel on the mountain of Las Isletas lit the beacon, the castle fired a gun and 28 ships were sighted. Later it was known that among them were six galleons of the queen of England's, the rest belonging to merchants, and that the generals by sea were Francis Drake and John Hawkins and the land-generals Nicholas Clifford and Thomas Baskerville. They first sent a launch with only eight soldiers to reconnoitre the harbour. This then returned to the fleet,[2] and another launch, bearing Francis Drake, came out together with a caravel. These arrived in the bay of Santa Catalina, where they left a buoy as a marker, and Francis Drake then returned to the fleet while the caravel went on to reconnoitre the whole shore as far as the bay of San Pedro.[3] They took 500 men out of the six

and the whole of the latter are printed in J. A. Rey, *Drake dans la Poésie Espagnole* (Paris, 1906). Cairasco was a canon of the cathedral of Santa Ana, Canary Islands, and a famous poet.

[1] Simancas, Guerra Antigua, *legajo* 448, printed in Rumeu de Armas, *Piraterías*, III, pt. ii, 954–6. Endorsed: 'To the king, our lord. To the hands of Andrés de Prada, secretary of war. Canaria. To his majesty, 8 October 1595. Prospero Casola. Recounts what happened when the English fleet [etc.]'. On the back of the letter is Casola's pen and ink sketch of the attack (plate I). Casola was one of two Italian military engineers who had been sent to the Canaries in 1589 to re-design the islands' fortifications. Leonardo Torriani, his companion, had already returned to Spain.

[2] This apparently remained anchored off Los Roques, near Las Isletas.

[3] To the eastward of the town.

galleons and some other large ships and distributed them into 27 launches with 27 standards. Fifteen warships set out with them and they reached the bay of Santa Catalina at about twelve o'clock. Three ships went in front of the launches and cast anchor twenty paces from the shore and began to bombard the men at the defence-works. A little later two field pieces arrived and with them they held the enemy. While they were fighting a shot was fired from the fort[1] which hit one of the three ships, carried away the bittacle[2] and killed five men. As they realized the damage that could be done them from there they withdrew about 300 paces farther down, where Governor Alonso de Alvarado was, with four more field pieces, which fired more than eighty shots. One round of 36 shot hit a launch, killing an English captain and four others. They moved a little farther down to the stream of Hornillo, where three shots were fired at the same ship that had been damaged by the fort. One of the ships was holed near the water and was sinking, as was clearly shown by their stopping the leak and manning the pump. Fourteen English came out in a boat, bringing a cable, with the aid of which, and of the tide, they saved the ship. Thereupon they left that position and the launches made seawards with many wounded and returned to their ships.[3] The fifteen ships went on to the bay of Santa Ana, where the fort fired a great number of shot at them, four of them being damaged. They for their part fired at the fort of Santa Ana and at the city, where their shot fell among the bishop's company without harming a single christian or heretic. Thence they departed that night and moved to Arganeguín, where Drake

[1] The fort called Santa Catalina, here 'el castillo del puerto'.

[2] 'La abitacolo de la agufa' – a variant not given in A. Jal, *Glossaire Nautique* (Paris, 1848–50) – literally, the little room of the needle. The bittacle was a large wooden cupboard stationed on deck in front of the helm, housing the steering compass, a lamp for reading the same at night, and running glasses. See W. E. May, 'The Binnacle', *Mariner's Mirror*, 40 (1954), 21–32, and D. W. Waters, 'Bittacles and Binnacles', *Mariner's Mirror*, 41 (1955), 198–208.

[3] 'They stayed fighting and keeping up this pressure for a little less than an hour and then withdrew with some damage, coming to a position directly opposite, out of range of fire from any direction, and rejoining the rest of the galleons which had remained anchored out at sea.' (Alvarado to the king, 12 October 1595, Simancas, Guerra Antigua, *legajo* 448).

landed with 500 men; and because the water was not to his liking he preferred not to take it from there but to go to Gomera.[1] Apart from the ten killed, there were fifteen English wounded in this conflict, and in Arganeguín nine, among them a captain called Grimston. Two were captured and two got away, and later a Polish mariner called Gasparan escaped. These gave account of all that had happened.[2]

It now remains for me to warn your majesty that the hand of God was at work in these events; if God had not ruled it so, it would have gone very hard for us. For the troops of this island are raw, and when they saw the launches coming they were much dismayed, except for Alonso de Alvarado, the provincial, Gerónimo de Aguilera and myself. We four were of one mind: to fight the enemy on the beach and to fight to the death – contrary to the regent, who did not want us to fight and ordered his secretary to retrieve the guns that were being taken to the defence positions. They made the oxen turn back, causing much harm and the danger that the enemy might take the opportunity to disembark. The governor and I repaired to the spot and in spite of the regent and his secretary we had the guns loaded into the carts; and by a miracle of God the oxen, without a driver, began to run like horses and arrived at the right place with the guns, to the amazement of everyone. Then, when Alvarado had ordered the companies to march immediately towards the position with the other four pieces, Melchor Morales, late governor of this island, arrived and ordered them to remain, saying that the regent's orders were not to fight on the shore, but to go and defend the city walls, because so powerful a fleet with so much artillery and the terror of the 27 launches could not fail to destroy any force that should attempt to resist their landing. There was such an uproar about this that we went over there, and the governor said they should tell the regent that what he had ordered was for the benefit of his majesty's service and that anything contrary was not to be done, and in great anger he told Morales to go away. These orders were carried out, and the troops and the governor himself reached their positions. Thus it would be

[1] There is no other evidence that the English touched at Gomera.
[2] See document 22.

advisable for your majesty to give express orders that the *audiencia* should not interfere in any military matter, for they are not soldiers. On the day in question they did not go out bearing arms, but in their black cloaks on horseback, though without getting as far as the shore; they took no pains to encourage the troops nor to provide necessaries and they obstructed all Alvarado's orders.

Your majesty should command that the fort of the port of Las Isletas must regularly keep twelve quintals of powder, the *alcalde* being bound to do so on pain of losing his post immediately he is found without such a supply. It should be requisitioned from the council and each *regidor* should be under penalty of 200 ducats if the powder is not delivered. This should be enforced by the governor, since it is for the benefit of the island. That day there were 200 quintals available and when the governor sent to ask the *alcalde* whether he was supplied he replied that he was, but later said that he was not. He fired no more than four guns during the fighting. It was because the fort did not fire and because the guns had not enough balls to bring down the ships' topsails that the enemy left not a single ship behind . . .[1]

22. *Statements of prisoners captured at Grand Canary*[2]

(a) *Vincent Bluq*

At Canaria on 10 October 1595 [statements were received before the *audiencia* from two prisoners in the manner following].[3]

---

[1] The *alcalde* in charge of the fort was later criticized for his parsimony in the use of powder. He was saving it for later use (Rumeu de Armas, *Piraterías*, ii, pt. ii, 710–11). The remainder of the letter shortly considers the future defence of the island and of Fuerteventura.

[2] Simancas, Guerra Antigua, *legajo* 432. Extract. The document consists of depositions attached to the *audiencia*'s report. The first three statements, by Spaniards, merely corroborate the official report. The text then continues as given here. Following the three prisoners' statements come depositions by the peasants who captured them and finally certain statements relating to a petition protesting against the *informaciones* inspired by Alvarado and calling for the preparation of the *relación verdadera* by the *audiencia*.

[3] The passage omitted rehearses the events of the English descent and the capture of the prisoners.

22. STATEMENTS OF PRISONERS

For the purpose of this inquiry Paul Reynaldos, Frenchman and citizen of this island took the oath as interpreter and one of the prisoners took the oath [etc.].

Asked his name, age, position and birthplace, he said, through the interpreter, that he was Vincent Bluq, aged 23, born in the city of Angers in France, and came as a soldier in the service of an English captain called Grimston in a ship of 200 tons called the Salomon Bonaventure.

Asked what fleet this was and who commanded it, he said it was a royal fleet set forth by the queen and private persons. The old man Francis Drake was general, who brought a brother and a nephew[1] with him (their names he does not know), the admiral being Sir John Hawkins – he who was at San Juan de Ulúa twenty years ago.

Asked how many ships there were, of what burden, and how many men they carried, he said that 27 ships left England from the port of Plymouth; en route they met another English ship which joined the fleet and remained in company until they arrived at this port, wishing to share in its capture; on the night of their withdrawal, seeing that they neither did nor could succeed, the ship asked permission to go on its way and was allowed to do so. Twenty of the ships were of 200 to 400 tons, carrying about 2,000 men, all English. The rest were small, with few men, and he does not know their burden.

Asked what artillery these ships carried, he said that the six great ships of the queen's each carried 50 guns large and small, of brass and iron, and the rest ten to fifteen ordinary guns of brass and iron.

Asked how long ago they left Plymouth, what route they followed and whether they called anywhere, he said that they left 35 days ago and came straight to this island, though on the way they sighted land which he understood to be Madeira. They also saw certain ships to windward, but took nothing from them, and made their voyage direct to this island without taking anything on the way.

Asked if he knew whether Drake came straight to this island by order of the queen of England to sack it, as he attempted to do on

---

[1] Unidentified. The brother was Thomas. The phrase used of Drake is 'Francisco Draque el viejo'.

Friday the sixth of this month, he said that they well knew they were coming straight here and that from the way they were sailing he inferred as much, but of General Drake's intention he knew no more than that he came to replenish his victuals and other supplies in this island.

Asked how many launches and men took part in the assault the day they attempted to take the island and how they were arrayed, he said that he and his master stayed in the ship they came in and did not leave it because they had no boat; had they had one, they would have gone. He did not count the boats nor the men, but they had orders to land the first boat-loads and to return for the rest up to the number of 1,200 men in twelve companies. The general of the assault force was Sir Thomas Baskerville, an Englishman and a great and valiant soldier, who had commanded in France under Vendôme.[1]

Asked why, having launched such a large force of boats, men, ships and artillery against this city, they withdrew without landing and turned tail, he said since he saw the great resistance facing them ashore, the damage done to their ships and men, the power of men there was upon the beach and the good order in which they fought, it seemed to the general that he would risk losing many men, and he therefore withdrew.

Asked how many men in the ships and launches were killed and wounded, he said that he only knew of three English killed and two wounded in all; since he was not in the launches he did not know what damage they suffered nor how far the ships were damaged by gunfire.

Asked about the quality of the men in the fleet and whether there were men of rank among them, he said that they included many gentlemen and men of rank, whose names he did not know.

Asked where they stopped when they set sail and withdrew on the Friday night, he said that they went to the place where the fleet anchored on the other side of this island, where he was captured, and that they went there to water because they had none, but because the water did not seem good they took little of it.

Asked what men went ashore at the said port, he said he did not

[1] Henry IV, who was also duc de Vendôme.

134

know the number, but that many did land, including Francis Drake and the said admiral, and that in the evening they returned to the ships.

Asked what persons went ashore with him when he was captured, he said that he left with eight others in a boat, including Captain Grimston, his lieutenant and sergeant, two other gentlemen and two other soldiers, all men of rank. The captain was on his way to visit Francis Drake, who was ashore with the rest of the men as he has stated; after landing they were proceeding on foot to where Drake was when they met twelve islanders, who killed his master and took himself and his companion Daniel prisoner.

Asked what course this fleet was to take, whither it was bound and whether it had sailed from its last anchorage, he said he knew it was going straight to the Indies to destroy La Margarita, Santo Domingo and other places; he did not know whether it had set sail, but he had heard the men ashore being told that they should depart, and in the fleet he had heard it said that they were to sail that night.

Asked how long Francis Drake intended to stay in the Indies and for what length of time he was victualled, he said that he was carrying supplies for ten months or a year.

Asked what other fleets or squadrons had left England or were waiting to leave, he said that various private ships came and went every day on missions of plunder and that some ships of the queen's were guarding the coast and that he did not know of any others. [The interpreter and the deponent then took oaths as to the truth of the statement. Deponent said he could not write and the statement was signed by the interpreter, Dr Arias, Luis de Guzmán and Gerónimo de la Milla. Before me, Miguel Gerónimo Fernández de Córdoba.]

(b) Daniel Equisman[1]

On the same day the said regent and *oidores* called before them a man who said his name was Daniel Equisman. The oath was

---

[1] *Sic.* This was the *Salomon*'s surgeon, whom the author of the Hakluyt account supposed to have 'disclosed our pretended voyage as much as in him lay'. In fact his deposition suggests that he did his best to conceal what he knew. But he and his companions may have been re-examined under duress.

administered to him orally by Jorge Parca,[1] who also swore in form of law to do the office of interpreter faithfully and lawfully, and the following questions were put.

Asked his name, age, position and birthplace, he said he was Daniel Equisman, aged 23, born in London, and that he was a barber-surgeon.

Asked what fleet this was and who commanded it, he said that Sir John Hawkins and Francis Drake were in equal command as leaders of equal squadrons, each with his own men, and that there were six of the queen's ships. He understood that the charge was borne by Sir John Hawkins and Francis Drake, and also, as some suppose, by the queen.

Asked how many ships there were, of what burden, and how many men they carried, he said there were 27 ships and one joined them on the way, which came to Canaria and was present at the action and departed that day. Four of the ships were of 800 tons, two of 500, and the rest of 200, 100, 80 and less. He thought that four of the queen's ships carried about 400 men each, and the rest 180 or 150 according to their burden. In his opinion they had at least 4,000 men and left Plymouth, England, about three weeks ago.

Asked what guns these ships carried, he said that the large ships had about 40 brass pieces and the rest had brass and iron guns. The ship he came in had 22 pieces, and the other ships would have been equipped proportionately, but he did not know the details.

Asked what course the fleet followed on leaving Plymouth and whether they stopped anywhere, he said that they sighted an island called Lanzarote, but neither stopped anywhere nor robbed any ships. At Plymouth it was not known where they were going because this was kept secret. When they were at sea, some supposed they were coming to Canaria to take the island and sack it, but he did not know where they intended to go after leaving here, except that some supposed they were bound for the Indies, though for which part of the Indies he did not know.

Asked whether it was on the queen's orders, or anyone else's,

---

[1] Sounds like a hispaniolized Englishman, which would not be surprising in the Canaries.

22. STATEMENTS OF PRISONERS

that they came to sack this island, he said he did not know, for there had not been a voyage so secret as this. Even the masters of the ships did not know, for they were simply told to follow Francis Drake's flagship and Sir John Hawkins' vice-admiral.

Asked how many launches and men made up the assault force, he said that some ships brought two launches and some one and that he thought there were about fifty in all. He did not remember the number of launches and men, but the ship called the *Salomon*, in which he came, sent 35 men, and he supposed that after landing the first boat-loads the launches were to return for the rest of the men to the ships, which for this purpose approached the land. Deponent did not go in the launches, but remained in the ship and he did not know how many men were to be landed.

Asked who was general of the assault force and from which squadron the assault force was drawn, he said that it came from both squadrons equally, and that the general was Sir Thomas Baskerville, knight, who had served the queen of England in Flanders and in France on behalf of Vendôme. They also had another general (for each squadron had its own) called Nicholas Clifford, an Englishman who had also served in France.

Asked why, having launched such a large force of boats, men, ships and artillery against this city and against the men defending the city at Santa Catalina bay, where part of the fleet anchored, they did not land, but withdrew, he said the reasons were that the condition of the sea was not good enough for throwing a slender force ashore, that they saw many men in the trenches and artillery obstructing access, and that such great resistance would have caused the loss of many men. They did not expect to find this island so defended, but rather to have been able to sack it with ease. After the retreat they remarked to each other that they had not expected so much resistance and well-ordered defence at Canaria, and this had made them afraid.

Asked how many men in the ships and launches were killed and wounded, he said that three were killed and two wounded, that some shots went through the sails, and that he had no knowledge of any other damage done by the artillery.

Asked about the quality of the men in the fleet and whether there were men of rank among them, he said that there were many gentlemen and men of war and that the four generals he had named were the chief.

Asked where they stopped when they turned tail and withdrew on the Friday night, he said that they went thence to Arganeguín, where they anchored to take water and in fact took some.

Asked what men went ashore at the said port, he said that many disembarked – he did not know how many – among them Francis Drake and Sir John Hawkins and many other gentlemen and men of rank. They stayed there Saturday and Sunday and fired two shots for the withdrawal and so departed on the Sunday night. Some thought they were to touch at one of the other islands and others said they were to pursue their voyage; he did not know for certain whither they were bound, except that it was for the Indies.

Asked where he was taken prisoner and what men came on land with him when he was captured, he said that about eight men came in a boat, including Captain Grimston, two or three other gentlemen and soldiers, himself and Vincent, his companion. Captain Grimston was going to meet Sir John Hawkins. Certain men of this island set upon them and took deponent and his companion prisoner. He did not know who else was killed, but they killed Captain Grimston, a valiant man.

Asked what course this fleet was to take, whither it was bound and whether it had set sail, he said he did not know whither they were bound, as he said before, but that on the Sunday night the ships fired two pieces, which was the signal for departure, and so they must have gone.

Asked how long the fleet intended to stay in the Indies and for what length of time it was victualled, he said that as far as the destination was concerned he had already deposed, and that the fleet had victuals and supplies for a year.

Asked what other fleets or squadrons had left England or were expected to leave, he said he had no knowledge of any apart from the present fleet. And that this was the truth upon the oath he had taken [signed by deponent, interpreter, Dr Arias, etc. before me Fernández de Córdoba].

(c) Gasparian

Two days later on 12 October of the said year a man was brought to the *audiencia* by Melchor Ramírez, *alcalde* of Agaete, who said the man had come to the village of Nicolas by way of a cliff overlooking the sea, and that from Arganeguín to where he was found was more than four or five leagues of bad road.

[An interpreter and the prisoner took the oath in presence of the regent, *oidores* and Captain Alonso de Alvarado, governor[1]].

Asked his name, age, position and birthplace, he said he was Gasparian,[2] aged about 22 and a mariner, born in the city of Danzig, which was a free city in the kingdom of Poland, giving assistance when necessary to the king of Poland.

Asked what fleet this was which arrived on Friday last and who commanded it, he said that it was an English fleet, six of the ships being the queen's and the rest paid for half by Francis Drake and half by Sir John Hawkins.

Asked how many ships there were, of what burden, and how many men they carried, he said that including large and small there were 28 ships; he thought the queen's were of 500 tons, others of 300 and others less, and that the men numbered 4,000 or 5,000.

Asked what artillery these ships carried, he said that Drake's ship carried 48 brass pieces, one of the others 46, and the lesser ships about 20.

Asked the place and time of their departure, the course they followed and whether they stopped anywhere, he said that they left from Plymouth and took 29 days on the way, steering always SSE. They did not stop anywhere on the way, though they sighted an island near this one – he did not know its name.

Asked if he knew whether Drake came straight to this island with the queen's orders to sack it, as he tried to do on Friday the 6th of this month, he said he did not know, but had heard that they came to Canaria for fresh supplies.

Asked how many launches and men took part in the assault and

---

[1] Alvarado, as he bitterly complained (to the king, 12 October 1595, Simancas, Guerra Antigua, *legajo* 448), had not been invited to attend the examination of the first two prisoners.

[2] 'Gasparan' in document 21. Otherwise unidentified.

how they were arrayed, he said he did not know the numbers, but thought there were 1,000 men and that they intended to take the city and the supplies there. In Drake's ship, where deponent was, there was a Spanish pilot who had been captured in a boat by an Englishman. This Spaniard, whose name he did not know, told them that the city would fall as soon as they reached it.

Asked why, having launched such a large force of boats, men, ships and artillery against this city and against the men on the shore, they turned tail and put out to sea, he said it was because they saw so much resistance ashore, with numerous men so well deployed; they withdrew to avoid losing their men and because they received some damage from the islanders.

Asked how many men in the ships and launches were killed and wounded, he said he knew ten men were killed, among them a captain of much repute, secretary to Drake, who was wounded in the head by a musket ball and died in the ship the next day;[1] in one ship five men were killed by a ball fired from the fort at Las Isletas and another 14 or 15 men in the launches were wounded by gunfire from ashore.

Asked about the quality of the men in the fleet and who they were, he said that there were many of rank and quality in the fleet; in particular he knew one Gaspa Host,[2] who always wore a gold chain about his neck and dined at Drake's mess. The rest he did not know.

Asked where they stopped when they set sail and withdrew on the Friday night, he said that they tacked to windward that night and in the early morning made for Arganeguín, where Drake and many of the men went ashore to take water because they were in great need of it. They filled about 100 barrels, but took no more because it was not good.

Asked how many men came ashore with him in his boat, he said he came together with 20 men from his ship to take water.

Asked how he was taken prisoner and by what order he came to this city, he said he was captured by the English in a ship and taken to England, where at Plymouth he was compelled to sail as a

---

[1] The incident is mentioned nowhere else. Jonas Bodenham, who was Drake's secretary, survived the voyage, but Drake may have had more than one.
[2] *Sic.* Unidentified.

mariner in Drake's ship, whence they removed him to another which had a broken top-mast. He came ashore (as he has deposed) with the others to take water and fled into the interior because he did not wish to remain with the English. Then he met the man who brought him to this city.

Asked whether he knew about the men killed by the islanders at Arganeguín, he said he did not.

Asked what course this fleet was to take and whither it was bound, he said it was intended to come to this island for water and thence to make for the Indies, to a great city, he did not know which.

Asked how long Drake intended to stay in the Indies and what victuals he carried, he said that Drake had provisions in the fleet for ten months.

Asked what other fleets, squadrons or ships had left or were expected to leave England, he said he only knew that on the departure of this fleet four ships were being equipped and provisioned to follow it,[1] and that some 18 or 20 corsair ships had gone out, he did not know whither. And that this was the truth upon the oath he had taken [deponent made a mark; signed by the interpreter, Dr Arias, etc. before me Fernández de Córdoba].

23. *Part of a letter from Grand Canary*[2]

Since it seems to me that owing to this ship's delay the letters I wrote you dated 5 and 15 October, which will be in Licenciado Palaños' bundle, will in any case be out of date, I have decided to draw up

[1] There is no mention of this elsewhere.
[2] Simancas, Guerra Antigua, *legajo* 448. Headed 'Capitulo de una carta de Canaria' and endorsed 'Treslado de lo que se escrive de Canaria en carta particular'. Printed in Rumeu de Armas, *Piraterías*, III, pt. ii, 986–9. The document is a contemporary copy of the original letter (or rather of part of it) and is clearly corrupt, particularly in those places where the author used Latin. The text is made no easier by the number of private allusions and witticisms and by the author's deliberate obscurity, adopted for reasons hinted at in the first paragraph. Mr John Jones of the department of Spanish in the University of Hull was able to solve a few of these problems, but others remain unsolved, as the footnotes indicate.

this new account of what happened subsequently as an appendix to our record, ciphering as much as possible. Wherever, *propter metum Judeorum*,[1] certain matters had better remain in the inkwell, I think brief notes alone must suffice, leaving the substance to the imagination of the discreet reader.

So many and so varied were the alarms and excursions that occurred upon the arrival of Drake in this cursed, disloyal island...[2] that those of Rome and Carthage at the time of the Punic wars[3] were not half so impressive, and if the Córdovan Lucan could come alive today I think myself he would consign his Pharsalia to oblivion to undertake this farce of ours. For there is among my countrymen a certain captain who, along with Alexander the Great, is sighing at the tomb of Achilles, as Petrarch says, with envy and sorrow at not having Homer to chronicle his exploits, holding them more worthy of his sonorous lay than you might. But the fact is, he has had ten or twelve English cannon balls, which fell some half a league away from him, collected and gilded to be sent to court sheathed in velvet, like the horns of our friend,[4] so as to have them for his coat of arms, like the flags of the *Gran Capitán*[5] – but nothing whatever surprises me now. This is to be an addition to an escutcheon that until now has been blank, like the arms of Italy, though not for the reason Alciati gives in his *Emblemata*.[6] You will yet see another captain prove with

[1] This may perhaps be taken literally as an expression of anti-semitism, for there were doubtless Canarians, as there were Spaniards, who conceived of something like Rumeu de Armas's 'international Jewish organization, in intimate alliance with masonry and protestantism for the defeat of Spanish power' (Rumeu de Armas, *Piraterías,* II, pt. i, 50).

[2] Text: 'lo mas atento estoi que un santilario . . .'

[3] Text: 'la guerra publica'.

[4] Text: 'Como los cuernos del amigo' (not 'enemigo' *pace* Rumeu de Armas). Perhaps refers to Don Rodrigo de Cabrera, who awoke on 22 October 1592 to find his front door hung with horns. Instead of concealing these and their imputation from public view, he wrapped them in crimson velvet and had them ceremoniously carried to the *audiencia,* from whom he demanded justice upon the perpetrator of the insult. See Rumeu de Armas, *Piraterías,* II, pt. ii, 609.

[5] Gonzalo de Córdoba.

[6] Andreas Alciati, *Emblemata,* first published 1531, with many subsequent editions. The first Spanish edition appeared in 1549.

a hundred witnesses that he took one of the galleons on his shoulders as Atlas[1] did the sky, preventing it by main force from landing men on the beach; and that Telamonian Ajax could not have done as much the day he unaided saved the Greek ships from the Trojan flames. God knows that the ship which came nearest to the beach was 150 paces away, and you can imagine what pair of arms could have reached it, even had they been the ecclesiastical and the secular. There is another who has proved, as if it were some famous deed, that in the presence of the launches he went fearlessly walking above the trenches.[2]

Although I do not believe you can wish for more than that, the fact is that the Dominican friars, wishing to carry off the honours of the day for themselves alone, are going around shouting to the poor folk (and such were most of those who rallied to face the danger) 'Alas the old colonists have departed',[3] claiming to have done more in the event than . . .[4] And to make sure everyone knows it, they held a festival in their monastery and in the cathedral, with a procession and a sermon *in laudem*, reviving the memory of Aljubarrota.[5] On top of all this there are so many opinions and disputes that I for my part hold that his majesty should send an investigator to pacify us as Aubeda and Bacca did the factions of Benavides and Carvajales.[6] But to recount here the pretensions of other potentates of the cloth would be to weary you and never finish, for there is not a rochet-wearing priest nor other ecclesiastical dignitary but imagines himself preferred. One wants to be archbishop of Toledo, as if the cardinal, God keep him, were ninety or so, and

[1] Text: 'Atlante'.
[2] Refers to Baltasar de Armas.
[3] Text: 'Het mea sumt beteres migrate coloni', perhaps should read 'Heu me absunt veteres migrati coloni'.
[4] Text: 'mas que la ,ornera de Aluandos' – a private allusion?
[5] The battle of 1385 in which the Portuguese defeated the Castilians. Many Canarians must still have had strong Portuguese affinities, presumably to the disgust of the author of this letter.
[6] May be an allusion to the two brothers Carvajales who were charged with the murder of Juan Alonso Benavides at the court of Fernando IV of Castile. See Antonio Benavides, *Memorias de D. Fernando IV de Castilla* (2 vols., Madrid, 1860), I, 242–3, 686–96.

as if, even should he die, they would confer the see on this person. Some seek presidencies, others bishoprics . . .[1]

But Captain Morales, . . . ,[2] is expecting the courier from Seville to bring him an appointment worth 500 escudos, which should rather be lashes for his refusal to go to his wife and for having openly repudiated the service and friendship of one who did so much for him. He aspires to the permanent captaincy of the castle of San Francisco,[3] which will be constructed two hundred years hence, not to mention that the wretched old man is about a hundred himself. But I think this ambition is inspired not so much by Mars as by Venus, so enraptured is he by Madalena, and even though it fades already, she, like Circe, detains this Ulysses forgetful of his return to Ithaca. I do not know what oracle has given him these hopes – although I say it not you will understand – and he deserves this prize so much that if his advice had been followed (which was to await the enemy on the walls and not in the trenches at Santa Catalina), the island would have been overwhelmed that day. For if they had been allowed to land and form up the 2,500 men from the launches and galleons, our small force would not have been sufficient to resist them. Although that opinion was accepted, that fine captain and *corregidor* Alvarado opposed it, taking some of the men almost by main force to the trenches – and those not the chief people, who followed at a distance like the Marys.[4] In the end God willed that with less than 200 men there, and the little field-pieces known to you, the enemy did not venture to land.

The everlasting Captain Martel, though he had been in bed for days (whether from fever or the coldness of his lady I know not) did excellent service, taking up his position in the place for lovers, so that if battle should break out he would distinguish himself above all others, as the sermon on the aforesaid Aljubarrota relates.[5] In

[1] Text: 'como si andubiesen agueno'.
[2] Text: 'entremetiendose como doblon de plomo entre paños', literally, 'intruding like a leaden doubloon among cloths'.
[3] A fortress planned by Torriani.
[4] Text: 'y no de la mas principal que esta sequebantur a longe como las marias'.
[5] Text: 'como dize el sermon de la prealegata Aljuba'.

addition to all this grasping and gallantry there have been a thousand rivalries – so much so that because disputes arose among the captains and lieutenants over the best seats, the right reverend Figueroa[1] did not allow the companies to march in the victory procession as had been agreed, for unless some of them had swallowed some bitter medicine a rumpus was expected on the day. It was not fair to place some on the right and some on the left without making distinctions, and so their government had to tell them 'nescitis quid petatis'. Thus the gallant gala went ahead, though less successfully than had been intended.

Military poems abound, for with this deluge and *indacio aquarum* hitherto unknown poets have been born. I promise you the battle of Roncevalles, though bloodier than this bloodless affair, was not so much sung nor made the theme of so many romances. There was such a mob of sonneteers that the *audiencia* ordered – and with reason – that they should cease, and that all epigrams and ballads on this subject should be handed in so that the wheat might be winnowed from the chaff. Among them was a romance by Argote,[2] which although unfinished took up five *pliegos* of paper, and which was so crude and ragged that . . .[3] These are accompanied by a thousand controversies and I am not sure but that the latter are the cause of their suppression. On the other hand, despite the *audiencia*'s ban they go on multiplying. Every day new ballads appear, which caused Francisco de Pineda, whom they call 'el cortesano', to remark that one could very well make a Montemayor's *Diana* out of this war.[4] As a very ignorant servant of mine said to me at Salamanca: 'Señor, however much he knows, master Leon is no Lorenzo Valla.'[5]

There has been a schism comparable to the English secession over the privilege of taking this message to the king. The devil of a

[1] Bishop Fernando Suárez de Figueroa.
[2] Gonzalo Argote de Molina, a notable Canarian poet. The romance appears to be lost.
[3] Text: 'que no parece prouincial ni aver corista'.
[4] The poet Jorge de Montemayor's pastoral 'novela' *Diana,* published c. 1559, was his greatest work.
[5] Text: 'como sauiendo tanto el maestro leon no haze un Laurenzio Uala'.

dust has been raised, as if it were an embassy to Rome, with a thousand claimants, each wanting to be the messenger. That is what has held up this ship so long, for the dispatches could have been at court on 20 October. The triumvirate would like it to be Alonso Cabrera de Rosas, *regidor* of Tenerife, who is here on legal business. You will know the outcome. The governor wants to send his lieutenant[1] as the most trusted servant of Don Luis, which would cost that poor gentleman not a little. The *regidores* combined to contest the messengership, and one of them would make the journey. With all this confusion it was agreed that no-one should go, and so the dispatches are simply being sent by courier.

And because I can see myself enlarging too much and you will already be weary of reading, I will say in sum that what they call a victory here was chiefly the work of the Almighty, whose will it was to save this poor island. But to come down to earth, you must understand that Drake's commission did not authorize him to sack this city except at his own risk. He could have done it, but disturbed by some resistance he withdrew and as I have said God blinded his eyes to the fact that if he had sent the 31 launches and 14 galleons half an hour earlier they would not have found a single man on the beach, for such was the disagreement about awaiting them there or in the city, that no-one had arrived, and the enemy could then have landed and overwhelmed the country. And he could have done this, moreover, because he was three hours at anchor hove down, during which time some forces gathered from the countryside. He was also wrong in thinking that all our men were either in the trenches or behind under cover, for in fact there were no more than 150 men there. It is laughable when I think how Canaria escaped. The women all took refuge in the eating houses at Tafira and La Vega, but the lieutenant and *oidor* Guzmán remained in the city to protect it from robbers, which they did with great diligence.

---

[1] Pamochamoso.

24. *William Stallenge to Cecil, 27 November 1595*[1]

Right honourable with the remembraunce of my moste humble dutie, hit maie please you to be adverticed this Laste night here arived an englishe Barke which departed from Tenariff aboute vj weekes past, where (as the Master reporteth) there was certaine newes that her Majesties Fleete arived at the gran Canaries about the beginning of October laste and presentlie the Generalls disimbarked certen of their companies intending to have landed betwene the towne and the Forte which is aboute half a League distant, but by reason of contrarie windes, the sea went so highe, as themselves could not come neare the shore with anye savetie of themselves and furniture, so as they were constrained to retorne aborde, and passe to the Calmes on the backside of the Islande where they remained vj daies, and watred at their pleasure without attempting any further matter and thens departed on their voiage Onlie with the losse of ten men that stragled abroade in the countrey wherof vj were slaine, and thother fower were taken and examined by the spanyardes; but coold not reporte anie more of the Generalls pretence then that they were bound for the Indies. Whiles they remained at the Canaries the spanyardes dispatched three Carvells of aviso to the Indies, to weete one from the Canaries; another from Tenarif, and the third From Palma: Thus muche I have thought meete to advertice, And so beseeching thalmightie for the long continuaunce of your honours prosperous healthe, Do moste humblie take my leave Plymouth the xxvij[th] of November anno 1595.

your honours most humble comaundement
William Stallenge

[1] Hatfield MSS, 36, no. 31. Endorsed: '27 November 1595. William Stallenge to my master.'

25. *William Holliday to Cecil, St Michael's, 20 December 1595*[1]

Right honorable my dutie most humbly done yt maye please your honor to be advertized yt the vth of october Sir frances Dracke was at the Canaries wher he Landed as yt is said on thowzand men, only for to tacke in freshe water at which Landing he Loste 8 men wherof som wher sleane & three of the same eight being saved are sent for the meane for to be examyned of Sir francis his intencion, frome whence he departed the 8 of october, since which tyme ther is no newes of him in speane, for this daie the 20th of December is come to this towne from Cyvill a flybote which hayth bene in the waye but tene daies who sayth that ther is no newes of Sir francis and the letterse frome Cyvill of the vjth of December declare no Lesse.

They wryt frome Cyvill that the king doth gether all the men he cane gett of all sortes of nacyons & that ther is 17 gallyons in St Lucar 8 at Lishbourne 23 at farroll all which they wryt should have gon after Sir francis but nowe comanded for to stey till marche. Yt is wryten that ther is comeing & come to Lyshbourne thre score and tene gallyes [for invasion of England. He had arrived at St Michael's on the 2nd and has not yet found passage for Lisbon. Has freighted a Bristol bark which had come there 'in the name of a Scot' and proposes to sail to Lisbon in her]

[1] P.R.O., S.P. 12/261, no. 16. Holliday dated this 20 December 1596 and Cecil's secretary endorsed it with a date that might be 1593; internal evidence leaves no doubt that the correct date for the letter is 1595.

V. *Puerto Rico*

The momentous capture of the *Francis* by Pedro Tello near Guadalupe is told by the Spanish admiral himself (document 26) and by one of the English crew (document 27). Taken together, these accounts show the extent of the Spaniards' luck, but the prisoners either could not or would not say what Drake's objectives were after Puerto Rico – a point confirmed by the official *relación* (document 29). Thus the warning relayed from Santo Domingo cannot have been as precise as was later suggested.[1] Even so, the news of Drake's presence and the certain knowledge of his immediate objective were of immense value to the Spanish.

Judgement of the Puerto Rico action itself must depend in large measure upon an assessment of the defences, the geographical basis of which may be seen in the accompanying map.[2] Antoneli's 'plat' unfortunately cannot be found, but the remarks he attached to it were translated by Baskerville, who added his own comments (document 28). Antoneli, who had inspected the position in 1589, pointed with admirable clarity and brevity to the essential needs: command of the approaches to the eastern end of the island by the establishment of gun-posts at El Boquerón and El Puente; and command of the entrance to the harbour by the building of the fort called El Morro on the western headland. Baskerville here tends to overstate (by implication) the difficulty of developing an attack from the east and neither English nor Spanish sources suggest that the eastern defences were adequately reconnoitred or tested while the fleet lay in that quarter. Similarly Baskerville in his

---

[1] By Ruiz Delduayen, for example (document 32). Rodrigo Díaz, who left Cartagena shortly after the arrival of the message from Santo Domingo, reported that the objectives were said (by Pedro Tello's prisoners) to be Puerto Rico, Santo Domingo and Cartagena (Museo Naval, Navarrete MSS, xxv, no. 67, ff. 279–281).

[2] Map 1, p. 150. This is based on a recent admiralty chart, the contemporary details being drawn chiefly from Menéndez de Valdés' description (see next footnote).

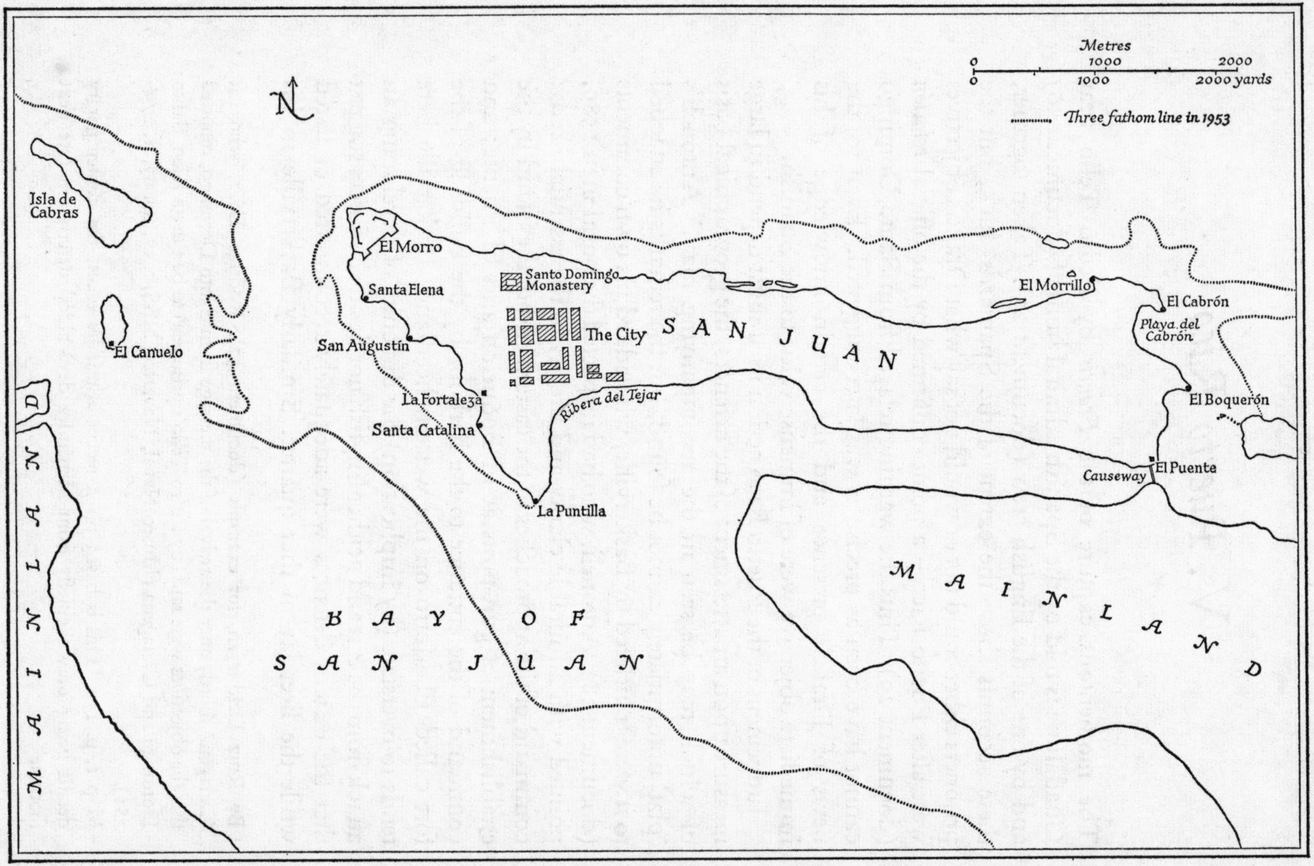

MAP 1. San Juan de Puerto Rico in 1595

'discourse' (document 20) appears to exaggerate the strength of the Morro and its supporting bastion, Santa Elena.

In fact the defences of San Juan were the subject of much controversy among the local officers of the crown throughout the 1590s. In 1587 Diego Menéndez de Valdés, then governor, drew up a detailed scheme[1] and his report of 1590[2] indicated that he had begun the construction of the Morro. The next year, however, Captain Pedro de Salazar took over responsibility for defence and reported that he had 'levelled all the fortifications, redoubts and trenches that Governor Diego Menéndez built, since I do not think they were of much value'.[3] Work did continue on the Morro, but progress was slow. It was later alleged that in 1597 'not a stone had been laid there for its defence nor a ditch dug; there was only a platform at the water's edge to protect the port'.[4] The statement is obviously biased and exaggerated, but perhaps no more so than Baskerville's picture of a castle of quarried stone with three platforms. Sancho Pardo and Pedro Tello both affirmed that the other works built by Menéndez, including the important redoubt of Santa Elena, which played a major part in Drake's defeat, were dismantled by Salazar and not re-established until Sancho Pardo himself took the defence in hand.[5] Pedro Suárez Coronel, who succeeded Menéndez as governor in 1593, repeatedly complained of lack of manpower, building materials, tools, guns, powder and ball,[6] and closed his report on the English attack with the remark that 'if it had not been for the munitions, powder and match from

[1] A. de I., Patronato, 18, no. 13, *ramo* 2. Another copy in A. de I., Indiferente General, 1887, no. 37.

[2] *Principal Navigations*, III (1600), 559 (X (1904), 161–3).

[3] A. de I., Patronato, 176, *ramo* 3, printed in *Boletín Histórico de Puerto Rico*, IV, 317–23.

[4] Deposition of Antonio de Mosquera, 18 March 1600 (A. de I., Escribanía de Cámara, 134, no. 2). His statement, which was essentially an excuse for his defeat at the hands of the earl of Cumberland, was corroborated by Juan de Texeda.

[5] *Información* for Diego Menéndez de Valdés, completed in June 1596 (A. de I., Santo Domingo, 155, *ramo* 4).

[6] For example, letter to the king, 8 June 1595 (A. de I., Santo Domingo, 155, *ramo* 4).

the frigates and the Tierra Firme flagship this island would have been utterly unable to defend itself'.[1] Early in 1595 Puerto Rico, for lack of men, guns and sound policies, would probably have fallen to such a force as Drake's. What gave it the strength to repel the attack when it came was not a steady advance in its fortification, but the successive arrivals of Sancho Pardo and Pedro Tello with the ships that were themselves of vital importance in the event, the guns and gunners that actually inflicted the defeat on the English, and the timely warning that put the island on its guard at precisely the right moment. Even so, San Juan was probably not so impregnable as Baskerville's observations suggest. The unexpectedness of the resistance must have made it appear to the English stronger than it really was, and Baskerville clearly had sufficient motive to overstate the opposition. As Maynarde's account implies, the decision to abandon the attempt was doubtless influenced by the thought of easier prey elsewhere. As for San Juan, it ceased to be a powerful stronghold as soon as the surviving frigates departed, leaving it with but a few additional guns and its natural advantages. These proved insufficient to repel the earl of Cumberland in 1598.[2]

Of the six major *relaciones* which describe the events of November 1595 the official report (document 29) is the best. The governor wrote two accounts, one for the king and the other for Juan de Ibarra, secretary of the council of the Indies.[3] Two were written from the point of view of Pedro Tello.[4] Another occurs in a lengthy MS narrative, by Andrés de León, of the travels of a certain

[1] Pedro Suárez Coronel to the king, 19 December 1595 (A. de I., Santo Domingo, 155).

[2] The only relevant modern studies are two unpublished works in the library of the San Juan National Historic Site, Puerto Rico: Ricardo Torres Reyes, 'The Harbour Defenses of San Juan in the Sixteenth Century' (1955); and Julio Marrero Nuñez, 'Puerto Rico and the Elizabethan Age' (1960). I am much indebted to Señor Nuñez for making them available and for his advice on the topography of San Juan, without which the accompanying map would have been much the poorer.

[3] Both are dated 19 December 1595 and both are in A. de I., Santo Domingo, 155. The one addressed to the king contains some matter lacking in the other.

[4] See document 26.

'El Huérfano' (the Orphan).[1] Two shorter reports take the form of letters by Francisco Gómez de Cid[2] and Diego López de Ribera.[2] The notes to the official *relación* indicate significant variations or additional matter in the other accounts, but the differences are not substantial. In general the Spanish sources are, as might be expected, least illuminating on English intentions, movements and losses, even when based on information from English prisoners or from Spaniards who had been in contact with the enemy. Thus neither the report that Drake had intended to make an English base at San Juan, nor the assertion that he had proposed to renew the assault and could find no support, is acceptable in the light of the English narratives.

26. *Report on the voyage of the five frigates*[3]

His majesty's five frigates set forth from San Lúcar on Monday, 25 September 1595. In command went Don Pedro Tello and as

[1] Biblioteca de la Real Academia de la Historia, Colección Muñoz, t. 43, ff. 183–6. The dedication was dated Granada, 28 August 1621, and the travels, which are apparently those of the author himself, began in 1580. The narrative of the Puerto Rico events is circumstantial and interesting, but the occasional examples of romantic invention or exaggeration which can be detected are sufficient to cast a shadow of suspicion over every statement that cannot be checked.

[2] To Ibarra, 15 December 1595 (A. de I., Santo Domingo, 169, *ramo* 4).

[3] From the Alba MSS (Archivo y Biblioteca del Palacio de Liria, Madrid), printed in Maria del Rosario Falcó y Osorio, Duquesa de Berwick y de Alba, *Nuevos Autógrafos de Cristóbal Colón y Relaciones de Ultramar* (Madrid, 1902), pp. 72–80. The document is headed: 'Relacion del viaje de las cinco fragatas y suceso de Puerto Rico en que demas de contener en ella todo lo de la primera Relacion mas cumplidamente, se ponen otras muchas cosas y particularidades que despues aca se han savido y la carta de Francisco Draque al gobernador y lo demas que hizo en aquella ysla.' It may well have been written by or on behalf of Pedro Tello, in which case the other *relación* referred to in the title may be the much briefer 'Relacion de la jornada que hizo Don Pedro Tello a Puerto Rico y de lo que suzedio en aquel puerto con la armada Ynglesa que fue sobre el.' The latter was transcribed by Engel Sluiter from 'Manuscritos Peruanos, Espejo historial (1642)' at the Biblioteca Nacional, Lima, Peru, a few months before

vice-admiral Gonzalo Méndez Canzo;[1] captain of the frigate *Santa Ana* was Marco Antonio Becerra, commander of the infantry; of the *Santa Isabel*, Pedro de Guia; and of the *Magdalena*, Domingo de Ynsaurraga. The said frigates carried 250 soldiers and 300 seamen and gunners. They reached Alegranza, one of the Canary Islands, on Sunday 8 October, having encountered some contrary winds and bad weather. Thence they followed their course making for Deseada and on Tuesday 7 November sighted land, which all the pilots said was Barbuda. Accordingly they set course south until close on daybreak and seeing no land, made westwards in the morning seeking it. At nine o'clock land was sighted, and the pilots, being asked what land it was, said that Deseada lay on the left and Antigua on the right. In view of what happened later it was a marvel that so many pilots and men well acquainted with these coasts should have been deceived; and it was no less remarkable that Don Pedro Tello, deciding, since the frigates were short of water and ballast, to make for Guadalupe to determine the matter by approaching and viewing the land, changed his mind, anticipating some misfortune that would cause delay, and ordered a northwest course to disembogue between Nevis and Redonda. Next day at dawn he found himself off Los Santos and Guadalupe, and realized that the land sighted the day before had been Martinino and Dominica, and that if he had steered west-southwest to seek Guadalupe, as he had intended, it would have been impossible to make the Virgin Passage and the

the library was burned, and I am most grateful to him for bringing this document (hereinafter called the Lima *relación*) to my notice and supplying me with a copy. In 1596 an amended and abbreviated version of the Alba MS was printed in Seville with the title *Relacion del Viage que hizieron las cinco Fragatas de Armada de su Magestad, yendo por Cabo dellas Don Pedro Tello de Guzman, este presente Año de Noventa y cinco*, described and partly reproduced in Kraus, *Sir Francis Drake*, pp. 174–5, 202–3.

[1] Gonzalo Méndez had served in Atlantic armadas for many years. Earlier in the year he had sailed in Coloma's fleet from Havana as captain of a galleon which was damaged in the storm that nearly wrecked the *Begoña*, but Gonzalo Méndez managed to bring his ship home. He was rewarded for his services in 1595 with the governorship of Florida, which he held for eight years. – A. de I., Santo Domingo, 232, no. 39.

little white island[1] in order to reach Puerto Rico. While everyone
was marvelling and joyful at this good fortune, two sails appeared,
which they pursued until three in the afternoon, when the vice-
admiral, having got to windward of one of them, closed with and
subdued her. Then, while the *Santa Isabel* remained with her, the
flagship and the rest gave chase to the other ship. At this juncture,
about four in the afternoon, the vice-admiral fired three guns in
warning to the flagship; order was given to watch the sea and nine
sails were sighted coasting Guadalupe, whereupon the pursuit was
abandoned and the flagship brought the frigates together and spoke
with the vice-admiral Gonzalo Méndez, from whom he heard the
statement made by the prisoners, of which the following is a copy:

First, that they left Plymouth on 8 September of that year in the
company of a fleet commanded by Francis Drake and John
Hawkins, and that this ship and her companion lost company of
the fleet four days before. They had orders that those who lost
company should rendezvous at the isles of Bayona, Puerto Santo
and Guadalupe, and if they failed to find the fleet in any of those
ports they should go on to Puerto Rico, where they said they would
stay ten days. Having arrived the previous afternoon at that island,
they had seen and counted 19 sail, but were not able to draw near
and speak with them, and believing the frigates to be ships of their
company, they had approached to join them. Asked about the
strength of the fleet, they said there were 26 sail, among them six
of the queen's, five of these being of 500–800 tons and the other of
300, and that among the 20 other, private ships some were equal
in strength and size to those. All of them came at the queen's
expense. The fleet carried 2,900 mariners and gunners and 3,000
soldiers, including many captains and gentlemen.[2] The generals
for the land were Thomas Baskerville and Nicholas Clifford, but

---

[1] *Isleo blanco.* The contemporary matter printed in *Principal Navigations,* III (1600),
613–27 (X (1905), 306–37), advised ships to negotiate the Virgin Passage keeping
this 'white litle Island' to starboard. The unpublished rutter in B.M., Sloane
MSS, 2292, ff. 34–40 gives similar advice to 'goe betwixt the Ilandes called
virgines and the Iland called *Blanca*'. These instructions, and the statement in
Principal Navigations, loc. cit., that the island 'seemeth like a ship under saile' suggest
that this island was the modern Sail Rock.

[2] Spanish *caballeros entretenidos.*

all were under the command of Francis Drake and John Hawkins, who were commissioned by the queen with equal powers.

Asked with what design this fleet set forth from England, they said they knew no other design than to go to Puerto Rico and seize the silver, though judging from the provision of victuals and other supplies they believed it would stay a long time in the Indies. Asked when they thought the fleet would leave Guadalupe, they said it had orders to stay three days there, and so they thought it would set sail that night or the next day unless the want of some necessity should detain them. Having heard all this, Don Pedro Tello discussed the whole matter with the vice-admiral and the captains, who unanimously agreed that in his majesty's service the best course was to get to Puerto Rico as quickly as possible, to await the enemy there and to defend not only the treasure of his majesty and private people, but also his land and Spanish prestige. This decision made, they acted upon it: orders were given that night for all the frigates to set new sails and extinguish their lanterns, so as to make themselves invisible to the enemy should he set forth in pursuit. Thus, with these and other very necessary precautions, they made their way to Puerto Rico with great care and attention, arriving there on Monday 13 November, having sent a bark ahead to discover whether the enemy had reached the port first. The royal ensign Pedro Vázquez went in the bark, and when it was learned that the land was safe, the frigates entered . . .[1]

27. The confession of John Austyn[2]

(a) Covering letter[3]

Right honorables my dutye humblye remembred, maye it please your lordships to be advertized that here arryved yesterdaye in the

---

[1] From this point the narrative covers the same ground as document 29. Significant differences between the accounts are noted there.

[2] P.R.O., S.P. 12/256, no. 111.

[3] Endorsed: 'for her Majesties affaires. To the Right honorables the lords and others of her majesties most honorable privie Councell. From Plimmouthe the xxv[th] daie of March 1596 att vj of the clocke in the afternowne. haste haste post haste with speede. 25 March 1595 [sic] Deputie Mayor of Plymmoth, to y[e] lords.'

eveninge John Austyn of London maryner of the Compaynye of a Barcke one of the Fleete under the Conducte of Sir Frauncis Drake & Sir John Hawkins kneightes in theire viadge & attemptes lately made to the Southwarde, who discoursed what hath happened in the sayd viadge, theffectes wherof appearinge in the inclosed, I thought it my dutye to signifie, leavinge the farther Consideracion therof to your lordships. Besides, this presente daye here arrived a Barcke of Garnesye [which had been plundered by Spanish ships hovering off this coast; he suggests sending out the queen's *Dreadnought* to attack them] ... most humblie take my leave From Plymouthe the xxv^th of March 1596

    Your honors most humbly att commaundement

      George Baron deputie to James Bagge Maior of Plymmouth the said Maior beinge nowe absent.

(b) Enclosure[1]

The Confession of John Austyn of London marryner taken the xxv^th daye of Marche 1595. whoe was one of the late Compaynye of Sir Frauncis Drake and Sir John Hawkins kneightes taken before George Baron depute to James Bagge Maior of Plymmouthe.

The said John Austyn sayeth that there was direction geiven to the whole Fleete that if anye lost compaynye they shoulde beare for Gwarda Lopa in the Indias, and the Barcke wherin this Examynate with xxvj^tie other persons were, by meanes of the lost of her Rother lost the Companye of the Fleete and so directinge theire Course toward the foresayd place & doenge what they meight to seaze the same, for want of theire Rother they coulde not, but felle with a place three leagues from it, where they were chasted with fyve frigettes of the kinges with the which they fought, but in the ende they soncke theire Barcke, and then for safegarde of theire lives (twoe of theire Companye beinge kylled) the rest lept into the Frigettes which carried theym to the Isle of St John deportaricho

---

[1] Endorsed: '25 March 1596. Declaracion of John Austyn before ye Deputie Mayor of Plymmothe. Concerninge ye service at St John de Porto rico.' Where it is dependent on what the Spaniards told Austyn, this report is of course unreliable.

where they were all imprisoned & kept in verie stricte sort, this was
on a soundaye att which tyme Sir Frauncis with his Fleete (havinge
lost the Compaynye of Sir John Hawkins the frydaye before) rode
afore Gwarda Lopa, where as the Spaynyardes that touke this
Examynate & his Compaynye meight see the toppes of his shippes,
but Sir Frauncis coulde not see the frigettes, howebeit theire was a
Barcke of his Companye that rode meane the waye (the whole
distance beinge aboute three leagues) which did see the feight and
takinge of the sayd Barcke, which acquaynted Sir Frauncis with
the myshappe. After this uppon examynacion taken of this
Examinate & divers of his Companye threatninge one of theym
with the racke, and understandinge of the Englishe forces they
begane presentlye to fortifie and soncke the greate shippe that
foundered there with the Treasure, a frigett and Three other
shippes in the mouthe of the harbouroughe to hinder the Commynge in of the Englishe forces, presentlye hereapon Sir Frauncis
Drake summoned the Fort & Towne to yelde, offeringe theym to
departe with bagge & baggage, whoe aunswered that they woulde
not accept his offer, but if he woulde have anye thinge he shoulde
comme a shoare and fetch it, then did Sir Frauncis and Sir John
Hawkins who was them comme also with his Fleete sende xv
Pynnaces & boates full manned into the harbouroughe in the
neight tyme to borne the Frigettes supposinge that if they coulde
have bournt theym they rest woulde have yelded the soner, which
Pynnaces & Boates bournt one of the Frigettes & sett one other on
fyer which was fourthwith quenched, butt here begane the bane of
ye Englishe, for by the leight that the fier worckes gave they were all
playnelye seen to the Spaynyardes, who hadd thereby advantage to
playe uppon theym at theire pleasure, and did, and kylled maynye.
The Englishe boates receavinge this sharpe intertaynement put
backe agayne to the shippes which rode without, fearinge to enter
because of the souncken shippes, but the daye before this the
shippes hadd shotte a shoare and throwen downe the one side of
the Castell, the next daye after this repulce, the Garlande wherin
Sir John Hawkins was came & rode verie neere to the Fort & shoat
att the same & they agayne to the shippe, in the which feight Sir John
Hawkins (as the Spaynyardes reported) was kylled, shewinge

8

divers signes & markes of him. Then Sir Frauncis Drake with
the rest havinge stayed att this place in all three dayes departed
therehence & went to the southwest of the sayd Islande at a place
called Agwano, where he stayed three dayes and touke in Freshe
victuals such as the Countrie yelded & watered and then departed
thence elonge by Carthagena for this was made knowen by twoe
smalle Pynnaces that followed theym to discover where they went,
who never gave theym over untill they brought theym within sixe
leagues of Numeratheus,[1] and then they retorned to Porterico
agayne to the Frigettes, which presentlye laded the Threasure there,
which was in valewe as it was generallie reported 4. myllyons, and
came for Spayne, and arryved therewith in St Lucar, which
Frigettes were sent out of Spayne for this purpose, all the Englishe
men were broughte awaye from Porterico in theise Frigettes, and
remayne all (this Examynate onlye escapinge awaye in an Irish-
man) in prison untill the kinges pleasure be knowen, it is to be
noted that in bourninge of the Frigett att St Porterico, there were
fyve Spaynyardes taken which Sir Frauncis newe appareled & sent
theym a shoare, wishinge the governer to use the Englyshe men well
& to send theym into theire Countrie uppon the which the
Englyshe men receaved some favour, both in theire imprison-
mentes & theire dyett, he sayeth that it is generallie reported, that
there are Two Fleetes wherin are in eche xxvtie shippes, Dun Pedro
Devaldes beinge generall of thone Fleete & Dun Frauncisco
Colomo Captayne of the other gone to followe Sir Frauncis Drake,
and were past out of theire Countrie before the Commynge fourthe
of the foresayd Frigettes, wherein are 5000. men in eche Fleete.

28. Baskerville and Antoneli on San Juan de Puerto Rico[2]

the discription of the porte and forteresses of St Jhon de porte rico
drawnen by the Ingenier Baptista Antonella wherin he shews as
aperithe written by hymself upon the said platt the strengthe of the
sayd place.

[1] Nombre de Dios.
[2] B.M., Harleian MSS, 4762, f. 85. In Baskerville's hand. The 'platt' mentioned
has not been traced, but was presumably one of those Baskerville promised to

The sity is situatid upon the sid a a¹ holow hyle which goes
falling downe towardes the porte of Teshar,² and frome the sea No
house cann be seen, only the Aby of St domyngo which standes
upon the very heyght of the hyle, which by them Lykwise is
fortefyed.³ This Cyty and porte is only to be asawtid 2 ways: the
one is by the causy thatt Coms from the mayn of the Iland,⁴ and
making ther a lytel forte as Is determynid, and allredy donn thatt
place is asurid; the other is by the mouthe of the porte, the which
the forte callid the moro that was then amaking and now fynyshid
will asure the comyng in of the sayd harboro. The which is very
difficult, by reason of the sholls and rokes of both sides, and the
shipping going in receaving certain contrary calme of wind growing by dubling the poynte of the moro; and of nessescity they must

show Cecil (document 45). The paragraph following the heading appears to be
a translation of what was written on the map, but the dating of this passage ('In
Porte rico the 25 of aprill 1595') creates a problem, for Antoneli was in Panama
in April 1595 and had not visited Puerto Rico since 1589 (Diego Angulo
Iñíguez, *Bautista Antonelli: las Fortificaciones Americanas del Siglo XVI* (Madrid,
1942), pp. 20–8, 61). The explanation that either Baskerville or Antoneli
carelessly wrote '1595' for '1589' is not acceptable because Antoneli left Puerto
Rico before 25 April 1589. Moreover the words 'the moro that was then amaking
and now fynyshid', unless interpolated by Baskerville, suggest that the description
was written long after the drawing of the map. It seems likely, therefore, that
Antoneli drew the map in 1589 and wrote the description in 1595, not at Puerto
Rico but at Porto Belo, the place-name being misread by Baskerville. On this
assumption Baskerville could hardly have obtained the map from Puerto Rico,
and indeed he had little opportunity to acquire any such materials there. On the
other hand it could have come into English hands from Alberto Ojeda, Antoneli's
assistant, when he came aboard at Nombre de Dios. The passage following the
date consists of Baskerville's own comments on the defences of the eastern end of
the island, and seems to show more detailed knowledge than the English could
have acquired in the course of the brief and necessarily superficial reconnaissance
carried out by the caravel which approached the Boquerón. It seems likely that
this information came from the Spanish seamen who were taken prisoner during
the night attack on the harbour. The document as a whole should be compared
with the description of the defences given in Baskerville's 'discourse' (document
20). Both appear to be based partly on information gathered after the event and to
contain an element of exaggeration which in the circumstances is only to be
expected. See also map 1, p. 150.

¹ *Sic.*   ² El Tejar.   ³ Caleta de los Frailes.
⁴ The causeway called 'El Puente'.

goe In by a wind with their shettes in their handes quatering their Trinkettes,[1] and If by chaunce they pass the porte with difyculty they cann retourn to fech itt. In porte rico the 25 of aprill 1595.

Tuching the cassy ther is a Lytell mouthe betwen tow Landes wher of upon the one standes 4 pecis of ordenance In a trenche the mouth having only 2 fadom water[2] and a quartir of a League of to the sea is shallows and rokes and with greatt diffyculty a bote can enter thatt way.

The causey hathe a forte mad for the keping of thatt way then from the mouth of the sayd Causey to the Callette of the Carborn[3] is all sholls, and In the Callett wer at thatt tym 2 pecis and now many more; in this place was Sir Nicolas Clyfford slayn; from thens to the other callett[4] is all sholls upon which ther is Lykwis ordenance placid nott to defend the Landing, for ther is[5] hope of putting fote ashore In any of those placis, butt to offend all shippes thatt would rid in thatt place, and to fors them to goe to the westward of the porte, from whence with greatt diffyculty the porte cann be recoverid.

29. Official report of the events at Puerto Rico[6]

Report of what happened at San Juan de Puerto Rico in the Indies, with regard to the English fleet under the command of Francis Drake and John Hawkins, on 23 November 1595.

[1] Spanish *trinquete* = foresail.
[2] The 'mouth' and the fort on its western side were both known as 'El Boquerón'.
[3] El Cabrón.
[4] Probably refers to El Morrillo. Here and throughout the Spanish material the term *caleta*, though sometimes used in its normal sense of bay, cove or beach, seems more often to mean something like 'gun emplacement'.
[5] The word 'no' (or 'small') appears to have been omitted by mistake.
[6] One version of this *relación* was printed in Alejandro Tapia y Rivera, *Biblioteca Histórica de Puerto Rico* (Puerto Rico, 1854), pp. 400–13. The document was said by Tapia to lie in 'Varios', número 2, ff. 203–9, Bibilioteca de la Real Academia de la Historia, Madrid, but has not been traced there. As printed it appears corrupt, and may well be, like many of the materials in this archive, a copy of much later date. A copy of this kind is the MS in B.M., Additional MSS, 13964, also corrupt, which was rather inaccurately reproduced and

General Sancho Pardo y Osorio[1] left Havana for Spain on 10 March of this year, in command of the flagship[2] of the Tierra Firme *flota*, escorted by Don Francisco Coloma's armada. On disemboguing from the channel[3] on the 15th in $28\frac{1}{2}°$ he ran into a storm, and found himself without a main-mast, his rudder broken, and his ship badly leaking, separated from the rest and unable to continue the voyage. In order to save the lives of the 300 people aboard, as well as two million in gold and silver[4] belonging to his majesty and private persons, he put in, with the advice and agreement of Martín Romero Caamaño, *veedor*,[5] and of the pilots and other experienced persons present, to Puerto Rico, where he arrived, miraculously enough, on 9 April. There he landed the silver and deposited it in the city fortress.

The said general at once dispatched first and second advices to his majesty making known his arrival so that he might receive instructions,[6] and it would seem that divine providence (to which

translated in Cooley, *Sir Francis Drake his Voyage*. For the present version I have collated the two available Spanish texts and made a new translation.

[1] Fernández Duro, *Armada Española desde la Unión*, III (1897), 109–10, provides the following information on Sancho Pardo: in 1590 he wrote to Don Juan de Idiáquez asking him to intercede with the king for him to be admitted to the order of Santiago, stating that he had served for 36 years without receiving *merced*. He commanded the squadron of transports in the armada of 1588, led an expedition to Brittany in 1590 and afterwards commanded Atlantic *flotas*. He had been governor of Havana in 1572.

[2] The *Begoña*, 800 *toneladas*, belonging to Agustín de Landecho, according to the Lima *relación*.

[3] The Florida or Bahama Channel.

[4] Sancho Pardo's report of 3 June 1595 to the crown (A. de I., Santo Domingo, 169) gives an inventory of the cargo, valuing the whole of it at 2,164,836 *pesos*.

[5] Inspector of the fleet. Each *flota* carried such an officer, whose job it was to supervise, on behalf of the king, all aspects of the conduct of the fleet. Romero's letters to the king (3 June 1595 and 22 July 1595) and to Ibarra (3 June 1595), reporting on Sancho Pardo's situation at Puerto Rico, are in A. de I., Santo Domingo, 169.

[6] This appears to be a deliberate falsification. As Pedro Suárez Coronel's letter of 8 June (A. de I., Santo Domingo, 155, *ramo* 4) relates, the governor tried to persuade the general to report to Spain, but without success. He later complained that the record of these proceedings (A. de I., Santo Domingo, 155, *ramo* 4) was ignored (Suárez Coronel to the crown, 19 December 1595, A. de I., Santo

PLATE 11. Plan of the Morro at San Juan by Pedro de Salazar: 1

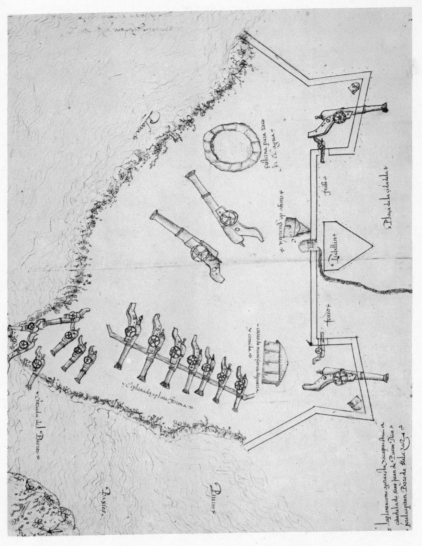

PLATE III. Plan of the Morro at San Juan by Pedro de Salazar: 2

many thanks are due) arranged, for its secret ends, that the orders, which might have come earlier, arrived at the right moment to save not only the silver, but also the island, and even perhaps all the Indies, as will be seen later. A few days after the dispatch of these advices, the governor of this island, Pedro Suárez Coronel, received those of his majesty, informing him that a great fleet was fitting out in England to come and take this island during the winter, since it was thought that then it would be least expected. On receiving this intelligence the general and the said *veedor* met together with the governor and Francisco Cid, captain of the infantry of the garrison here.[1] Having discussed the precautions to be taken to secure the island and his majesty's silver so that if the enemy came he should not capture everything, they all agreed that the places where the enemy might attack and land men should be inspected and that the general should have some of the guns of his flagship planted where he should think best, and the ship itself laid athwart the mouth of the harbour to be sunk on the arrival of the enemy so as to bar the entrance, for this seemed to be the most vulnerable point, where the enemy would attack and where our men should keep most careful watch. Meanwhile the general awaited his majesty's orders to proceed on his voyage.

Domingo, 155). The earliest known report by Sancho Pardo to Spain is dated 3 June 1595 (A. de I., Santo Domingo, 169). He had meanwhile written at length, on 22 May, to Don Luis Fajardo, *veedor general* of the *armada de la guardia de las Indias* at Havana (A. de I., Santo Domingo, 128, no. 50; another copy in Santo Domingo, 169, and another in Museo Naval, Navarrete MSS, XII, no. 98, ff. 357–63). Here he gave a dramatic account of the ordeal of the Begoña and argued that he be permitted to patch her up and proceed home with the treasure. It was with this intention in mind, he explained, that he had refrained from notifying either Spain or Havana of his presence in Puerto Rico, since any advices sent by sea might fall into English hands. For this reason, too, he had prevented the departure from Puerto Rico of any vessel that might report the fact. Fajardo replied refusing permission to move until instructions had been received from Spain, and at the same time reported the whole matter to Spain (Fajardo to Ibarra, 8 June 1595, A. de I., Santo Domingo, 128, no. 50). Thus nearly two months elapsed between Sancho Pardo's arrival in Puerto Rico and the departure of the official dispatch reporting the event.

[1] Francisco Gómez Cid. He wrote a brief account of the action to Ibarra, dated 15 December 1595 (A. de I., Santo Domingo, 169, *ramo* 4).

On 13 November of this year Don Pedro Tello de Guzmán arrived here with his majesty's five frigates, in which general Sancho Pardo was to lade the silver and return to Spain, with Pedro Tello as his vice-admiral. Having delivered his dispatches, Pedro Tello told the general that in the course of their voyage they had encountered at Guadalupe two English ships that had lost company with the English fleet, and that his vice-admiral, Gonzalo Méndez de Canzo, had beaten and sunk one of them, taking 25 English prisoners; and that he, Don Pedro, going in pursuit of the other vessel, discovered nine sail of the enemy fleet, and as soon as he descried them tacked about to continue his voyage; and that the English prisoners had declared that near there, on the southern side of Guadalupe, preparing launches, lay the queen of England's fleet, consisting of 25 ships, including six galleons of the queen's, of 600 tons each, and two private ships of the same burden, the fleet being divided into two squadrons under Francis Drake and John Hawkins, with Drake and his lieutenant for the land, Sir Thomas Baskerville, directing the fleet's course and proceedings on land; and that the fleet carried 3,000 soldiers and 1,500 sailors well furnished with guns and was bound straight for Puerto Rico, as appeared from the instructions taken from the captain of the English ship. These ordered him, if separated by any mischance, to proceed to Puerto Rico, where they would wait ten days for him, leaving orders there for his further direction, but the instructions did not specify any further design. In view of all this Don Pedro came on here, fearing lest the enemy should have arrived ahead of him and taken the island. Since they had not yet come, he was sure that they would descend on the port the next day, and in view of this the general should arrange his departure as he thought fit.

When general Sancho Pardo heard the report of Pedro Tello and his vice-admiral, since the news found him in bed of a sickness that had kept him there several days, he notified the bishop and the governor, asking them to come and meet him, together with the frigate captains, Marco Antonio Becerra, captain of the harque-busiers, Pedro de Guia, of the order of St John, Domingo de Ynsaurraga, Francisco Gómez, captain of this garrison, Martín

Romero de Caamaño, *veedor*, and Juan de la Vera,[1] purser for the frigates. They met in his house and the general presented for their consideration the report he had received concerning the enemy, and the best means available for the defence of the island and the treasure, bearing in mind that the enemy fleet was large and to be expected within a very short time, that the frigates badly needed re-fitting and fresh supplies of wood and water, all which, together with the lading of the treasure, would take eight days at least; and that, whether they thus busied themselves or not, the enemy, knowing from the other ship sighted that these frigates were on their way to collect the silver they already knew to be here, might lie in wait to intercept it, or else capture the island and establish there a base for the conquest of all the Indies, whence would ensue great injury and loss of reputation for his majesty. All were agreed that the guns and men should go to fortify the island, that the Tierra Firme flagship and another belonging to Pedro Milanes[2] should be sunk in the harbour channel to block the entrance and that the silver should not be moved from the *fortaleza* until it was seen how the situation was shaping, for it was thought it would be safer there, and could (if, for our sins, it were so determined) thence be cast into the sea to save it from the enemy. This decided, they proceeded to carry into effect every possible measure of defence, working day and night with great alacrity and zeal.

General Sancho Pardo, as a man of great experience who had also examined the defence positions and approaches, assured Pedro Tello and the others that it was impossible to lose the island so long as our men fought and did their duty. It was only necessary to be careful of the harbour, lest the fleet should enter it all at once. To prevent this it would be as well to sink the two ships as agreed, with the frigates behind them, their bows turned seawards to oppose entry. These measures would secure both the land and the treasure of his majesty, who would thus be well served, and in whose name the general called on them to set about their tasks. Accordingly Pedro Tello himself undertook the defence of the harbour.

[1] Juan de la Rea (Lima *relación*); Roa (Alba MS).
[2] The *Pandorga* (Suárez Coronel to the crown, 19 December 1595, A. de I., Santo Domingo, 155).

The bishop offered to say mass the next day and to preach a sermon to the people, as he did in fact, charging them as christians to serve God and their king; and he continued to discharge this duty night and day throughout, visiting the men at their posts, at each of which he stationed a priest, and encouraging them with great spirit.

The same day the governor and the general sent an advice boat to Santo Domingo to warn them to keep watch, so that if the enemy went there (the president having been informed by letter that he would), the news should be sent at once to Cartagena and Santa Marta.

All the local men were immediately mustered and some of the men of the frigates were sent ashore, being needed there. In all there were 10,300 persons, including 700 fighting men and 800 from the frigates and the Tierra Firme flagship, apart from the garrison and foreigners, and fifty of them were horsemen with lance and buckler. The whole force was distributed as follows:[1]

At the *caleta* of El Morrillo, Captain Pedro de Guia, of the order of St John, with soldiers ... 150

At the *caleta* of El Cabrón, Alonso de Vargas, with soldiers ... 100

At El Puente and El Boquerón, Pedro Vázquez, royal ensign, with soldiers ... 150

At the mouth of the Bayamón, Captain Ortega,[2] with soldiers ... 50

In the frigates, under the command of Don Pedro Tello, men ... 300

[1] See map 1, p. 150. The numbers here are obviously corrupt. Pedro Suárez's report to the crown (19 December 1595, A. de I., Santo Domingo, 155) gives a total shore strength, including men from the frigates and the *Begoña*, of 806. He also gives 28 or 30 as the number of men left in the *Magdalena*, which suggests about 150 as the number remaining in the frigates, a figure compatible with other references to a 'small' force in the frigates. The Alba MS gives larger figures: ashore, 1,215, including 225 from the frigates; in the frigates, 325. These figures, deduced from those in the Alba MS, depend on the assumption that the entire original complement of the frigates took part in the action, which is of course very unlikely. As to the quality of the defending forces, 'El Huérfano' remarked that the troops in the frigates had been collected from the streets for the expedition. On the other hand the *Begoña* and the frigates must have supplied most of the gunners, who, apart from the sailors in the frigates, were the only Spaniards to play any effective part in the fighting.

[2] Both texts give 'Otega', but other sources 'Ortega'.

All the rest of the men were in El Morro and at the parade ground, under Captain Marco Antonio Becerra, with the governor taking command of the cavalry, each of whom was to give support with his party wherever it should be most useful or necessary.

ARTILLERY PLACED[1]

At El Morro, very good brass pieces	27
On the platform of the said Morro, pieces	5
At Santa Elena, pieces	4
At the *caleta* of Los Frailes, next to the fortress, pieces	3
At Santa Catalina *caleta*, pieces	5
At El Tejar, pieces	9
At the mouth of the Bayamón, pieces	2
At El Puente and in a ship placed there, pieces	6
At El Boquerón, pieces	4
At the *caleta* of El Cabrón, pieces	2
At the *caleta* of El Morrillo, pieces	3
	70

The frigates were also well gunned, apart from the abovesaid seventy pieces, manned by good gunners at each post, with Vice-admiral Gonzalo Méndez de Canzo in general command of the forts of El Morro, El Morrillo and Santa Elena.

On the 15th of the same month news arrived from the governor of Canaria to the governor of this island to the effect that the enemy fleet had gone there and, putting men ashore to take water, had been repulsed with the loss of 25 men, and that it was making for the Indies. The advice-boat reported that on passing by the island of San Martín it had sighted the fleet at anchor, twenty-five sail of them. Immediately, that same day, General Sancho Pardo forwarded this dispatch to the governor of Havana, requesting him to send it on to New Spain to General Pedro Meléndez, who was there with his *flota*.

These measures having been taken and all the men being eager to confront the enemy, a council was held, consisting of the general,

[1] As to the disposition the sources vary, but not significantly. For the total, Alba MS gives 73 and Suárez Coronel (to the crown, 19 December 1595, A. de I., Santo Domingo, 155) 66.

Pedro Tello, Vice-admiral Gonzalo Méndez, Captains Marco
Antonio Becerra, Pedro de Guia and Domingo de Ynsaurraga,
and Martín Romero de Caamaño, *veedor*. They discussed whether
it would be as well to embark the silver into two of the frigates, so
that in case the enemy should capture the port, they, being the
nimblest craft, could escape by night, with the other three following
as a rear-guard, and remaining if necessary to hold the enemy in
fight while the two pursued their voyage. The majority opinion
was that the silver should not be moved, because that would dis-
courage the men on shore, who were in good heart to fight, but,
seeing themselves so deserted, would weaken, so that his majesty
would lose not only the country but his reputation, which was
more important to him than treasure. The right thing to do was
to face the enemy, trusting in God to give us victory. When the
general perceived the majority opinion, he ordered Pedro Tello to
prepare the frigates speedily, so that the silver might be laded whenever it should be expedient. Meanwhile, in case the enemy should
give some sign of whether he would lie in wait for the treasure, he
sent a caravel to make a search fifty leagues to sea. This was done
and the silver remained in place, which was the prudent course.

At dawn on the 22nd of the same month of November the
enemy fleet was sighted from the land. It comprised 23 sail and a
lateen-rigged caravel, the six galleons of the queen being of 800 tons,
with two other ships of the same burden, the rest being of 300 and
150 tons and less, together with 40 launches, all sailing in close
order. At once the call to arms was sounded and all hastened to
their posts with a will to fight. There was little wind, and so they
approached slowly until a breeze got up. The caravel came ahead
together with some boats, taking soundings and signalling with
white flags. When one of them came opposite El Boquerón, the
men there fired a gun at her, making her withdraw seawards,
whereupon she put out coloured flags. And passing further on,
after mid-day the whole fleet anchored off El Cabrón beach, where
no ship has ever been seen to ride, for it was not known to be
possible until after the enemy's departure, when the general sent
to have the place sounded and it was found to have twenty or thirty
fathoms of clear water. It was understood that he intended to land

men there under cover of his guns, expecting to take us unawares and to meet no resistance to his invasion, wherein he was mistaken.

While the fleet remained at this place our men fired many pieces of artillery from El Morrillo[1] and El Cabrón beach, so that several balls did damage, and it was afterwards learned that they killed John Hawkins, general of one of the squadrons, and two of the chief gentlemen accompanying him, as well as others, and that one ball carried away the table at which Francis Drake was eating and struck one of his companions, who, as is known, will not escape with his life.[2]

Seeing the damage he was receiving from the shore, the enemy sent the lateen caravel with an islander pilot (a mulatto who is said to be well acquainted with these parts) and five boats towards the harbour to reconnoitre and take soundings off the islet called Isla de Cabras, which is on the western side. After the soundings, one of the boats returned to inform the fleet, which immediately moved off at five in the afternoon, not having fired a gun nor even a musket all the time it was there; it ran out to sea and stood off and on that night until the next day.

At eight o'clock in the morning on Thursday (the following day) the whole fleet came to anchor to the leeward of the islet they had sounded the day before, close to the port, which was another new anchorage not known until then because it was 60 fathoms

---

[1] Lima *relación*: 'del Morrillo viejo'.

[2] Alba MS is fuller on this incident: 'And the governor, thinking that the enemy might, because the sea was calm, land men, took 80 men from the reserve, and, with Captain Lanzarote de Viera, who for this occasion was appointed captain of horse (of which there were fifty), began firing at the enemy from the Morrillo. However, because the distance was great, some shots reached the target and others not, and so the governor brought up two guns, one of them a demi-culverin, which was manhandled to position. With this they fired only five shots, as it was already late in the day. The first cleared the whole fleet; the next three struck the great ships, whereupon they at once began to weigh, in order to get away from that place. The next shot, at sunset, was fired at the flagship and struck her stern, where, so they say, it killed John Hawkins and two of the leading gentlemen of his company, and bore away the table at which Francis Drake was dining – they say he was very lucky not to have been killed.' Pedro Suárez Coronel (to the crown, 19 December 1595, A. de I., Santo Domingo, 155) gives a nearly identical account of this episode.

deep over rocks,[1] so that a vessel might easily be lost on the coast in the event of bad weather. There they remained, the weather being favourable, beyond the reach of our artillery, and that night they sent two boats to reconnoitre the beach of Bayamón and the shallows as far as El Canuelo stockade, to see if it were possible to land men there. In one of the boats, which was well covered with an awning, went Francis Drake, as was subsequently learned.

Don Pedro Tello, who was responsible for the port, noticed the enemy's activity, and thinking that an attack was to be made on El Canuelo, to force it with boats that night and put men ashore, he reported this to the general and asked for men to be sent to resist such an attempt. The general ordered that Captain Agustín de Landecho with 30 soldiers should be there that afternoon, and that 50 soldiers under Martín Romero de Caamaño, *veedor*, should go there that night, with instructions to withdraw by boat to the frigates in the event of enemy superiority, there to consolidate their position.

On the same Thursday, the 23rd, St Clement's day, at ten o'clock at night, under cover of darkness, the enemy attacked the harbour with 25 boats, each containing 50 or 60 well armed men, with the object, as was seen later, of burning the frigates. These all drew near the platform of El Morro, ranging themselves under the guns, and from what was learned afterwards, it appears that Francis Drake came in one of the boats to the harbour mouth to guide the rest. Although it was dark, the boats were seen, and the guns at El Morro and the fort of Santa Elena and the frigates at once began to fire rapidly. Most of the boats attacked the flagship, the *Texeda*, setting fire to her at the bows and throwing many fire-balls and shells into her, but our men with great alacrity extinguished the fires before they caused any damage and fought back with artillery, muskets and stones.[2] At the same time they set fire to the *Isabel*, the *Magdalena* and the *Santa Clara*. These fires were put out, but the

[1] Both texts give *sobre bajos* – in fact sharp rocks in deep water, as 'El Huérfano' makes clear.

[2] Alba MS says that the frigates were so ill-supplied with hand-to-hand weapons that Pedro Tello put quantities of large stones aboard. These, according to 'El Huérfano', were hurled down upon the English when they came alongside, and were responsible for much of the damage.

third time the *Magdalena*, under Captain Domingo de Ynsaurraga, was set alight, the blaze could not be quenched, for she took fire at the stern and burned furiously. The captain and his men did all they could to keep a foothold aboard, and fought the flames until she was almost burned down and twelve men had been killed by enemy musket fire, besides as many burned. The captain escaped by swimming through the midst of the boats to the *Santa Isabel*, which was under the command of Captain Juan Flores de Rabanal in place of Captain Pedro de Guia, who had charge of a shore post, where he gave every assistance the situation demanded. The fighting – the most bitterly contested that was ever seen – lasted an hour, and the whole harbour was lit by the flames of the burning frigate, which favoured the others, for they could see to aim their guns, which, together with those of the forts and the muskets and stones fired from the frigates, wrought so much injury that the enemy withdrew after an hour's fighting, as I have said, having lost nine or ten boats and more than 400 men, not counting many others wounded.[1] On our side we lost no more than the frigate and forty men dead and burned, besides some wounded by musket fire.[2] It was good to see how well the frigates fought and how well they were backed by the guns of the forts, particularly those of Santa Elena, which were in the best position to injure the boats.

On Friday the 24th, considering that the enemy would repeat the night attack and land troops, our men did not from daybreak cease their preparations, placing guns at various points ashore, as for example all along El Tejar, which was under the command of the governor and of Captain Marco Antonio with the men of the guard company. Captain Guia moved to Santa Catalina *caleta*, having formerly been at El Morrillo with 50 harquebusiers, and two other guns and 30 soldiers under Martín Romero, *veedor*, were stationed at the *caleta* of Los Frailes near the *fortaleza*. Everywhere

[1] Lima *relación*: 'with the loss of many Englishmen and several boats, which were found on the shore next morning'. Alba MS and Suárez Coronel (to the crown, 19 December 1595, A. de I., Santo Domingo, 155): eight or nine boats were sunk and 200 English left dead and wounded. 'El Huérfano': over 300 bodies of the enemy were found on the shore.

[2] Lima *relación*: 14 dead, 18 wounded. 'El Huérfano': over 30 dead. Alba MS: 15 of the *Magdalena*'s men killed.

trenches and defence works were constructed and everyone set to with a mattock, without a single Negro to help, for all the citizens had sent them into the bush with their women and goods as soon as the enemy appeared.

However, about eight in the morning when the land breeze got up, the enemy fleet stood to sea, working to windward of the port, and so continued until the afternoon, when Don Pedro Tello, thinking that the enemy's object was to run straight into the harbour, went ashore to tell the general his opinion that the enemy was about to bear directly down upon the harbour, that the channel was not completely blocked by the two sunken ships and that two frigates should be sunk in the part that remained open in order to obstruct the entrance completely, since the security of the port was as important as the two frigates, for many reasons and for the good of his majesty's service.

General Sancho Pardo immediately held a council with the governor and the other officers, and it was agreed at once that a frigate should be sunk in the channel if a ship of Pedro Sedeño's, laden with merchandize, and another of lesser burden, should prove insufficient; these two were to be sunk as they were, since there was not time to unload them, and the frigate should be sunk whenever Don Pedro thought best.

At four o'clock in the afternoon the enemy came running down with the breeze towards the harbour, and Don Pedro, believing that he was making straight for the entrance, sank the two ships of Sedeño and Juan Díaz de Santana as well as the frigate *Texeda*, not having time to take out all the provisions and guns, although some were removed. Thus the entrance to the channel was completely closed, and at vesper time the enemy came to anchor between El Morro and the Isla de Cabras, where he had anchored the night before.

The sight of the fleet anchored so close to the harbour tended to confirm the suspicion that the enemy that night would attempt to finish burning the frigates and to land troops. Don Pedro therefore, with the general's consent, had the three frigates withdrawn into the harbour and stationed them at El Tejar with a guard to secure them. He did not fear that the enemy might land men, for he saw that our men were in good heart and that all the posts and landing places were well trenched and strong. The removal of the frigates took place at night, when the enemy could not observe it, so that the next morning he concluded that they had all been sunk. That night passed quietly, without any sign on our part that we were keeping careful watch.

On Saturday the 25th in the early morning the enemy sent seven or eight boats to reconnoitre the port and the coast as far as El Boquerón. They kept clear of the land to avoid our artillery and at ten o'clock rejoined the fleet, which lay at the place before mentioned.

That day at two in the afternoon appeared our caravel, which had gone out in search of the enemy eight days before. As soon as our people sighted her they fired a gun from El Boquerón warning her to bear up without approaching the port. Some boats from the fleet followed her as far as Cangrejos beach, where she ran aground and some of the cavalry hastened forward to assist the crew. Francisco González, pilot and captain of the caravel, scuttled her so that the enemy should not take her, and so the boats moved off and returned to the fleet without a prize.

The same Saturday during the night, the whole fleet set sail unobserved and stood out to sea, and when our people found in the morning that it had disappeared, they sent men at once by land along the coast westwards to discover whether it had been seen or had passed that way, making, as they supposed it was, for Santo Domingo. On Monday word came back from Arecibo, fourteen leagues from this port, that the fleet had passed by there on its course. That day the governor sent another messenger to San Germán, who returned within six days with the news that the fleet was lying in the bay of Azúcar, beyond San Germán, and had put ashore five companies of pikes and muskets, who were obtaining meat, water and wood, and constructing four pinnaces (which they did in four days) to carry their fresh stores.[1]

On receipt of this news, considering that the enemy might have some stratagem in mind – that he might be lying in wait there for

[1] Alba MS relates that they came to the port of San Francisco, 29 leagues from San Juan, and took some victuals at a place called Guayano, where they stayed four days and built four pinnaces, departing on 4 December.

the frigates, or waiting until they had gone in order to return to a defenceless Puerto Rico to capture it and carry out his design of establishing a base there – the general took counsel about what to do, and decided that they should not leave the port until it was known for certain that the enemy had passed beyond point Aguada, and that Captain Juan Flores de Rabanal should go out in an advice-boat and search 70 or 80 leagues northwards, during which time the silver should be embarked. He returned eight days later, having seen nothing. On 9 December news came from San Germán that the enemy fleet had gone southwards.

On the 11th of the same month there arrived at this city Lope Sánchez, boatswain of the frigate *Magdalena*, together with four of her crew, all of whom had been taken prisoner in the water by enemy boats on the night of the burning of the frigates. These had been put ashore at the bay of Azúcar, with a letter from Francis Drake for the governor of this place. The following is a copy of it:

Letter from Francis Drake to Pedro Suárez Coronel,
governor of Puerto Rico[1]

Understanding your lordship to be a gentleman of rank and a soldier, I write this letter to give you to understand that whenever I have had occasion to deal with those of the Spanish nation, I have always treated them with much honour and clemency, freeing not a few, but many of them. Thus, when our men set fire to the frigates, certain Spaniards escaped from the fury of the flames and they received no harm after their capture, but honourable usage of war.

From them it is learned that Don Pedro Tello's flagship captured a small vessel of our fleet with 25 or more Englishmen aboard. Provided they receive good and fair treatment, I shall be my usual self, but otherwise I shall be obliged to act against my nature. But as there are soldiers and gentlemen in that city, I do not doubt that our men will fare well and be given liberty by virtue of the rules of war: so much I expect, and will myself perform. I remain your servant in all things apart from the matter that lies between us.

[1] Several Spanish versions of this letter exist, but do not significantly vary: the Alba MS and El Huérfano's account include copies, and another accompanied the Lima *relación*; two further copies lie in A. de I., Santo Domingo, 169.

From the flagship of her sacred majesty the queen of England, my mistress, the 23rd November 1595, English style.

Francis Drake.

From the report of the boatswain and the other mariners, who accompanied the enemy for eight days, it was ascertained that they had departed thence making south or south-south-west, bound for Santo Domingo and thence for Panama,[1] for they said they were going where there was much gold and silver, and so indeed one might gather from the number of boats carrying provisions of war. These men confirmed the death of John Hawkins and the sorrow felt on his account, as well as the great damage the enemy had received: so great that when one day they went from the flagship to another galleon they found nearly all the men therein wounded and sick. They much bemoaned the damage caused by the stones fired from the frigates. So much were they harmed that when, on the day after the fighting, Francis Drake held a council to determine whether they should renew the attack, he found no one to agree with him, especially because these men had told them that our forces were very strong – stronger than formerly. Drake was amazed when he learned how few men were aboard the frigates on the night of the fire, and plucked his beard for not having taken the treasure and the island. For two days he would not be seen and complained about John Hawkins, who had opposed their pursuing the frigates from Guadalupe as soon as it was learned that they had captured the ship and were making for Puerto Rico. He intimated that otherwise we would not have had the chance to strengthen our defences as we did during the eight days while they dallied preparing their boats and watering. All this was ordained by God, to whom many thanks are due, since, by his grace, besides obtaining such a victory with so small a force as ours opposing such a powerful fleet, saving the island and two million of silver, notable services to his majesty have ensued, together with general benefit to his subjects.

In the first place, from what has been gathered, it appears that

[1] Alba MS: the returned prisoners reported the English as saying they were going to Santo Domingo and Cartagena; they also 'heard much talk of Panama'.

the enemy intended to maintain this base, which he might easily have done at small cost, for the corsairs of all nations who frequent these waters would have resorted hither and would have assisted in its defence. It would have been necessary to fit out an expedition expressly to retake the place, because the port is strong and from hence further damage can be done to the *flotas* and the coasts, all of which lie to leeward.

Secondly, this enemy, who until now has met no resistance at sea, has here had his head broken, for as has been related, one of the two commanders died, together with 400 others, apart from many wounded.

Thirdly, two million in silver, gold and cochineal has been saved, with which the queen could have organized fresh forces and caused us further trouble.

Fourthly, the engagement of the enemy in these islands until 3 December gave time to warn the places suspected to be in danger, and advices were dispatched, as has been said, to Santo Domingo and Havana, and thence to Cartagena and New Spain, so that we may expect their safety.

Last, and not less important, are the morale and esteem our men have gained with the knowledge of the enemy's weakness, and on the other hand his loss of prestige, which plays a great part in success or failure. And since so many benefits hence ensue, his majesty should reward those who were involved in order to encourage the beholders to serve him on like occasions.

After the events related the general, having been advised that the enemy had gone on, that provisions were scarce because much had been consumed during this episode and the island was too poor to supply more, and that he had better hasten his departure, made arrangements to set forth. He ordered the artillery to be collected with all speed from the shore positions[1] and the silver to be embarked in the frigates; and with the latter and a ship and an advice-boat, carrying some of the men and guns of the two lost frigates and of the Tierra Firme flagship, he left Puerto Rico in good weather on 20 December 1595.

[1] He left the governor ten of the ships' guns (Suárez Coronel to the crown, A. de I., 19 December 1595, Santo Domingo, 155).

Instructions given by Francis Drake to the captain of the Francis, *one of the vessels of his fleet, which was taken at the island of Guadalupe*

The instructions and orders to be observed by the whole fleet, which is departing from the port of Plymouth on 29 August 1595.

The first is to observe divine worship and to keep this rule twice daily unless for some special reason you are unable to do so.

Secondly, you are to take great care to keep company and to come up to speak with your flagship twice daily, and if you cannot do it more than once, do it each day; and take great care to observe the orders given you to remain always in company, as the weather shall allow.

And if any ship or pinnace from stormy weather or other cause whatever should lose company, she should seek us first at the isles of Bayona off Galicia, where the fleet will wait until it is time to proceed and you shall have found us; thence, if you should not find us, make for Puerto Santo and wait there three days; should we not be there, make for the island of Guadalupe, a small island near Dominica towards the northeast, where we shall stay three days, leaving some sign whereby you shall know whither we are bound, which will be for Puerto Rico, where we shall stay ten days.

If in our course we meet any contrary wind or storm at night, you are to take in all sails until the morning, unless you should see one of the flagships carrying sail, in which case you should do the same.

And if the weather should change or contrary wind should develop during the night, your flagship will put out two lanterns, one above the other, the height of a man apart, so that you may steer by them.

And if we should all shorten sail at night on account of the weather and it should be necessary to make sail that same night, you must before we set sail show a single lantern with a light at the poop at the foretop.

You shall keep no light in any ship (apart from the flagship) except the light in the bittacle, and that with great care that it be not seen; and on account of the dangers from fire, you are not to carry any candle or light about the ship unless it be in a lantern; and without fail you must take great care with the fire in the galley.

177

No ship, bark nor pinnace shall go ahead of the flagship at night, particularly in rough weather, nor get under the lee of the great ships, tacking from one side to another.

And if any vessel of the fleet should by mischance lose a main-mast, a yard, a pump or other important item, she should fire one or two guns, according to the gravity of her need, so that the other ships can speedily assist her and so that no ship shall lose company without succour according to her need.

And should any vessel of the fleet go off her course and collide with any other vessel, the signal shall be to hoist and lower the topsail three times, and the other shall do likewise in recognition.

You shall not permit gambling in the ship, neither with cards nor dice, by reason of the many quarrels which usually arise from this.

You shall take the greatest care to conserve victuals, following your own discretion in this until you receive further orders.

Finally, so that you may keep company the better, you shall see a light at the poop of the flagship once or twice.

Francis Drake

VI. *Tierra Firme*

Drake's three weeks at Río de la Hacha evoked a substantial spate of letters and *informaciones,* but the Spanish material is unusually free from controversy. The governor, Licenciado Francisco Manso de Contreras emerges, not only in his own letters[1] and *información,*[2] but also in the city *cabildo's* reports,[3] as the hero of the occasion. Comparison with the English narratives suggests that he exaggerated the strength of the initial resistance to the landing, but that his account of the ransom negotiations was essentially true,[4] though the men of Río de la Hacha, preoccupied as they were with their own troubles, failed to notice that Drake had other reasons to pause at this stage: he had probably at least fifty wounded, and no extensive re-victualling had so far been possible. It must be allowed that the English accounts likewise omit to point out the relevance of these facts. In any case the value of the time thus gained and lost was great in view of the situation at Panama, but the governor's messages to the westward were not, as he claimed, vital to the safety of Cartagena and the Isthmus. For Don Pedro de Acuña, at Cartagena, had already received Pedro Tello's warning on 5 December[5]

---

[1] To Ibarra, 14 January 1596 (A. de I., Santo Domingo, 81); to the king, 15 January 1596 (document 30); to the king, 24 March 1596 (A. de I., Santo Domingo, 193).

[2] A. de I., Santa Fe, 190.

[3] Letter to the king, 15 January 1596 (A. de I., Santo Domingo, 81); *información* of January 1596 (A. de I., Santo Domingo, 51).

[4] Cp. 'Full Relation': '*December* the third, being tuesday the *Spaniards* came to parley with us for a certain sum of Treasure for ransome of the said towne. The fourth of *December* they brought Pearle, &c. but lesse in value than was compounded for, which our Generall Sir *Francis Drake* refused, and thereupon ordered that it should be set on Fire and burned, which accordingly was done at our departure.

'The fifteenth of *December* being Friday, the Enemy made faire promises to our Generall, which was onely to have us to stay as we supposed, till they had sent word to other places, as afterwards the Governour confessed.'

[5] Letter of Juan de Yzurrieta, 9 December 1595 (A. de I., Santa Fe, 92).

and, on the 13th, a report by a trading vessel which had sighted 25 enemy ships off Cape de la Vela on the 11th.[1] These reports reached Panama on 12 and 16 December respectively, whereas it was not until nearly the end of the month that Sotomayor heard of the sack of Río de la Hacha.[2]

Spanish evidence concerning the passage of the fleet from Río de la Hacha to Nombre de Dios is unfortunately meagre. Maynarde implies that some attempt on Cartagena had been contemplated, the idea being finally abandoned during the brief visit to Santa Marta. The bad weather experienced there, which continued during the following night, may have contributed to the decision, as Manso de Contreras and two of the English prisoners thought.[3] Bad weather also probably caused the separation of the *Phoenix* and the *Garland*'s pinnace,[4] though the Spaniards, who captured the latter, believed that the two vessels had been sent ahead to discover whether Cartagena had been warned.[5] In fact Pedro de Acuña had made intensive preparations and the morale and defences of the city were reported to be in good shape,[6] but it seems rather unlikely that Drake was deterred from attempting Cartagena by fear of the galleys, as Avellaneda alleged.[7]

[1] 'Relacion de Rodrigo Diaz', Museo Naval, Navarrete MSS, xxv, no. 67 (ff. 279–81). This deposition was made at Seville by the master of a *patache* which had left Cartagena on 15 December 1595.

[2] 30 December, according to the *relación* in Biblioteca de la Real Academia de la Historia, Salazar, F. 19 (ff. 1–10).

[3] Pp. 193, 214, 222 below. Raleigh and his men, it will be remembered, had evidently envisaged Cartagena as an important target to be attempted after the sack of Panama (see above, p. 15).

[4] VTD. On Piers Lemon's capture and subsequent adventures see also Kraus, *Sir Francis Drake*, p. 154.

[5] Pedro de Salazar to the king, La Margarita, 1 May 1596 (A. de I., Santo Domingo, 184): 'He made for Cartagena and sent two launches ahead to find out whether it had news of him; a galley gave chase to them and captured one, from which was obtained an account of the events.' A transcript and translation are available in B.M., Additional MSS, 36317, ff. 94–8, 100–3.

[6] 'Relacion de Rodrigo Diaz', Museo Naval, Navarrete MSS, xxv, no. 67 (ff. 279–81).

[7] In a letter of 1 March 1596 (A. de I., Santa Fe, 93) Avellaneda enthusiastically described the Cartagena galleys and concluded: 'Francis Drake feared the

The events from the arrival of the English at Nombre de Dios on 27 December 1595/6 January 1596 until their departure from Porto Belo on 8/18 February were the subject of no less than five major *relaciones*. Two of these were apparently written by or on behalf of the campmaster, Don Gerónimo de Çuaço Casasola and deal respectively with events before and after the English departure from Nombre de Dios on 5/15 January.[1] The first is in some respects the best account of the earlier period, for Çuaço was more immediately in touch with the situation at Capirilla than the authors of the other *relaciones* and was less concerned than they with the glorification of Don Alonso de Sotomayor. On the other hand this narrative, with its sometimes tedious recapitulation of the campmaster's every action, has already been published. Miguel Ruiz Delduayen's *relación*, which covers the same period from Sotomayor's point of view, lacks some of Çuaço's detail but is on the whole clearer and more lively, with better detail on some episodes. Since it has not been published before, it takes a well deserved place herein as the main Spanish report on the first part of the Isthmus campaign.[2] The much shorter account by Sotomayor is remarkably uninformative on the chief events, devoting much space to his quarrel with the *audiencia* and to recommendations of leading participants. The prisoners' statements he enclosed are, however, of major interest.[3] Another narrative, which appears to be a copy of the official *relación* presented to the king on Sotomayor's behalf by Licenciado Francisco Caro de Torres, may have been written by the latter, who accompanied the general throughout the campaign.[4] Although this is plainer and more accurate than the account he published in his *Relacion de los Servicios que hizo . . . Sotomayor* (1620), it is generally less reliable and interesting than Ruiz Delduayen's. Finally the only *relación* which covers the events

galleys and the governor of Cartagena, and said as much at Río de la Hacha to the governor there and to Licenciado Bravo.' This judgement, particularly since Cartagena possessed only two galleys at this time, reflects more upon Avellaneda than upon Drake.

[1] Museo Naval, Navarrete MSS, xxv, nos. 64 (ff. 258–66) and 66 (ff. 269–77), published in *La Dragontea*, 11, 149–68 and 171–92.   [2] Document 32.

[3] A. de I., Santo Domingo, 81. The depositions are in document 33.

[4] Biblioteca de la Real Academia de la Historia, Salazar, F. 19, ff. 1–10.

after 5/15 January in detail is Çuaço's second instalment, which is therefore given below,[1] with the omission of certain passages of minor interest which may be found in the Spanish edition. A sixth *relación* is the short description written on 13/23 January,[2] which, while adding nothing important to the other sources, claims special credit for Don Francisco de Valverde y Mercado, one of the commissioners for Porto Belo, and for Juan Bautista Antoneli. Further commentary is provided by numerous letters, several of which constitute minor *relaciones*,[3] and by various *informaciones*.[4] Antoneli's excellent description of the terrain, which is relevant in more ways than one,[5] and Baskerville's note to Drake after the battle of San Pablo[6] complete the present selection.

The most impressive feature of this wealth of evidence is the large measure of agreement, even in matters of detail, between the various reports. This is not to say that controversy was absent. As Dr Diego Villanueva Çapata, *oidor* and Valverde's fellow-commissioner for Porto Belo, wrote shortly after the events, 'this place [Panama], with its few and quarrelsome citizens, is full of passionate disputes ... they are all attacking and contradicting each other'.[7] The main parties in these quarrels were the *audiencia*, Soto-mayor, Antoneli and Diego Suárez de Amaya, the *alcade mayor* of Nombre de Dios. The *audiencia* was vehemently criticized by all the other factions for dilatoriness and neglect of elementary pre-

---

[1] Document 37.

[2] A. de I., Patronato, 265, *ramo* 58, headed, 'Relacion de lo sucedido en Nombre de Dios a una armada Ynglesa y disposiciones que contra ella dio el Marques de Cañete Virrey del Peru con auxilio del Yngeniero Juan Bautista Antonelli. 1596.' A copy, with a different title, appears in Navarrete MSS, xxv, no. 65 (ff. 267–8) and is printed in *La Dragontea,* II, 168–71.

[3] Notably Dr Juan del Barrio to Ibarra, 24 January 1596 (A. de I., Santo Domingo, 81); marqués de Cañete to the king, 18 May 1596 (A. de I., Panama, 44); Baltasar Pérez to the king, 18 January 1596 (A. de I., Panama, 44); Licenciado Antonio de Salazar to the king, 6 March 1596 (A. de I., Panama, 14).

[4] Those cited herein were compiled for Captain Juan Enríquez Conabut (A. de I., Panama, 44), Fray Bartolomé de la Barrera y Castroverde (A. de I., Indiferente General, 2988) and Captain Gerónimo Ferrón Barragán (A. de I., Panama, 46).

[5] Document 31.   [6] Document 36.

[7] Letter to the king, 20 May 1596 (A. de I., Panama, 14).

cautions before the operations. Antoneli and Amaya, though openly in conflict over the relative importance and defensibility of Porto Belo and Nombre de Dios, were at one in condemning the amateurism of the civil government and in advocating its replacement by military rule.[1] Sotomayor and his following (notably Ruiz Delduayen, Caro de Torres and Conabut) resented the *audiencia*'s unwillingness to accept his commission as captain-general and emphasized the consequent delay and the inadequacy of the measures previously taken, maintaining that it was only Sotomayor's arrival in the nick of time that saved the country from disaster. Dr Juan del Barrio de Sepúlveda, the senior *oidor*, made no attempt to deal with these attacks in his own report,[2] and the absence of serious defence together with the unanimity of the critics lends the case against the *audiencia* a high degree of credibility. Sotomayor[3] of course took the lion's share of the glory. His own report generously commended the *oidores* individually and even put in a word for Antoneli and Amaya, though reserving the highest praise for Conabut. Antoneli worked amicably with Sotomayor in the Río de Chagre and afterwards paid tribute to his leadership,[4] but he claimed most of the credit for the decision to defend the Capirilla pass, whereas neither Sotomayor nor Ruiz Delduayen connected him with this decision and Conabut implied that he had nothing to do with it.[5] Whatever their private feelings,

[1] See p. 201 below.
[2] Letter to Ibarra, 24 January 1596 (A. de I., Santo Domingo, 81).
[3] Don Alonso de Sotomayor, knight of the order of Santiago, having served in the Netherlands, was appointed governor of Chile in 1580 and left Spain with 600 men in 1581 to take up his command, sailing with the fleet of Diego Flores de Valdés, bound for the Strait of Magellan. In the event Sotomayor and his men disembarked at Buenos Aires and made their way overland to Chile, where Sotomayor continued to direct the war against the Araucanian Indians until 1592. He was in Lima when appointed captain-general of Panama in 1595 (Caro de Torres, *Relacion de los Servicios que hizo . . . Sotomayor* (1620)).
[4] Letter to the king, 24 May 1596 (A. de I., Panama, 44), cited below, p. 204.
[5] See p. 224 below. The *relación* in A. de I., Patronato, 265, ramo 58 (*La Dragontea*, II, 168–71) goes so far as to say that 'It was God's will that by the counsel and industry of Antoneli the Capirilla pass had been fortified', omitting to mention Sotomayor in this context, and giving the general impression that he was a mere figurehead.

Antoneli and the *oidores* probably took care not to insist too loudly in view of Sotomayor's position and prestige. Amaya evidently did not share that attitude. He claimed to be the true victor of San Pablo and organized his considerable local following to produce letters and *informaciones*.[1] He also had valuable connections in Spain and it was presumably their influence that caused the great playwright Lope de Vega Carpio to make him the hero of the epic *La Dragontea,* published in 1598. In that year Amaya was appointed governor of Cumaná, but his acrimonious dispute with Sotomayor continued until at least 1601.[2]

These dissensions, however, do not seriously complicate the historical interpretation of the campaign, for on the main events and issues the different parties are generally in agreement. It was not until the day before Drake's arrival at Nombre de Dios that work was begun to block the River Chagre and it was not until 30 December 1595/9 January 1596 that Conabut began fortifying the Capirilla pass. The Spanish commentators repeatedly stated or implied[3] that Drake would have met no serious resistance had he sailed direct to the Isthmus and reached it before Sotomayor's arrival or the receipt of Pedro Tello's warning. It is less clear why

[1] Amaya to the king, Cumaná, 2 January 1601 (A. de I., Santo Domingo, 187), referring to 'my *informaciones* and the letters accompanying them'. These documents have not been found, but Amaya's main arguments may be gathered from this letter and another dated Cumaná 15 June 1602 (A. de I., Santo Domingo, 187) and from Conabut's petition (document 34). He described himself as 'captain-general' of Nombre de Dios and claimed to have been in command of the forces at Capirilla. Sotomayor, he pointed out, did not set eyes on the enemy. A. de I., Santo Domingo, 584 contains a recommendation of Amaya, dated 5 March 1598, for the governorship of Cumaná, which also mentions the *informaciones*.

[2] Amaya's letter of 2 January 1601 (A. de I., Santo Domingo, 187) refers to accusations recently made against him by Sotomayor and to his own ambition to replace Sotomayor as president of Panama. On 1 June 1601 his brother Francisco Suárez wrote to him from Porto Belo (A. de I., Santo Domingo, 187) reporting William Parker's capture of that port and bitterly denouncing Sotomayor's incompetence and misrule.

[3] In addition to sources cited below, direct statements to this effect were made by Avellaneda (memorandum of 8 December 1596 on Avellaneda's report, A. de I., Panama, 1) and Hernando del Berrio (letter to the king, Panama, 23 January 1596, A. de I., Panama, 44).

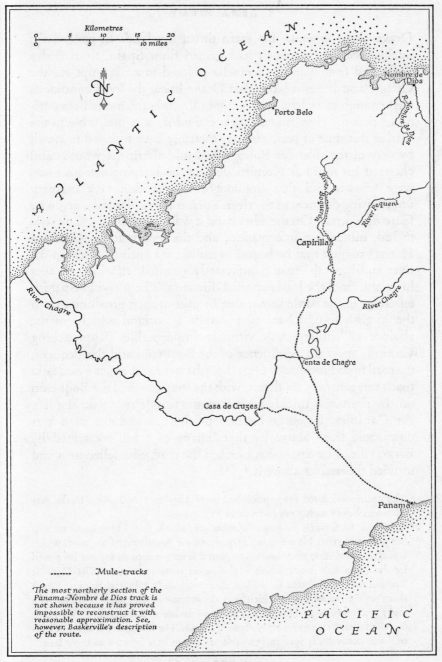

Kilometres
0 5 10 15 20
0 5 10 miles

ATLANTIC OCEAN

Nombre de Dios

R. *Nombre de Dios*

Porto Belo

River *Boqueron*

River *Pequeni*

Capirilla

River *Chagre*

River Chagre

Venta de Chagre

Casa de Cruzes

Panama

------- Mule-tracks

*The most northerly section of the
Panama-Nombre de Dios track is
not shown because it has proved
impossible to reconstruct it with
reasonable approximation. See,
however, Baskerville's description
of the route.*

*PACIFIC
OCEAN*

MAP 2. The Panama Isthmus in 1596

Drake chose to make his main thrust overland. In general the intelligence the Spaniards had gained from Spain, from Pedro Tello and from Río de la Hacha pointed to an attempt via the Chagre and it seems likely that Drake knew the local conditions well enough to realize, even without the aid of Antoneli's exposition,[1] that the river route, unless defended, was preferable to the road at this time of year. He may therefore have planned to attack by way of the river (as Raleigh had told Berrío he would) and changed his mind at Nombre de Dios on learning that his plans were known and that Sotomayor was at that very moment improvising defences in the river. Such is the explanation given by Caro de Torres.[2] On the other hand it was very much Drake's style to leak misleading information, and the reports from Río de la Hacha[3] suggest that he hoped to induce the enemy to defend the river and leave the road insufficiently guarded, attacking, as was his wont, from the least expected direction. The plentiful Spanish reportage of the battle shows that in spite of their gruelling march the English fought hard to penetrate a position which, in the absence of artillery, was virtually impregnable. Approaching Capirilla, near the confluence of the Boquerón and the Pequeni, the road from Nombre de Dios (here the same as the later Porto Belo road) ran generally southeast, with the steep gorge of the Boquerón on the right and thickly-grown mountainside rising on the left. At Capirilla the gorge became precipitous and the road was dominated from above by that 'knape of a hill' described by Baskerville. The Spaniards blocked the road with felled trees and fortified themselves above it.[4]

[1] The description dated 1587, published by Hakluyt in 1600, which Drake may have seen before setting out (document 31).

[2] *Relacion de los Servicios que hizo . . . Sotomayor* (1620).   [3] Document 30.

[4] See map 2, p. 185. No surviving map shows the Nombre de Dios road, which was abandoned soon after these events, but this stretch appears to have been used for the Porto Belo road, which is shown on some later maps. The Caro de Torres *relación* (Biblioteca de la Real Academia de la Historia, Salazar, F. 19) describes the site as 'a pass which is at the summit of Capira, where there is a rocky precipice on one side and thick forest on the other'. It is clear from Maynarde that the forested side rose steeply above the road. The alternative spelling 'Capireja' was occasionally used in 1596 and appears to have become standard later.

Among other issues of interest raised by the Spanish commentaries is the problem of Drake's intentions after leaving Nombre de Dios. The Spaniards' speculations, based on prisoners' statements, suggest that had he lived he might have attempted a desperate attack by way of the river. It was probably fortunate for the English that no such venture was launched, for in the three weeks before Drake's death the already weakened force had been sadly reduced and enfeebled by disease, the most effective of Panama's defences.[1]

30. Manso de Contreras to the king, 15 January 1596[2]

It was a long time since I had learned that the fleet, which according to your majesty's advices was being prepared in England, might be coming to these parts; and the last dispatch, which arrived in November, ordered only the collection of the royal treasure for delivery to the fleet due in September, without mentioning the English force. Nevertheless I took care to have munitions brought from Cartagena at my expense and to do whatever else was necessary in the light of the position of this place and the few men it has to set against a fleet which would inevitably comprise many ships and men. For our numbers were insufficient to defend this port, which in fact is not a port, but a low-lying land and beach, on which for more than eight leagues to leeward and windward one can disembark without the slightest trouble; and it seemed impossible to defend so wide a front with some fifty citizens and as many soldiers at my disposal, the few others being stationed at the pearling

[1] Antoneli to the king, Panama, 24 May 1596 (A. de I., Panama, 44): 'He cannot bring many men and the long voyage spoils and consumes his manpower, besides which, after the arrival and landing of his force, the injurious quality of the country and its air, together with the change of climate, must cause much sickness, and the water must infect them. Of this we have much experience, and lately have observed it upon the arrival of the English this year at Nombre de Dios, Panama and Porto Belo, when the worst obstacle they encountered was the evil condition of the country and its waters, which were the reasons why the beaches were peopled with dead bodies.'

[2] A. de I., Santo Domingo, 81.

settlement and at a country outpost for operations against the rebel Indians.

On receiving news from Santo Domingo on 6 December that ten ships, suspected to be a squadron of the English fleet, had been sighted at Guadalupe,[1] I gave orders for the women, the unfit and the valuables to be placed in hiding, and for the treasurer, with a sufficient guard, to remove your majesty's treasure to a very secret place. I ordered that the defence works, which I had caused to be constructed when the first warnings arrived, should be repaired, and sent Captain Jaime Jinobarte, a thoroughly experienced soldier, to train the men and serve as sergeant-major at Santa Marta, where for this occasion I had appointed as my deputy Don Francisco Flores, who had recently retired from the governorship of La Margarita with great credit. Leaving Santa Marta thus with the best defence I could manage, I came here, for this place seemed to be in greater danger and more in need of my presence, my greatest anxiety being that the Indians were in revolt and the whole country in a state of war and insecurity, with especially serious peril if the forces of this fleet should compel us to withdraw.

On the eleventh the canoes came fleeing in great haste from the pearling station with twenty ships in pursuit of them, put into the river and scuttled themselves and sank to the bottom. One of them I sent at once to Santa Marta and Cartagena with this news. A little later I had information that the ships numbered 56, large and small, and thinking that if they found some resistance they might proceed on their way without bothering about so unimportant a matter, I distributed these 100 men in a central position a quarter of a league off, personally inspected the artillery posts, weapons and munitions and exhorted all to do their duty in the service of your majesty and in defence of our homes and property. I stationed them in advanced positions from which they could neither flee nor retreat, for the whole country was in a state of war and we would have fallen into the hands of the cruellest Indians of these regions.

At nine that night 22 small vessels appeared off the mouth of the

[1] Pedro Tello's report, relayed by Santo Domingo, reached Cartagena on 5 December (letter of Juan de Yzurrieta, 9 December 1595, A. de I., Santa Fe, 92).

river within sight of the settlement and attempted to land men. We resisted them with three pieces of artillery and musketfire for the space of two hours,[1] but having sent thirty men to the ravines about half a league from this settlement, I now had word from their leader that they had been unable to hold the enemy there, and that roughly 2,000 men had landed and were marching along the beach and the highway in two columns. I gave orders for the men to be collected from their various positions, and since this settlement has no means of defence, consisting of no more than fifty houses on the shore, twenty of them roofed with tile, the rest thatched and all alike weakly built, and since we would have been attacked on all sides (for our few men – as indeed the enemy intended – no longer held a central position), we were then compelled, after consulting about it, to withdraw all the way to the place where the valuables and unfit people remained, in order to defend them.

Most of the soldiers disregarded the order and took flight into the bush, which I could not prevent because this happened at night; and some abandoned their weapons and returned to the settlement,[2] where the enemy now lay, and informed them of the state of the country, of its weak defences and of the ease with which they could pillage everything of value, especially your majesty's treasure, and take me prisoner, offering to serve as their guides for all these purposes, as indeed they did. Forthwith two squadrons of 400 men each set out that same night in different directions, and within an area of a league around the settlement they left not a thicket, not a track, not a hiding place unsearched. No resistance was possible because I had not six men left who had not deserted me and their weapons. Some had absconded and others were attending to the burial of their valuables, and if with the few men at

[1] Cp. the *relación* preceding the depositions in the *información* drawn up for the city of Río de la Hacha, dated 24 January 1596 (A. de I., Santo Domingo, 51). This states that in resisting the attempt to land at the mouth of the river the Spaniards sank an English launch, forcing the enemy to put to sea and make his landing about half a league from the city. English accounts do not mention any losses incurred in the landing operations.

[2] The *relación* of 24 January 1596 (A. de I., Santo Domingo, 51) says that 'they held it a better course, in order not to die at the hands of such cruel Indians, to surrender to the English'.

my disposal I had not made haste to remove the majority of the women and the leading citizens, these would undoubtedly have been taken prisoner with all their families that night, for when I made them leave a house in the country, where they were gathered, they had not moved more than a stone's throw from it when one of the enemy's squadrons arrived in search of them.

These two bands returned to the settlement with various prize-goods and in the morning three more came out, again guided by our soldiers, and ransacked all that was left. They began to kill the cattle and to carry off or destroy the food supplies, digging up the valuables and treasure and leaving no stone unturned. Many Negroes employed at the pearling station and by the local citizens joined the enemy voluntarily. These and the majority of the remainder stole what there was to steal and gave Francis Drake information about my plans and where to find our people and your majesty's treasure, which to obtain was his whole object. He sent to me offering, in exchange for its surrender, to restore all he had taken from me and the other citizens, to leave the Negroes to their masters and to refrain from burning the settlement. Although the royal treasure did not amount to 10,000 pesos, whereas my own and others' private property in jewels and valuables were worth over 150,000 ducats, I sent him a message that I would lose my head rather than see your majesty's treasure reduced by a single *real* for this purpose of ransoming the settlement. I issued an edict forbidding the citizens to have any dealings in this connection, on pain of heavy punishment.[1]

Seeing, however, that there was nothing further to lose and that it was in your royal interest that Cartagena and other places should have notice not only of the fleet's arrival, but also of its strength and purpose, I decided to try to obtain some account of these things under colour of negotiating a truce and pleading for some moderation of this warfare and spoil. And since I had in my company throughout this episode Licenciado Bravo, *oidor* of Santo Domingo (who was awaiting a passage thither and had done his duty in all respects, having lost more property than anyone, in the shape of the

[1] The text of this edict is given in a document dated 20 December 1595 in A. de I., Santo Domingo, 207.

goods he had ready for his voyage), trusting in his diplomatic skill, I persuaded him to go and see Drake, who had many times invited me to go or send someone to treat with him. At this meeting,[1] where other citizens were present, nothing whatever was agreed, but it yielded the fruit I had hoped for, which was definite and true information about the strength of the fleet and the troops it carried, the ports and places it had instructions to attack, the parts where men were to be landed and how this was to be arranged and ordered. For since Drake is extremely conceited and confident and saw that no advice could be sent by sea and thought it would be a slow matter by land, there was nothing he did not tell. I also learned further useful particulars from one Simón de Morales,[2] a Portuguese, who had been a prisoner for nine months and fled from this fleet. He came before me and made a statement about the fleet and all the rest.

At various times during the eighteen days that the fleet remained in this port I sent five messages to Cartagena by land and sea. Fearing, however, that some of them might not arrive in time, all of them being important, I decided to delay Francis Drake by going to meet him, for he had many times invited me. And so, with neither hostage nor security apart from his word, putting myself,

---

[1] According to the *relación* of 24 January 1596 (A. de I., Santo Domingo, 51), Licenciado Francisco Bravo de Cavañas asked Drake to moderate his severity, 'who replied that this was war and that he could not omit to carry out the orders of the queen, his mistress . . . it was his final purpose that to him should be surrendered the governor and the royal treasure, which was the substance with which the king our lord made war on England, and that his majesty should pay for it and not his subjects, and that if they did this he would leave them in peace'.

[2] This was evidently Simón Moreno, a copy of whose declaration, dated Río de la Hacha, 24 December 1595, made before Manso de Contreras, appears in A. de I., Santa Fe, 1, no. 140. Here he is stated to be a Portuguese pilot and to have fled from the English fleet. He deposed that he had been captured near Terceira in the previous March by an English captain called 'Legas', being handed over to Hawkins on reaching England. His account of the fleet and of the voyage was inaccurate, but he did reveal the English intention of taking Santa Marta, Cartagena and Nombre de Dios and of proceeding by river in launches to Panama. He added that the English had strict orders to return in full strength to England because a Spanish offensive was expected.

as everyone thought, in the greatest peril, and subordinating my personal liberty to the interests of your majesty, the common good and the defence of Cartagena and other places, I went to the town. There Drake tried to persuade me to ransom it by means of various offers and many threats, but he could not make me submit, nor lose sight of my duty to your majesty and the observance of royal decrees. These and other facts are established by an affidavit of the whole proceedings made out by a notary whom I took with me. Francis Drake, realizing that he could not obtain the ransom by any means, resumed the devastation of the country. His men ravaged the country ten leagues about and did unprecedented damage to the town, sacking it and leaving it burnt and razed to the ground, its citizens poverty-stricken, stripped of everything and in extreme want, without any kind of provisions. This was his revenge for my having detained him so long there and informed the other places, as will appear more fully from the *relación* and testimony being sent on behalf of this *cabildo*.[1] He set sail on the 29th, taking 100 Negroes and Negresses from the pearl station, who for the most part joined him voluntarily, and some citizens and other prisoners. [There follow three paragraphs on the problems now facing Río de la Hacha.]

I have just received a letter from Santa Marta advising me that the fleet came to that port, burnt the settlement and took Don Francisco Flores prisoner. They did not seize any of the citizens' property because they had hidden it, having received my messages; and these, they tell me, have been sent on to Cartagena, where in

---

[1] The *relación* of 24 January 1596 (A. de I., Santo Domingo, 51) says that Drake personally supervised the sacking of the pearling station and that afterwards, when approached by several leading citizens to arrange some composition, he refused to consider anything less than the ransom of the city, threatening to hand it over to the rebel Indians and to hang all his Spanish prisoners. The full record of the interview between Drake and Manso de Contreras, compiled by a notary, occurs in A. de I., Santa Fe, 190, which is a comprehensive account of the governor's services, including a series of *informaciones*. According to the *relación* of the interview (ff. 149–52), the governor refused to ransom the town and boldly admitted that the object of the earlier exchanges had been to delay the English while intelligence was collected and forwarded to Cartagena. He was then given two hours to get clear of the town before the English burned it.

consequence the governor is fully on the alert.[1] I am certain it will
go well with him, for his courage and carefulness promise as much.
I will do all in my power to rebuild these two settlements quickly,
though re-peopling them will be no simple task. [He asks to be
rewarded for his services.] From Río de la Hacha, 15 January 1596.
El Licenciado Manso de Contreras.

31. Antoneli's report on the defences of certain places in the West Indies, 1587[2]

A relation of the ports, harbors, forts and cities in the west Indies
which have bene surveied, edified, finished, made and mended,
with those which have bene builded, in a certaine survey by the
king of Spaine his direction and commandement: Written by
Baptista Antonio, surveyour in those parts for the said King.
Anno 1587.

[1] In a letter to the king dated 24 March 1596 (A. de I., Santo Domingo, 193)
Manso de Contreras gave further details concerning Santa Marta and Cartagena:
'It appears that on the 30th he took the settlement of Santa Marta, burned it and
carried off as a prisoner Don Francisco Gutiérrez Flores, who was there for this
emergency with no more than sixty men. Just as the English began to overrun
the country, such a storm blew up that the ships of the fleet, unable to withstand
it, dragged their anchors and left the harbour, and as they passed the River
Magdalena in the heavy storm they lost several launches and barks with the men
in them, and in the morning the rest of the vessels found themselves widely
scattered, the fleet being almost completely disrupted. According to some of
Drake's prisoners this, together with the strong counter-measures taken at
Cartagena [two or three words illegible: perhaps 'on receipt of my'] messages,
was the reason why he changed his mind and passed by to Nombre de Dios and
Panama . . . [Prisoners have reported that] Francis Drake and his men said that
these losses and their failure to achieve their object were due to my messages and
to my having guilefully delayed them so long, for they thus missed the good
weather and continued their voyage in January, which is a very stormy month
on this coast, and if they had gone on, as they intended, within four days, they
would undoubtedly have taken Cartagena and Panama.'
[2] *Principal Navigations*, III (1600), 549–57 (X (1904), 135–56). Antoneli visited
Cartagena and the Isthmus briefly during his first expedition to the Indies in
1586–7. It is not known how Hakluyt acquired this document, but the marginal
notes, which take no account of the experience of Drake and Baskerville in 1596,

...[1]   *Nombre de Dios*

Nombre de Dios is builded upon a sandy Bay hard by the sea side,
it is a citie of some thirtie housholdes or inhabitants: their houses are
builded of timber, and most of the people which are there be
forreiners, they are there to day and gone to morrow: it is full of
woods and some places of the land are overflowen with water
continually by reason of much raine which doth fall upon the hils.
It is a very bad harbour, neither is there any good water: and it is
subject to Northerly winds and Easterly windes, which continually
doe blow upon this coast: many of the great ships which doe come
to this place doe unlade halfe their commodities betweene the two
ledges of rockes, for that there is but little water in the harbour: and
after that a ship hath unladen halfe of her goods, then shee goeth to
the second rocke, as it doth appeare by the platforme, but the small
ships come neere unto another rocke on the West side. If the winde
chance to come to the North and Northwest, and that it overblowe,
then such great ships as then be in the roade must of force more
themselves with sixe cables a head, especially in a storme, and yet
nevertheless sometimes they are driven ashore and so cast away, and
all because they dare not vier cable ynough, because of so many
shelves and rockes which are in both those places: also the shippes
doe roule very much in the harbour, by reason in foule weather the
Sea will bee mightily growen, which is the cause that their cables
do oftentimes breake, and their ruthers are unhanged, the cause
thereof is by reason the shippes doe ride but in little water, yet goeth
there a great sea.

The citie is builded and situated very well if it were a good

suggest that it was already in his hands (and annotated) before Baskerville's
return. Indeed, it is not unlikely that the notes were written before the voyage,
whether by Hakluyt or someone else, specifically for the eyes of those who were
planning the Panama raid. Hakluyt himself may well have made such a contribution to Drake's 1585 venture (G. B. Parks, *Richard Hakluyt and the English
Voyages* (New York, 1928), p. 105). It seems to the present writer, in view of
Hakluyt's key position as a collector and distributor of intelligence relating to
Spanish as well as unoccupied America, that Drake probably had access to this
important report before he left England.

[1] Two sections describing Santa Marta and Cartagena are here omitted. The latter
makes reference to Drake's capture of the city in 1586.

harbour, it standeth upon the Eastside upon a rocke where they may builde a very good fort, according to the platforme for the safe-gard of this harbour: but seeing it is but a bad haven and shallow water, therefore I doe thinke that it is not needefull for your majestie to be at any charges in fortifying that place, but onely a trench to be made of earth or clay, so that these townesmen may defend them-selves from danger of 3. or 4. ships.

The citie of Panama is eighteene leagues from Nombre de Dios, the wayes are exceeding bad thitherwards; yet notwithstanding all the silver is brought this way to Nombre de Dios, as well your majesties treasure as other marchandize; so likewise the most part of those commodities which are caried to Peru, and the rest of the marchandize are carried to the river of Chagre which is some 18 leagues from this citie and it is brought up by this river within five leagues of Panama unto an Inn or lodge called Venta de Cruzes, and from this place afterwards they are transported to Panama upon Mules. The high way which goeth from Nombre de Dios to Panama may be very wel mended, only to remoove this way and to stop it quite up, and so to make it againe upon the side of a mountaine. This citie lieth in nine degrees and one tierce,[1] and if your majestie will give order that this citie should be plucked downe and newly builded againe in Puerto Bello, then you are to make a new way through the mountains of Capira, by reason it may not be frequented and because the high wayes are very bad: with little charges they may be broken and so shut up, and the channell of this harbour may bee stopt with the timber of those old ships which are laid up here every yeere, and then afterwards may be cast a great number of stones into the same, and so by this meanes to damme up the harbour: and here is great want of stones to ballast the shippes: wherefore they are faine to goe to an Iland three leagues from Cartagena called Isla de los Bastimentos, and this is a thing very needefull for this Countrey, as by experience I have seene.

Puerto Bello

Puerto Bello lieth five leagues from Nombre de Dios Westward: It is a very good harbour and sufficient to receive great store of ships,

[1] Marginal note: 'Nombre de Dios in 9. deg. and one tierce.'

and hath very good ankering, and fresh water . . . [praises the situation and resources of the place at some length and proposes the removal of Nombre de Dios thither]

Panama[1]

Panama is the principall citie of this Dioces: it lieth 18. leagues from Nombre de Dios on the South sea, and standeth in 9. degrees. There are 3. Monasteries in this said city of fryers, the one is of Dominicks, the other is of Augustines, and the third is of S. Francis fryers: also there is a College of Jesuits, and the royall audience or chancery is kept in this citie.

This citie is situated hard by the sea side on a sandy bay: the one side of this citie is environed with the sea, and on the other side it is enclosed with an arme of the sea which runneth up into the land 1000. yards.

This citie hath three hundred and fiftie houses,[2] all built of timber, and there are sixe hundred dwellers and eight hundred souldiers with the townesmen, and foure hundred Negros of Guyney, and some of them are freemen: and there is another towne which is called Santa Cruz la Real of Negros Simerons,[3] and most of them are imployed in your majesties service, and they are 100. in number, and this towne is a league from this citie upon a great rivers side, which is a league from the sea right over against the harbour of Pericos. But there is no trust nor confidence in any of these Negros, and therefore we must take heede and beware of them, for they are our mortall enemies . . .
[describes the city and its means of defence] . . .

When newes were brought to this citie of those Pirates which were come upon this coast, the Lord President and Judges commanded that there should a sconce bee made, and trenched round

[1] Antoneli wrote a rather similar report on Panama, dated 5 October 1595, a copy of which exists in the Cecil papers (Hatfield MSS, 35, no. 45). In this he seems to have used his first report as a basis, without adding to it significantly. This later version was possibly one of the documents Burghley received from Baskerville; if so, Baskerville may have obtained it from Alberto Ojeda, the old architect who went over to the English in January 1596. See p. 212 below.

[2] Marginal note: 'Panama hath 350 houses.'

[3] Marginal note: 'Negros Simerons mortall enemies to the Spanyards.'

about, made all of timber for the defence of this citie against the enemie, and to keepe your majesties treasure. So your officers caused Venta de Cruzes to be fortified, and likewise Chagre, and Quebrada, and fortified the garrison of Ballano: for all these are places where the enemy may land,[1] and by this meanes spoyle all this countrey.

There are three sundry places where this citie may without difficulty be taken, and spoyled by the Pirates. The first is on the North seas[2] in a certaine place which lyeth foureteene leagues from Nombre de Dios, the place is called Acle to the Eastwards, where once before certaine men of warre have entred into those seas. The other place is Nombre de Dios,[3] although this is a bad place and naughtie wayes, and full of waters and a very dirtie way: for three partes of the yeere the countrey people doe travell upon those waters, and an other very badde way, which is the going up of certaine rockes and mountaines which they must climbe, called the mountaines of Capira, which are of height three quarters of a league, so in this place with very small store of souldiers wee can defend our selves from the fury of the enemie, so these dwellers doe say that in Sommer the wayes are very good without either dirt or water.

The other entrance is up the river of Chagre,[4] which rivers mouth lyeth eighteene leagues from Nombre de Dios to the Westwards falling into the North sea, and this is the place which the citizens of Panama doe most feare, for they may come up this river to Venta de Cruzes,[5] and so from thence march to this citie, which is but five leagues off.[6] So up this river there goe boates and barkes which doe carry 320. Quintals waight. These are they which carry the

---

[1] Presumably a mistranslation. Hakluyt has the marginal note: 'Places good to land in.' – but seems to be referring to the places mentioned below.

[2] Marginal note: '1. Place.'

[3] Marginal note: '2 place. This was Oxenham.'   [4] Marginal note: '3 place.'

[5] Marginal note: 'The place of most advantage for the English.'

[6] The preceding passage corresponds substantially with the following passage in Hatfield MSS, 35, no. 45: 'Tiene esta ciudad tres partes por donde puede ser acometida por la mar del Norte: la una es por la ensenada de Acle por donde otra vez a entrado el corsario en esa mar; y la otra es por Nombre de Dios aunque este camino es muy mala y de mucha agua y lodos y con poca gente se podria guardar

most part of the marchandize which doe come from Spaine to be transported to Peru, and from Venta de Cruzes it is caried to Limaret which is three leagues off that place, and the dwellers doe report that it is a very good way: and if any men of warre will attempt to come into these seas, they may very easily come up this river as farre as Venta de Cruzes, and from thence march unto this citie, and if the enemie will, they may bring their pinnesses ready made in foure quarters, and so taken in sunder, may afterwards set them together againe: as it is reported that Francis Drake hath used it once before when he came that voyage; and so he may attempt us both by sea and land. And forasmuch as the most part of these people are marchants, they will not fight, but onely keepe their owne persons in safetie, and save their goods;[1] as it hath bene sene heretofore in other places of these Indies . . .

[proposes that Limaret be made a fortified refuge for the citizens and the treasure; describes the strategic situation of Panama, with further proposals for its proximate defences]

The river of Chagre

The river of Chagre lieth in 9. degrees and one tierce. The mouth of this river is in the North seas 18. leagues from Nombre de Dios, and 13. leagues from Puerto Bello:[2] there is caryed up this river certaine quantitie of those merchandize which are unladen at Nombre de Dios which come from Spaine. From the mouth of this river to Venta de Cruzes are eighteene leagues. From this place where the barkes unlade their commodities, they are carried upon mules to Panama, which is but five leagues off from this place.

This river hath great store of water in the Winter. And the barkes which belong to this river are commonly of 320. Quintals

esta entrada; esta otra entrada es por el rio de Chagre, que su boca esta 12 leguas de Nombre de Dios hacia el poniente en la mar del Norte, y esta es la entrada donde mas vezes puede ser offendida esta ciudad, porque se puede yr por el rio arriba con barcos hasta la casa de Cruzes, que esta cinco leguas desta ciudad; y siempre que hubiese nueva del corsario en el mar del Norte sera bien poner gente en la dicha casa de Cruzes y en la venta de Chagre y en el presidio de Vallan, como hiziesen cuando tuvieren nueva de Francisco Draque y de su venida.'

[1] Cp. John Arthur's statement (document 33) concerning Drake's views.

[2] Marginal note: 'These five leagues are very good ground or champion countrey.'

that is of 16. tunnes in burthen: but in the Summer there is but small store of water: so then the barkes have much to doe to get up this river: and in many places these barkes are constrained to unlade their commodities; and are drawn by mens strength and force a good way up the river . . . And therefore if it might please your majestie to command, that Puerto Bello might be inhabited, and the towne made neerer the Rivers side, every thing would be a great deale better cheape, if the commodities were caryed up the River: for it is a great danger to cary them up by the land, for it is daily seene that the mules do many times fall and breake their neckes with their lading upon their backs, as well the treasure as other kinde of commodities, because it is such a bad way . . . [expenditure on these improvements would much benefit the merchants] because the other is a most filthy way, as any is in the world.

32. *Report by Miguel Ruiz Delduayen*[1]

I have served your majesty here in this kingdom for sixteen years, seven as comptroller of the royal treasure, and I have rendered a good account of the treasure to your royal council. On this occasion of the defence of this kingdom against the English fleet which came to rob and occupy it I have been busy in serving your majesty from the first moment, personally accompanying the general Don Alonso de Sotomayor unfailingly up to the present and, as one of such long residence in this kingdom, experienced in matters of war and peace, advising him with the goodwill due from a good servant and vassal of your majesty. At his command I have been and remain serving in the capacity of captain of the unpaid volunteers in this war, paying my own expenses and those of many others.

[1] A. de I., Panama, 44. Endorsed: 'Panama. To his majesty. 1596. Miguel Ruiz de Elduayen on 22 January. To the king our lord in his royal council of the Indies, in the hands of Juan de Ibarra, his secretary.' An inaccurate copy, without the covering letter or the appended deposition and letters, is to be found in the Biblioteca de la Real Academia de la Historia, Colección Salazar, N.9, ff. 154–65.

As an eye-witness I have written the enclosed true and full report of this war and of the fortunate outcome Our Lord was pleased to grant, so that your majesty may know and take notice of the danger in which this kingdom stood had God not helped it. I assure your majesty it is pure truth, as may be seen from the existing records of proceedings, advices and measures taken. I have done this solely for the service of your majesty, to whom I am obligated in so many ways. May the Lord preserve your majesty for many years, as we your servants desire and Christendom needs. From this settlement of Casa de Cruzes, xxii January MDXCVI.

Miguel Ruiz Delduayen

Report of what happened upon the coming of the English fleet, general and captain Francis, to this kingdom of Tierra Firme and port of Nombre de Dios, from the time when his majesty sent warning that it was being made ready in England for the Indies and that they should take heed and be prepared.

At the end of June 1595 royal letters patent arrived at Panama, warning that in England a fleet was being equipped for the Indies with troops and generals of the sea and land, and that care should be taken and preparation made to prevent damage by way of the Río de Chagre and Nombre de Dios. Upon this warning the *audiencia* and royal officials agreed that a force of some fifty or sixty soldiers should be raised in royal pay to serve as sentinels at the mouth of the Río de Chagre and at Nombre de Dios, where they were in fact sent. In July came another warning to the same effect and nothing fresh was done nor was the least preparation made.[1]

From Porto Belo the commissioners Dr Villanueva Çapata and

[1] Dr Juan del Barrio de Sepúlveda, senior *oidor* of Panama, was the effective head of the government after the death of the president on 22 May 1595. On 24 January 1596 he wrote a short report of the events in the form of a letter to Ibarra (A. de I., Santo Domingo, 81). According to this, the first warning, dated 8 March, was received on 20 June, and the second, dated 14 June, on 23 August. It was only on receipt of this second warning that he requested help from Peru. His own report mentions no further measures apart from the listing of the arms and men in the city and the inspection of the munitions available. He does not comment on the dispute about his own and Sotomayor's status.

Don Francisco de Valverde and the engineer Bautista Antoneli wrote to the *audiencia,* asking that something be done about the defence of that port, which his majesty had ordered to be fortified and settled, this being their concern; and they said that apart from the great capacity and excellence of the harbour, it would be easy for the enemy to fortify it, and that the port, the works that had been begun and the equipment and stores there should be safeguarded. On this there were deliberations and varying opinions. And because nothing was decided or arranged in this matter Dr Villanueva and the engineer came to Panama and made the same request again in various petitions; and the engineer advised particular measures for the defence of this kingdom. On these there were deliberations at different times and a variety of views, as may be seen in the records of the proceedings.[1] Later, it seems, notice came from Castille that the *flota* was in preparation and that the silver should be made ready and with this came letters for Peru; and because enemies were not mentioned a discussion took place at the beginning of December 1595 on whether the soldiers at Chagre and Nombre de Dios should be dismissed; four out of the seven votes were in favour of dismissal and so it was done.

On 10 December there arrived at Panama his majesty's frigate, sent from Callao de los Reyes by the marqués de Cañete, viceroy of Peru, together with supplies of 150 jars of powder, quantities of lead, match for harquebuses and hemp and six pieces of artillery, for it seems the *audiencia* of Panama had notified him of the shortages and asked for help. In the same frigate arrived Don Alonso de

---

[1] A similar account is given in Antoneli's letter of 24 May 1596 to the king (A. de I., Panama, 44). The advice he gave in July 1595 – to fortify in the River Chagre, in the Sierra Capira and at Santa Catalina on Captain Magán's track from Porto Belo – is outlined in his letter of 11 July 1595 to the king (A. de I., Panama, 44). In the latter half of 1595 Diego Suárez de Amaya, *alcalde mayor* of Nombre de Dios, was likewise memorializing the *audiencia* to little effect (his letter to the king, 18 October 1595, A. de I., Panama, 44). He argued the importance of defending Nombre de Dios and the indefensibility of Porto Belo, whereas Antoneli made exactly the opposite case, but they agreed on the need for defence positions in the Sierra de Capira and the River Chagre and used almost identical phrases in condemning the civilian amateurism of the *audiencia* and in advocating military government (cp. Antoneli to the king, 20 October 1595, A. de I., Panama, 44).

Sotomayor, knight of the order of Santiago, who had been governor of the kingdom of Chile and a veteran of Flanders, where he served as captain of infantry and horse and was employed in matters of high importance; whom the viceroy sent as his lieutenant captain-general of this kingdom to defend it on this occasion. On 12 December a letter from the governor of Cartagena arrived at Panama, together with a copy of another from Lope de Vega Portocarrero, president of Santo Domingo, which gave notice that on 15 November Don Pedro Tello de Guzmán, coming to Puerto Rico with five royal frigates for the silver from Sancho Pardo's flagship, had encountered two English ships, one of which fled and the other he sank. From the latter he took 26 Englishmen; these were given torture and declared that they were of the company of Captain Francis Drake, who was coming with a fleet of 26 ships and six galleons of the queen; and they showed instructions from Francis that he was coming to Puerto Rico and thence to Cartagena and Nombre de Dios.

At this news Don Alonso de Sotomayor on 13 December exhibited in the *audiencia* the title of lieutenant captain-general which he brought from the viceroy, and they answered what appears in their reply and in effect did not accept him. Nevertheless, having asked his opinion, the *audiencia* gave him authority to raise men on pay with two pays in advance, which some, had they not been forced, would not have accepted, since on other occasions three pays have usually been given. On 18 December advice came from the governor of Cartagena[1] that off Cape de la Vela a frigate coming from Lake Maracaibo had sighted the English fleet, which had pursued it. Recruiting these men and other matters took until the 19th, Dr del Barrio (the senior *oidor*) performing the office of general; on which day the *audiencia* discussed the appointment of Don Alonso de Sotomayor as captain-general and drew up a decree which was communicated to him. He answered that he had been nominated by the viceroy to be his lieutenant captain-general, as appeared from the title he had exhibited; and that he was ready either to act in this capacity or else to give advice as an individual soldier on what he understood to be best for the service of his

[1] Sotomayor's report (A. de I., Santo Domingo, 81) gives 16 December.

majesty; and he made other points which appear in his reply. They then produced another decree in which, in spite of their excuses that they neither would nor had to admit him, they accepted him. He accepted what was proposed in the second decree, referring the *audiencia* in his reply to what had happened so far, pointing out how unprepared and disorganized everything connected with the defence of this kingdom was, for at that time no preparation or defence whatever had been arranged; and that wishing to obtain information about the north coast from Nombre de Dios to Porto Belo and Río de Chagre which he had not seen, he had been given very different accounts, so that he could not make provision or order in matters of importance until he had seen for himself the roads, places, river and other things; and that notwithstanding all this, to assist as always the service of God and his majesty he would offer his person on this occasion of such danger and travail. The title of captain-general was given him by the *audiencia* and published.

Then on 20 December he began to discharge that office, arranging and ordering what was necessary in Panama, with which he was busy until Tuesday 26 December. On that day at the hour of the angelus he left the city for Nombre de Dios to reconnoitre that place, Porto Belo and Río de Chagre. In his company went Don Gerónimo de Çuaço, campmaster-general appointed by him for this war, Don Francisco de Valverde, factor and inspector for Mexico and commissioner for Porto Belo, Captain Hernando de Ocampo, Francisco Caro Torres, cleric, the comptroller Miguel Ruiz Delduayen and some paid soldiers. On the first day the campmaster remained behind at the settlement of Chagre, by order of the general, to assemble the men coming, as ordered, from the city, and to send them on to the places indicated by the general. Also Don Francisco de Valverde was compelled to stay there because the illness he was suffering from had worsened and he had developed a high fever, for which reason the general would not consent to his leaving that place. The captain-general went on to Nombre de Dios, where he arrived on 29 December, and on the way he reconnoitred a strong defence position called Capirilla near the Quebrada, about a quarter of a league towards

Panama.[1] In Nombre de Dios he inspected the landing stages and so on and a fort the *alcalde mayor* had built. The place seemed to have no defence at all against a fleet much less powerful than this one, nor even against a few launches, and so with the citizens' agreement he commanded that the artillery be concealed and that, having done what damage they could to the enemy as he disembarked, they should withdraw, having previously evacuated valuables, women and those unable to fight. He also left orders that all the ships and boats the enemy might take should be sent after him to Porto Belo.

While he was there news arrived that the enemy had sacked Río de la Hacha and was on his way to Río de Chagre. On the morning of Sunday the last of December the general left by sea in a *patache* for Porto Belo, where he arrived that afternoon and spent until Wednesday 3 January 1596 inspecting that place; he thought both the port and the quality of the harbour very good. The work the engineer had constructed for its defence was defensible on the side facing the sea, but the general thought that because the enemy could disembark without being damaged and turn his back on it and march through the open country, the defenders (sixty soldiers ordered thither from Captain Mateo de Ribera's company who arrived on Tuesday 2 January) would be in danger of being cut off if the enemy came in strength. And so he ordered that on the enemy's arrival they should do what damage they could while he landed and after reconnoitring should retire to the bush, and having safely disposed their equipment, supplies and munitions, should

[1] Antoneli (to the king, 24 May 1596, A. de I., Panama, 44) claimed that Soto-mayor, on reaching Porto Belo, 'asked me how the road from Nombre de Dios to Panama could be defended and whereabouts the enemy might be intercepted, and since I had seen and considered the position carefully, I told him that he should immediately order the occupation of a pass which is on the road at the ridges of Capirilla ten leagues from Panama. And so the general forthwith ordered the occupation of this position'. The campmaster, Çuaço, said that Sotomayor reconnoitred the position and sent the order from Porto Belo after consulting Antoneli (*La Dragontea*, II, 154–5), which seems the likeliest explanation, for the idea of holding the pass was not Antoneli's secret. Conabut (document 34) suggests that the general made the decision before meeting Antoneli. Caro de Torres, *Relacion de los Servicios que hizo ... Sotomayor*, pp. 60–1, wrongly states that Antoneli travelled with Sotomayor from Panama to Nombre de Dios.

make their way towards Panama. On this the general had the agreement of Dr Villanueva Çapata, *oidor* of Panama and commissioner, and of Bautista Antoneli, his majesty's military engineer, who was there, both of whom he consulted, as appears by the record of their opinions signed with their names.

Having agreed that the Río de Chagre should be fortified so as to close it and deny the enemy passage, they took tools and supplies from those there belonging to his majesty to make the necessary defence works on the river. The engineer went with the general to inspect and choose the site and to plan and help to carry out what the general should command, since in his advices his majesty had ordered the defence of the river, and according to the news from Santo Domingo and Río de la Hacha by way of Santa Marta and Cartagena the enemy was bringing flat-bottomed boats to go up that river and it looked as if the entire enemy force threatened it. On Thursday 4 January in the morning the general left there for Río de Chagre, at the mouth whereof he found 25 soldiers with a corporal. He inspected all of it and the headland where, the engineer said, his majesty had ordered a tower or fort to be built to defend the entrance. The next day he left there, inspecting everything up the river, and at a bend in the river called Tornavellaco about five leagues from the mouth a satisfactory site was found for two forts, one on each side of the river, where guns and men could be placed and a boom of logs to close the river. They began clearing the site and on the following Sunday, 7 January, it was cleared. It was agreed that the engineer and Captain Miguel Ruiz Delduayen should remain there with a few men, so that together with those expected from Nombre de Dios and the soldiers ordered to retire from the mouth of the river they should continue fortifying, while the general should go to Panama or Cruzes to send what was required for this work. He being already embarked for this purpose at daybreak on Monday 8 January, there arrived a boat sent from Cruzes by Campmaster Don Gerónimo de Çuaço with the news that the enemy fleet, consisting of 23 ships and 30 launches, was entering the port of Nombre de Dios on Saturday, 6 January, the feast of the epiphany. This boat brought 22 smiths requested by the general for the work on the forts.

With this news, seeing that the work on the forts and defence
works intended there would be a lengthy matter and that if the
enemy came that way there would not be sufficient time, it was
decided to leave there and to look for a site higher up, where
defences might be established more easily and quickly and where
they might receive supplies by land. And so they all embarked,
sending this information on to the mouth of the river, with orders
that the few remaining sentries should withdraw and that the
patache should sail for Veragua and warn the coast. Making the
greatest possible speed he arrived that afternoon at Cruz de San
Juan Gallego, which is in the middle of the river, where he found
Captain and Sergeant-major Antonio Carreño with 44 soldiers,
sent by the campmaster at the general's command. On inspection
this site proved to be the worst in the river and so the general and the
engineer, taking the captain with them, went to examine a site half
a league further up at the Gallincoja bend. They then ordered the
men to be moved there, a work for guns and men to be built and
the river to be closed with tree-trunks, though these would have to
be manhandled into position. The engineer stayed there to see to
this and the general left him the boat, the forge, all the workmen and
some Indians.

Then making all possible speed, travelling by day and night, we
reached Casa de Cruzes about one o'clock in the afternoon on
Wednesday. Here we heard news that the enemy had advanced up
the Nombre de Dios road, that the *alcalde mayor* and the soldiers and
citizens there under Captain Pedro de Quiñones had withdrawn,
that the enemy had reached the Quebrada and that on the morning
of that day they had attacked in order to pass through. From Porto
Belo the general had ordered the campmaster to send Captain Juan
Enríquez Conabut with 40 soldiers of his company (then in
Chagre) to the place he had reconnoitred near the Quebrada at
Capirilla. Conabut arrived at the position on the Tuesday – the 9th
– on which day the enemy reached the Quebrada, and there he was
joined by the men retreating from Nombre de Dios, who in their
retreat had burned the inn at the Quebrada.[1] Of these many were
still in the bush and some forty or fifty arrived there that night. On

[1] Conabut (document 34) maintained that they had omitted to burn it.

Captain Juan Enríquez's orders they made what defence-work and fortification they could with trees and boughs thrown across the road above a gorge; and munitions arrived for them.

In the morning about eight the English arrived, with a mulatto cowherd named Amador, who went over to them, as their guide, without sending scouts ahead to reconnoitre. They were understood to be 800 men, led by Thomas Baskerville. They must have kept to the road to have crossed the Sierra de Capira and the Lajas, which have always been reputed most difficult to pass, and the general thought this another reason for holding that position from which to throw them back. They attacked the defences furiously and meeting resistance they maintained the fight with musket fire for two and a half hours with such courage that in spite of the height and difficulty of the gorge some climbed with their pikes so far as to lay hands on the mouths of the harquebuses above them which were shooting them down. And just as our men were running out of ammunition, seven having been killed – three Spaniards and four Negroes – Captain Hernando de Liermo Agüero came up in support. He is in charge of the garrison at Vallano, and on this occasion by order of the *audiencia* and the general he came with 30 soldiers given him at Chagre, and on arriving they charged, sounding drum and trumpet. The enemy perceived this reinforcement and began to weaken, and realizing this the said captain rushed down from the defences shouting 'ea Españoles, a ellos!'[1] and with him went Captain Pedro de Quiñones. And as, along with several others, they went into the attack, Agüero was hit in the right arm by a musket-ball, at which he and the others retreated, and the enemy then did likewise and fell back to the site of the Quebrada inn, in sight of the fort. There they re-formed, leaving many dead and carrying many more wounded. Of those that remained on the road many were dead, including, it is said, three of their chief captains. On their retreat they divided their men into two squadrons, and believing they would be pursued they left one in ambush while the other withdrew. Our men, being few in number – altogether about 120 – and those weary (some from fortifying all night and marching the day before, others from fast marching to

---

[1] 'Up Spaniards and at them!'

their support and from the fighting) and fearing some ambush, did not give pursuit. As far as can be known, the English dead numbered about 150 and the prisoners six, these being men of little importance, four of whom were wounded. Apart from these the wounded were numerous.[1]

When the general arrived at Cruzes he had news (as has been mentioned) that the enemy were eight and a half leagues inside the country that Captain Juan Enríquez Conabut was fortifying the place indicated to him, and that the *alcalde mayor* of Nombre de Dios and his men had joined Juan Enríquez. At once he sent warning to Panama, ordering that the force which was to have followed him should be hastened and that Dr Juan del Barrio, senior *oidor*, should come with it. He also commanded the captains and soldiers he found in Cruzes to follow the enemy's retreat, and he sent word to the campmaster, and through him to Juan Enríquez, that he was marching to their support, so as to encourage everyone. And he left without losing a moment, taking with him Captain Miguel Ruiz Delduayen and four other soldiers. On his way he received word that the enemy had been routed, and he pressed on to reach at two in the morning the inn of Pedro Cano about three quarters of a league from the fort. There he found the campmaster, who had gone there to bring help and encouragement to the men of the fort, and Don Francisco de Valverde who, although not fully recovered from his fever, had returned to be present on this occasion. He also found here an English prisoner from whom he took a statement, the translation of which accompanies this report. From this it was clear that this fleet was dispatched with the principal intention of taking Panama and that it was to be attacked by way of the river with 23 launches and 1500 men.

The general with his company and Don Francisco left at dawn for the fort, and when they had seen it and the English dead around it, they congratulated the men on the good work they had done and were well content. The general ordered what should be done there and commanded Captain Juan Enríquez with his men and the

---

[1] This account of the English losses is common to nearly all the Spanish reports, the only important exception being Conabut's first estimate (document 35).

alcalde mayor and Captain Pedro de Quiñones, with the paid men
who had withdrawn thither, to stay and guard the fort and complete its construction. Captain Luis Delgado and the men from La
Villa de los Santos, who had arrived after the English retreat, were
ordered by the campmaster to return to Chagre along with the men
who had come up with Captain Agüero. The general returned to
Pedro Cano and from there, taking with him the campmaster and
Don Francisco de Valverde, went on to Venta de Chagre, where
he ordered the companies of Nata, Veragua and La Villa to follow
him to Casa de Cruzes. He himself went there on the morning of
Friday 12 January, to wait there and see where the enemy might
attack. That same morning after the general had left Chagre, Dr
Juan del Barrio, senior *oidor*, arrived there with some citizens of
Panama who, having received news at Panama of the rout of the
English and the general's orders, came with forward readiness to
oppose the enemy should he attack from some other quarter. The
next day at midday the doctor and the men with him went on to
Casa de Cruzes. There the general was informed that a Negro of
his majesty's at the Porto Belo works called Agustín had gone
over to the enemy and that this man knew the road Captain Magán
had discovered between Porto Belo and Venta de Chagre and
could take the enemy to it. The general's enquiries about the road
yielded the information that at a place called Santa Catalina there
was a steep ridge which had to be crossed, and he ordered a strongpoint and a work to be built there to defend that pass. For this
purpose he sent thither Captain Juan Ramón de Vergara, sergeant-
major of Nata and La Villa, together with Captain Agüero's
company from Chagre (now led by Captain Diego Sánchez
Gatica, since Agüero was wounded) and some Negroes from
Santa Cruz la Real.

Further, being informed by all reports that the English fleet was
making ready to come to the harbour of Porto Belo, and realizing
that if it did the men there under Captain Mateo de Ribera would
be cut off, he ordered them to withdraw, taking all their supplies
and munitions, and to throw the guns into the water. And so they
withdrew, together with Dr Villanueva Çapata, *oidor*, who, as
commissioner, had remained there until then. Then he ordered

Juan Enríquez to go with his men to guard the pass at Santa Catalina, and he went. From Casa de Cruzes the general went down the river twice for about two leagues inspecting it, mostly on foot, taking with him on one of these occasions the engineer Antoneli who, having (as he said) finished the river strongpoint, had arrived at Cruzes on Monday the 15th. He intended to make some defence-work which his main force might if necessary occupy to withstand the enemy should the latter succeed in passing the forts. He took men and materials for this, but could find no suitable site and so returned. He had sent a soldier to the river fort, where Captain Carreño was, to look at the state of the place, and this man returned on Wednesday and reported that the works on either side fronted the river, but were open at the rear, while the country on the Nombre de Dios side was clear and easy for men to march through, there being a landing place and an open road some distance down-river. On learning this the general ordered the engineer to return there and close the fort on the Nombre de Dios side with traverses, transferring to it the guns and men from the other fort. He also sent two more guns which were in Casa de Cruzes, so that there were altogether four pieces of 13 or 14 quintals as well as two falconets and small pieces that Francisco de Valverde had caused to be brought from Panama for dispatch to Porto Belo.

On Wednesday the 17th the general reviewed the troops present in that place, and it appeared that, counting the paid men and the citizen volunteers, there were 325 soldiers, nearly all of them harquebusiers, under the following captains:

Juan Tinoco, captain *ordinario* of the city of Panama.

Captain Miguel Ruiz Delduayen, with the volunteers who came at their own charges to serve in this war.

Captain Diego de los Ríos, with the paid men from Nata.

Captain Luis Delgado, with the paid men from La Villa de los Santos.

Captain Francisco Despinassa, with another party of paid men from Nata.

Captain Montesdaca, with the men sent by the governor of Veragua, Iñigo de Arança.

On Thursday at midday the licentiate Don Francisco de Alfaro, *fiscal*[1] of the *audiencia,* arrived from Panama with 18 paid soldiers and 22 citizens of Panama, by order of the general. The *fiscal* had asked to be ordered up many days before, but because his presence in Panama was very important for the dispatch of all the provisions that had to be sent from there and of the men repairing thither from elsewhere, to all which business he had attended with great care and diligence, he had been indispensable there until that day.

During these days various reports were sent by Diego Mendes Torres, *regidor* and *depositario*[2] of the city of Nombre de Dios, who with a group of soldiers who had stayed in the bush was ranging the environs of that place and taking particular note of the enemy's movements. Reports were also sent by Juan de Tesada, governor of the Negroes of Santiago del Principe,[3] who was with them all the time. These stated that on Wednesday 10 January the enemy burned part of the city and embarked; that on receiving news of the defeat the enemy sent two companies to hearten and help back the retreating force and that having completed the burning of the town they all embarked; that the Negroes of Santiago del Principe would not allow the enemy to take water at the river Fator and killed some of them, including a captain of some importance, whom they buried with lowered flags; that angered by this the enemy sent ten manned launches against them and that the Negroes, who until then had stayed in their village, which is less than half a league from Nombre de Dios, now set fire to their huts and withdrew to the bush, from which they killed a number of Englishmen, about 25 altogether. On the feast of the epiphany the enemy disembarked on the beach near the slaughterhouse without meeting resistance because all the men withdrew to the fort. The English advanced by a cattle track to cut the road to Panama and if Captain Quiñones had not warned our men of this they would have been cut off. Thus they left in the fort all the munitions and supplies they had removed thither. The enemy took some Negro women belonging to Ana Gómez, a rich trader, and some poor Spaniards; some of these he set free and others ran away. Among them was one

[1] Attorney. [2] Councillor and public trustee.
[3] A Negro settlement of 30 houses half a league from Nombre de Dios.

Ojeda, who was in charge of the work at the fort of San Juan de Ulúa; he went away with the English and dined with Drake and was very friendly with him;[1] and he took Ana Gómez with him. Of the prisoners the enemy brought from Río de la Hacha some escaped and fled into the bush; these say that many of their men have been killed and that they took aboard many sick and disabled. They set sail from Nombre de Dios on Monday 15 January, making for the Bastimentos and standing well out to sea.

Today is the 23rd[2] and there is no news of them. It is presumed from the weather that they are not going back to Cartagena, but either have gone to the port of San Juan or the bay of Juan de la Borda on the coast of Nicaragua to refit and to burn some of their ships (as is said to be their intention), or they are making for Cape Camarón and thence for Cape San Antón, for they are exhausted and weak from their many reverses and are afraid of our lord the king's armada which is coming in pursuit of them.

The subjugated Negroes of both factions at Santiago del Principe and Santa Cruz la Real have rallied to his majesty's service with loyalty, hard work and energy, and the freed Negroes came to serve in this war under the banner of their captain Juan de Roales who is also one of them, and they worked very well in attendance upon the general's person. More loyalty was found among the slaves than was expected, for it was their disloyalty which was feared here and which the enemy counted upon: he relied upon it to bring him quick success.

Thus our lord mercifully delivered us from this enemy, for all

---

[1] Alberto Ojeda, an old man, had been architect of the fortifications at San Juan de Ulúa and was thus associated with Antoneli. Having joined the English at Nombre de Dios he stayed with them until they set him ashore at Porto Belo, and it was probably he who advised them to attempt to reach Lake Nicaragua. It seems likely that he supplied them with Antoneli's plan of Puerto Rico and possibly with other material, including Antoneli's report on Panama, dated 5 October 1595, a copy of which found its way into the Cecil papers (Hatfield MSS, 35, no. 45). See *La Dragontea*, II, 165, 186; Baskerville's discourse (document 20); Baskerville and Antoneli on San Juan de Puerto Rico (document 28); Baskerville to Cecil (document 45); Antoneli's report on the defences of certain places in the West Indies, 1587 (document 31).

[2] Ruiz Delduayen's covering note is dated 22 January.

the means of our defence arrived at the crucial moment – help from the viceroy in the shape of powder and munitions and the person of General Don Alonso – at the same time as the news of the enemy. God inspired the general to order Captain Juan Enríquez the veteran just in time to go and fortify the Capirilla post; and if he had not arrived there that night, or the enemy had marched a day before, the latter would have reached a defenceless Panama – his main objective which, according to some of the prisoners, he even thought of occupying.[1] Substantially Don Alonso de Sotomayor's arrival in this kingdom was its sole protection and means of redemption,[2] for he governed it with great judgement, valour and experience, working day and night himself without a pause. By his good measures he imposed a single will upon all the king's officers, which was very important, for with that everyone rallied with might and main to help the service of his majesty and to carry out the general's orders relating to the war. Glory be to God.

This report is certain and true, and as such is certified by me, Miguel Ruiz Delduayen.

Statement of Guillermo Hed, Englishman:[3]

At the inn of Pedro Cano on 10 January 1596 about two after midnight in the early morning of Thursday,[4] Don Alonso de Sotomayor, knight of the order of Santiago and captain-general of this realm of Tierra Firme for the king our lord, examined a prisoner, a young man aged about 22 years, to whom the general put the following questions, translated into Latin by Licenciado Osorio, advocate in the royal *audiencia* of Panama.

[1] Sotomayor's report (A. de I., Santo Domingo, 81) of 23 January 1596 makes the same point: 'from those they captured alive I learned that the enemy's plan was to settle in Panama', but this is not borne out by the depositions themselves.

[2] Sotomayor naturally expounded a similar view (A. de I., Santo Domingo, 81), as did Antoneli: 'if Don Alonso had not been in this kingdom, let not your majesty doubt but that the enemy would have sacked this city' (letter to the king, 24 May 1596, A. de I., Panama, 44).

[3] A copy. Follows directly upon the *relación,* in the same hand. A copy of the same deposition was the first of the three enclosed by Sotomayor with his report (document 33).

[4] Thursday was 11 January.

1. Asked his name and birthplace, he said his name was Guillermo Hed and he was a native of Mosfel[1] in England.

2. Asked in what company he left England, he said that he left England as a mariner in the fleet now anchored at Nombre de Dios.

3. Asked who set forth this fleet, for what purpose, when and whence it departed, what soldiers and sailors it carries, how many vessels there are and who is in command, he said the fleet was made ready and brought together in the port of Plymouth by order of the queen of England, and for what purpose he knows not. It left Plymouth on 29 August 1595; 27 ships sailed, with 2,000 soldiers and 3,000 sailors and gunners, all English; as generals, with equal power, came John Hawkins, of the queen of England's council, and Francis Drake.

4. Asked whether in these 26 vessels[2] there were any from Holland or La Rochelle[3] or any other place outside England, he said that the ships and soldiers and sailors were English, with no other help.

5. Asked what voyage they made after leaving England, what ports they took and what damage they did, he said they visited first the Canary Islands, then Guadalupe and then Puerto Rico; and attempting to take the latter they received much damage from artillery; 300 men were killed and among them John Hawkins, and there[4] they did not dare to enter the harbour. Thence they came to Río de la Hacha and sacked it without any resistance, thence to Santa Marta and thence to Nombre de Dios. And that wishing to take Cartagena, they were prevented by the weather.

6. Asked what they planned to do after anchoring in Nombre de Dios, he said that the plan was to come to Panama because they held for certain that they would find more than four million there. For this purpose Francis sent by the road from Nombre de Dios to Panama 900 men in three brigades under three captains, with a colonel called Baskerville in command of all. This deponent came

---

[1] The Sotomayor copy gives 'Mosfelt' – perhaps Marshfield, near Bristol.
[2] The Sotomayor copy gives '27'.
[3] Sotomayor copy: 'Holland, Zeeland or La Rochelle'.
[4] Sotomayor copy: 'thus'.

with them. The orders they had were that on taking Panama Baskerville should send word to Francis Drake who would then either send or lead in person up the Chagre 23 launches and other boats with 1,500 soldiers and sailors. And if Baskerville could not get through by the Nombre de Dios road and returned, the fleet and men on the day after his return were to leave for the Chagre together with Baskerville's men.

7. Asked whether the vessels which were to go up the Chagre were fenced and what means of defence and offence they carried, he said that he did not know whether they were fenced and that each one carried four small guns, two at the bows and two at the stern and that most of the men were musketeers.

8. Asked what design Francis has after taking Panama and whether he thought of holding it, he said that what he understands is that he has no further design than to rob and return down the river, bringing the captured silver to Nombre de Dios by mule-train.

9. Asked if they sent any vessels through the Strait of Magellan or landed men in any other place to invade the South Sea, he said that no vessel was sent, nor men landed in any other place.

10. Asked about the four vessels missing from the 27 which set forth from England, since not more than 23 anchored at Nombre de Dios, he said that Francis had abandoned and burned them as unfit for sailing, and that he took two ships[1] he found anchored at Río de la Hacha.

11. Asked how long Francis will remain on these coasts with his fleet, he said that the orders he had from the queen were to return to England by the end of May, and that his chief intention is to take Panama on account of the great quantity of silver there.

12. Asked what artillery the ships of this fleet carry, he said that the four large ships, which are admirals and vice-admirals,[2] each carry from 29 to 34 heavy pieces and the rest carry from 12 to 25.

13. Asked whether Francis Drake sent any report or ship to the queen of England, he said that he sent a pinnace from Río de la Hacha with a collection of pearls for the queen.

---

[1] Sotomayor copy: 'two small ships' (*navichuelos*).

[2] *Capitanes y almirantes*: another indication that Drake and Hawkins maintained distinct command structures.

14. Asked if Francis Drake has taken any ship or report coming from Spain, he said that he has not captured any advice-ship, but that near Guadalupe ships from Spain took a small ship of Drake's, and that these were the five frigates. With this the declaration ended. Before me, and signed by me, Francisco Riaño.

He was asked whether this fleet of Francis Drake's set forth to intercept the silver coming from the Indies and whether it waited any time on the plate-route for this purpose; how they used the time up to their discovery at Guadalupe; what island or land of the king our lord they first saw; and for what purposes this fleet set forth. He replied that the fleet left Plymouth on 29 August and did not wait for any Spanish fleet, but made straight for the Canaries, which it reached on 26 September; thence they came to Guadalupe, where they were until some time in November, when they reached the island of Puerto Rico; thence they came to Río de la Hacha and Santa Marta and thence straight to Nombre de Dios. And what this deponent understands and was public is that Francis had instructions from the queen to take Panama, and so he holds for certain, as he has said, that Drake will not depart without attempting it by way of the Chagre. Signed by me, Don Alonso.

The following is a copy of a letter which General Don Alonso de Sotomayor, knight of the order of Santiago, received at the inn of Pedro Cano that same day, an hour after the above statement was taken. It reads to the following effect:
Señor General, campmaster and royal *audiencia*,
Here in the river Cascaxas I captured an English lad and put him to torture. He divulged that having arrived at Puerto Rico the enemy attacked the fort with all his fleet and burned two of our ships. Our men sunk one of their ships and captured another, killing 100 of them, including a general, while another general of theirs died. Thence they came to Río de la Hacha and burned it and they also burned Santa Marta. They came to Cartagena, but did not take it because the weather did not give them the opportunity. And so they came to Nombre de Dios and then dispatched 900 men in six brigades of 100 to 150 men each, armed with pikes and hand-guns—those who had guns did not carry pikes. 500 remain

in Nombre de Dios to guard the town and 50 or 60 men remain in each ship. There are 22 ships in the harbour, not counting launches. They bring with them twelve negroes for the road – these are from Río de la Hacha. They also bring from Nombre de Dios Francisco Cano and his mules – they go under compulsion. Until now they have sent no men to Chagre and they say they will not leave for Porto Belo and Chagre until they know Panama is taken. On Monday, the day before yesterday, I was about to withdraw when I heard news that the English had begun their advance. I therefore came to this farm, where I have gathered together about twelve Spaniards, who at my request and summons joined me to inflict what damage we can on the English, who are still disorganized. Seven or eight of them have guns and others have swords, and with these I set forth this morning, Wednesday the 17th.[1] May our lord Jesus Christ favour us. I agreed to send this Negro of mine with this news. God be with your honours and with us. The English boy remains tied up here in Maldonado's hut.

     Diego Mendes Torres.

They say that they are all sick in Nombre de Dios and that from Puerto Rico they brought more than sixty wounded.

The writer of the above letter is a respected citizen of Panama who remained at the farm mentioned, which is half a league from Nombre de Dios. On 13 January the captain-general received another letter from Diego Mendes, which in substance reported as follows:

That on the afternoon of Wednesday the 10th the enemy began to set fire to the city of Nombre de Dios and the next day in the afternoon he resumed and burned it all. On the same day, Thursday, they all withdrew to the launches, taking with them all those of our people who had fallen into their hands, whites as well as blacks. A Negro who brought this report to Diego Mendes said he understood that the enemy was going straight to Porto Belo, confident that their men marching by the road from Nombre de Dios to Panama would take Panama and treat it as they had treated Nombre de Dios. Leaving their ships at Porto Belo, they were then

---

[1] *Sic.* The context indicates that this must be a slip for the 10th.

to make for the Río de Chagre in the launches. He likewise says that the enemy burned all the Chagre barks that were at Nombre de Dios; and that the retreating enemy force had then gone five leagues from the Venta de la Quebrada towards Nombre de Dios. The letter was dated Thursday the 11th from the farm where Diego Mendes was.

In addition to the statement of the Englishman above reported, similar depositions were made by three other prisoners. They only differed in that they affirmed that the English who gave battle at the fort of San Pablo de la Victoria (as it is now called) numbered 900, with five brigades and five captains under a colonel. Two Spanish soldiers of those who withdrew from Nombre de Dios, whom the enemy caught up and captured on the road, say the same, and so do two Negroes who were taken prisoner in Nombre de Dios. All four came from them after their defeat and say the same as the three Englishmen: that they numbered 900 men in five brigades with five captains and a colonel, and that Francis Drake told them he would follow by way of Río de Chagre when he knew Panama was taken.

33. Report by Alonso de Sotomayor[1]

Depositions of English prisoners[2]

At Casa de Cruzes, where his majesty's army is, on 13 January 1596 Don Alonso de Sotomayor, knight of the order of Santiago, captain-general of this kingdom of Tierra Firme for the king our lord and before me, Francisco de Riaño, his secretary, examined an English prisoner, a young man of 21 years or thereabouts, to whom the general through Pedro Gutiérrez, interpreter, put the following questions:

[1] A. de I., Santo Domingo, 81. Dated San Francisco de Cruzes, 23 January 1596, and addressed to the king, this letter gives a short account of the events which does not differ in any important respect from Ruiz Delduayen's, and ends with recommendations of most of the leading participants by name.

[2] Copies of three depositions are enclosed with Sotomayor's letter. The first of these, by Guillermo Hed, was included in Ruiz Delduayen's report and is therefore omitted here, minor variations in the texts being noted in document 32 above.

1. Asked his name and birthplace, he said his name was John Arthur and that he was born in London in England.

2. Asked in what company he left England and from what port, he said he left in the company of Francis Drake and from the port of Plymouth.

3. Asked who set forth this fleet, for what purpose, when and where it departed, what soldiers and sailors it carries, how many vessels there are and who is in command, he said that the queen of England set forth this fleet at her own expense; it left Plymouth on 21 August 1595; the generals were John Hawkins and Francis Drake, with equal power; it carried 2,200 soldiers and 3,000 mariners; 26 large ships left Plymouth, among them a caravel and a dozen pinnaces; in the fleet came 20 captains and many others of the queen's court – he does not exactly know how many.

4. Asked what voyage they made after leaving England, what ports they visited and what damage they did, he said that the first port they visited was Canary, where they watered; thence they came to Puerto Rico, where they burned one of the frigates of his majesty's fleet with fire-bombs and captured six men who threw themselves from her into the water; these they put ashore on the same island 20 leagues from Puerto Rico; and from these frigates they killed more than a hundred Englishmen of Drake's fleet; thence they came to Río de la Hacha and sacked and burned it without resistance and at Santa Marta they did the same; thence they came to Nombre de Dios, where the English armada is at present anchored.

5. Asked what design this fleet has and for what object it was set forth, he said that the chief object was to take Panama by way of the Nombre de Dios road and the Río de Chagre, for Francis had information that there were four million in Panama;[1] accordingly he sent up the road 900 men in six brigades with six captains and a colonel, among whom came this deponent; and because he was wounded in one foot he was unable to retreat with the rest and was captured on the road by some Negroes.

6. Asked how it was that the fleet went to Puerto Rico, since

[1] Cp. Antoneli to the king, 24 May 1596 (A. de I., Panama, 44): 'he would have found more than three million there'.

he said they had orders only to come straight to take Panama, he said that when the generals learned that there was much silver in Puerto Rico, they came in quest of it.

7. Asked from whom and from what port or ports the generals learned of the silver in Puerto Rico, he said that while the fleet was making ready in England to come to Panama, there arrived at Plymouth a ship bound from Puerto Rico which had been captured by the English; and a Portuguese citizen of Puerto Rico revealed to the generals that there was much silver of the king's at Puerto Rico; they then set about changing their route so as to go first to Puerto Rico before coming to Panama.

8. Asked what plan Francis Drake has after taking Panama and whether he is thinking of holding it, he said that he understands that he has no further design than to rob it and then return.

9. Asked what artillery the ships of this fleet carry, he said that the six largest ships carry 40 large brass pieces each; the rest carry 18, 20 or 22 and some 30, all brass.

10. Asked how many English remained in Nombre de Dios when the 900 came to take Panama, he said that there remained there 1,400 men, Captain Francis Drake among them.

11. Asked what person or persons came as guides to the road for the men who came to take Panama, he said their guides were a man of small stature and a tall mulatto.

12. Asked how they intended to take Panama with 900 men, he said that Francis Drake told them that there were not more than 500 men in Panama and that all the rest were merchants and not men of war.

13. Asked what provisions those marching on Panama carried, he said a little biscuit and cheese in the sleeves of their doublets, and nothing else.

14. Asked what ship or ships of advice from Spain they took on their way, he said they did not take any ships, but that his majesty's frigates bound for Puerto Rico sank a ship of theirs – one of two which had gone ahead of the fleet.

15. Asked what gold, silver, money or other goods the fleet took in Nombre de Dios, he said he had heard they had taken 20 barrels of silver and nothing else.

16. Asked what people they captured in Río de la Hacha, he said a number of Negroes and a few Spaniards.

17. Asked whether Francis Drake sent any vessels through the Strait of Magellan or landed any men elsewhere to occupy the South Sea or expected any reinforcement from England, he said that he had sent men neither by the North Sea nor by the South Sea, nor did he expect any reinforcement.

18. Asked whether John Hawkins, Drake's companion in the making of this force, is in the fleet, he said that while the fleet was in Puerto Rico he died of his sickness, and thus Drake remained in sole command.

19. Asked how long this fleet is to stay in these parts, he said he understood that when Panama had been robbed they were to return for England in the fleet, and he had heard that Drake was to stay two months in Nombre de Dios.

And being warned many times by the interpreter to tell the truth, the Englishman said that he swore to God that what he had said was true and that he knows nothing further; he did not sign because he said he could not write; and the general signed in my presence, Francisco de Riaño, secretary.

At Casa de San Francisco de Cruzes on 15 January 1596 General Alonso de Sotomayor examined an Englishman of 16 years or thereabouts, to whom through Latin (the interpreters being Licenciado Francisco de Vera, advocate in the royal *audiencia* of Panama, and another Englishman called Guillermo Hed, who knew Latin) he put questions in this form:

1. Asked his name and birthplace, he said his name was John Esbran and that he was born in Bristol in England.

2. Asked in what company he left England, he said he came in Drake's fleet as a grummet in the merchantman the *Susan Bonaventure*.

3. Asked who set forth this fleet and for what purpose, when and whence it departed, what soldiers and sailors it carries, how many vessels there are and who is in command, he said this fleet was made ready and brought together by order of the queen of England, that it left the port of Plymouth on 28 August last; he

does not know how many men came in it; 27 ships set sail, the six largest being the queen's and the rest private; the generals were John Hawkins and Francis Drake, with equal power.

4. Asked what voyage they made after leaving Plymouth, what ports they visited and what damage they did, he said that they visited the island of Gran Canaria and watered there and that the local people captured five Englishmen alive and killed two; thence they came to Guadalupe and thence to Puerto Rico, and the five frigates that came from Spain for the silver of Puerto Rico captured and sank an English ship which with one other was ahead of the fleet; the other ship made away and reported this to the fleet; in Puerto Rico they killed 47 and more men of the English fleet; there John Hawkins died of his sickness and Francis Drake remained in sole command; thence they came to Río de la Hacha and sacked and burned it without meeting any resistance, and they did the same at Santa Marta; thence they came to Nombre de Dios and they did not attempt Cartagena because the weather was bad.

5. Asked what design Drake had after anchoring at Nombre de Dios and what he did, he said he sent many men by the Nombre de Dios road to take Panama – 900 English soldiers; he does not know whether there were six or seven brigades; there were eight or nine captains and one captain went as colonel; his name was Baskerville and a brother of his went too.

6. Asked how many were killed in the retreat by our men, he said he did not know, because he was captured on the beach at Nombre de Dios where he had lost his way, and did not accompany those who marched overland for Panama.

7. Asked what Drake planned to do after taking Panama he said he did not know.

8. Asked whether Drake sent any ships to the South Sea or to the queen of England and whether he was expecting any reinforcement, he said he did not know.

Although he was asked many more questions he knew nothing concerning them; and being warned many times by the interpreter, the Englishman said he swore to God that what he had said was true and that he knew no more; he could not sign his name; and the general signed, before me Francisco de Riaño, secretary.

Agreed with the original, which remains in my possession. Dated at Casa de San Francisco de Cruzes, 23 January 1596.

Francisco de Riaño

34. Inquiry on behalf of Juan Enríquez Conabut[1]

Captain Juan Enríquez Conabut, Flemish corporal, states that his parents, citizens of Gorcum in the estates of Flanders, died in defence of our holy catholic faith at the hands of the heretic rebels when the said town revolted against the crown, losing all their property to the said rebels. Juan Enríquez and his three brothers continued to defend the faith and to serve the king [details of the services and deaths of his three brothers are given]. The said Captain Juan Enríquez, emulating his parents and brothers (having been brought up from the age of twelve in the service of Don Alonso de Sotomayor of the order of Santiago, who at that time was serving his majesty in those provinces), was employed, from reaching an age to bear arms, in the company of Don Luis de Sotomayor, Don Alonso's brother, whenever occasion arose in Flanders. When peace was made in those provinces, Juan Enríquez, not wishing to stay in Flanders, went in that company with the Spanish infantry to Sicily and thence to these realms. He then accompanied Don Alonso to pursue his duty in the province of Chile, and on the journey endured two years of numerous and great travails. Having arrived, he served the king with much spirit, valour and zeal, risking his life in three continuous years of war. [Details of his services in the Araucanian wars are given, including a reference to Don Beltrán de Castro's victory over Richard Hawkins, Juan Enríquez being one of the soldiers in the Spanish

---

[1] A. de I., Panama 44, *información* concerning the services of Juan Enríquez Conabut. The record of the proceedings, which were held in May 1596, comprises 82 folios. The translated extract is the petition, which prefaces a set of 18 questions with the replies of seven witnesses, followed by another set of questions and witnesses and a brief testimonial from Sotomayor.

flagship.] When the viceroy nominated Don Alonso de Sotomayor captain-general by land and sea of the kingdoms of Tierra
Firme, to defend them against the English fleet under Francis
Drake, having had information that the latter was coming to take
the city of Panama, Juan Enríquez was appointed captain of
infantry and assigned the troops he was to lead.

The captain-general, on leaving Panama on 26 December 1595
to reconnoitre the road to Nombre de Dios with a view to fortifying
and defending it, commanded him to proceed with his company
with all speed to Venta de Chagre, there to await further orders –
which he did. And having surveyed the road and the city of
Nombre de Dios, the captain-general wrote to the *audiencia* that he
had marked a very good position on the road suitable for fortification and that he intended to place Captain Juan Enríquez there
with forty or fifty soldiers, with which he thought he could hold it
against Drake's entire force. Accordingly the captain-general,
having received the final report concerning the English fleet, sent
orders from Porto Belo on 3 January to the campmaster that when
he obtained news of the enemy's arrival at Nombre de Dios he
should command Enríquez to go and hold that pass, taking picks
and axes to fortify it. When the said news arrived the campmaster
ordered Enríquez to proceed to the position, taking with him 23
soldiers of his company. In addition he gave him thirteen citizens
of Panama and eleven free Negro soldiers, making in all 48 includ
ing Captain Enríquez, who set out with all speed and diligence,
equipped with picks, axes and machetes. And on Sunday, 7
January at sunset he and his men crossed the Río de Chagre. All
that night was spent making bullets and preparing other necessities,
and on the Monday they marched, arriving at vespers at the most
suitable place for fortification, which the general had indicated.
Taking the advice of the most experienced men, he constructed a
large arbour to function as guard-house where the weapons would
be protected from downpours. He also sent in search of water to
sustain the men, this being difficult on account of the dense bush
and steep ravines, and to this end he opened up a path through the
bush. He set to work on this fortification with notable spirit and
energy and spent all that day at it. On the Tuesday at three in the

afternoon, when this work was nearly finished, there arrived Don Diego Suárez de Amaya, *alcalde mayor* of Nombre de Dios, together with 56 soldiers, tired, hungry and in disarray, powderless, their harquebuses wet and possessing neither picks nor other equipment for fortification. Captain Enríquez took them in and lodged them as best he could, feeding them with what he had and putting some heart into them. Had they not found Captain Enríquez established there, the *alcalde mayor* and his men could not have set up defences nor protected themselves and the enemy would have slaughtered them, for he came in close pursuit and had already captured four of them.

That same Tuesday Captain Enríquez assigned the positions to be held by the *alcalde mayor* and by Captain Pedro de Quiñones (who had come with the latter), together with their men, divided the powder and munitions and took other measures for defence, giving orders and instructions, as the responsible commander, to each one. He posted himself at the right hand of the work, since this was the most dangerous position, which was bound to be attacked. On the Wednesday morning he addressed the whole company, exhorting them and encouraging them with many arguments. Then at eight in the morning the enemy came into view before the defences, numbering over 900 men, and attacked fiercely, charging the fort. Captain Enríquez ordered that no shot should be fired until three ranks of the enemy had entered the open ground in front of the defences, so as to inflict the maximum damage. At the right moment, when they had entered, he gave the order to fire, calling with great verve and boldness upon Santiago. The enemy attacked vigorously for three hours, with great force on account of his numbers, but was held until he withdrew, having lost over 150 men dead and many others wounded. And all the time the battle lasted Captain Enríquez went about the fort sword in hand animating the soldiers and giving support at the most hard-pressed positions with all the courage expected of an outstanding captain. Thus to him was due a notable victory which saved this kingdom, with the loss of only seven men killed at the fort. And since he wished in all respects to serve his majesty well, he treated Don Diego Suárez de Amaya with respect and told his men to do likewise, although he recognized no other general than Don Alonso de Sotomayor, whose orders he observed ; and how the *alcalde mayor* carried himself in the engagement is established by the opinions and statements herewith. Although he had passed by an inn where the enemy could find shelter, he had not ordered it to be burned, and so Captain Enríquez at once sent two soldiers who did burn it.

After this victory Don Alonso ordered him to take his company to what they call Magán's road, there to build a fort, because he had information leading him to suspect that the enemy might return that way. Accordingly he went thither and stayed there many days, until the enemy set sail. [He asks that the reward of an annuity of 400 pesos already granted to him by the viceroy for this service should be raised to one of 2,000 pesos, or to 3,000 if a mining concession granted him for former service should prove unprofitable.]

35. *Juan Enríquez Conabut to Fray Bartolomé de la Barrera y Castroverde, 11 January 1596*[1]

My Good Sir,

I have received all your letters, and with them more aid and comfort than I know how to express. The bullets you made and blessed with your hands must have been well made, for we have had great success in punishing those accursed men. Yesterday, which was Wednesday the day of St Paul, three brigades of Englishmen attacked us, each containing 200 men, all musketeers, harquebusiers and pikemen. They engaged me and my company so violently that if we had not by the grace of God been reasonably fortified, and myself granted the strength and courage to resist so powerful a force, I do not know what would have become of us or

[1] A. de I., Indiferente General, 2988. Extract from an *información* made in 1604 for Bartolomé de la Barrera y Castroverde, a dominican friar who served as chaplain to the troops at Venta de Chagre in January 1596. The petitioner claimed he had played a vital part in the battle of San Pablo by supplying the Spaniards with bullets and by persuading Juan Enríquez to go up to the pass earlier than he would otherwise have done. The translated text is one of several letters produced in evidence.

of this kingdom. The fighting lasted two and a half hours and on their side sixty men were killed, among them their captains and chief leaders, and a hundred badly wounded, so that, God willing, they will neither recover nor return this year. On our side two Negroes died, one being Antonio López, a corporal, and the other Simancas; of the Spaniards, two members of the other company were killed and three of mine were wounded, one badly, while another died of a wound. After the battle an Englishman came to us asking for mercy and we sent him on at once to Don Alonso, who took a statement from him, containing many things you will already have heard. This morning Don Alonso visited us and gave us the congratulations due to such loyal subjects of his majesty and defenders of the catholic faith . . .[1] From this fort of San Pablo, 11 January 1596 . . . Juan Enríquez Conabut.

36. Baskerville's note to Drake after the battle at Capirilla[2]

Sir we have found a most troblesom way and som encounters which I Leav to resitt till I speek with yow. I pray yow ther for thatt yow will atend us att ‿ for ⴶ and ♄ will nott suffer L K. I comend me to yow and rest redy to do yow servis

    Tho: Baskervile

I pray Lett som 100 or 200 men
mett us som Leagu or 2 upon the
way with vittualls and as many
horsis as may

this wensday att 3 aclock

[1] A short passage follows, giving no further significant information about the battle.

[2] B.M., Harleian MSS, 4762, f. 103. Written on 31 December 1595/10 January 1596. This is the actual note sent, which Baskerville presumably retrieved from Drake's papers later. Endorsed: 'to my Honorable frend Sir frauncis drake general of Her majesties Army'.

37. *Report on the return of the English to Porto Belo and subsequent events*[1]

Relation of the return of the English fleet, general Francis Drake, to Porto Belo 24 days after departing defeated from Nombre de Dios; of the fresh measures of offence and defence carried out in Tierra Firme by Don Alonso de Sotomayor; and of the death of the said Francis, with a further account of the losses of ships, seamen, landsmen and officers suffered by the enemy until, disillusioned as to their ability to attain their objects, they set sail from that port for England. The year 1596.

[After the departure of the English fleet from Nombre de Dios on 15 January, various military precautions continued to be taken by Don Alonso, but for 24 days there was no news of the said fleet.] Which, so far as could be guessed after much discussion among those skilled in matters of the sea and of these coasts, would not take the usual course to return home by way of Cartagena, thence crossing to Cape San Antonio to disembogue, because the weather would be rough and dangerous, it being the worst time of year on that coast; but might set course towards Nicaragua, sailing to Escudo de Veragua, Bahía del Almirante[2] and Puerto de San Juan del Desaguadero,[3] where it could refit and wait for better

---

[1] Museo Naval, Navarrete MSS, xxv, no. 66 (ff. 269–77), extracts. The whole document is printed in *La Dragontea*, II, 171–92. It appears to be a sequel to Navarrete MSS, xxv, no. 64 (ff. 258–66), printed in *La Dragontea*, II, 149–68. Both belong to the great collection of maritime materials copied from various archives by Don Martín Fernández de Navarrete, now deposited in the Museo Naval, Madrid. According to Navarrete's notes the originals were found in the Archivo General de Indias, among the papers drawn from Simancas, in *legajo* 6 of various papers of the secretariat for New Spain, and were copied on 23 October 1794. Both are *relaciones*, dealing respectively with events after and before the English departure from Nombre de Dios on 5/15 January, and from internal evidence they seem to have been written by or on behalf of the campmaster, Don Gerónimo de Çuaço Casasola. For the second period there is nothing comparable to Çuaço's second *relación*, of which all the parts bearing directly upon English fortunes are here translated.

[2] Laguna Chiriqui.   [3] San Juan del Norte.

weather in which to make the voyage; and if it went that way it would find difficulty in returning to this coast on account of the winds. Alternatively he might make for Cape Camarón and Jamaica, there to revictual and refit until the weather improved sufficiently for disemboguing. But from what has been gathered since from English prisoners taken from the fleet and from Spaniards who went with it and then fled or were put ashore by the enemy, it would appear that the latter had different intentions, for the fleet went to Escudo de Veragua, stayed there and prepared four new launches, and attempted various projects, sometimes to make for New Spain and sometimes to go up the Desaguadero[1] to Granada, crossing to the South Sea with launches. With these, and such ships and vessels as they could capture in the South Sea, they would come to Panama and do what damage they could in the South Sea, and they were discussing the City of the Kings, its forces and defences. But what in effect is certain is that Drake's intention was to deceive Tierra Firme by so long an absence into neglecting its defences (to which end he bided his time to an extraordinary extent, without making an appearance anywhere), and then to return and go up the Río de Chagre in person with launches and a strong force of men to carry through his purpose of reaching Panama, even though he knew how obviously he was risking himself and his fleet in such an attempt. For there seemed to him no other way of saving his reputation or justifying himself to the queen, since he was much grieved that all he had done with so powerful a royal fleet he could have achieved with a single ship and two launches, the anguish of which thought caused him to fall sick, of which sickness seven days later he died as he entered the harbour of Porto Belo with his fleet. The fleet anchored in the harbour on Wednesday, 7 February, and there were 21 sails, apart from the launches and the *patache* of Captain Melchor Juárez, captured at Escudo de Veragua.

[The military dispositions made by Don Alonso and Çuaço are described in detail.] On the night of the twelfth the two soldiers, Pedro Cano and Tomé, who had been sent to Porto Belo, returned and reported that the enemy fleet was at anchor. There were 21

[1] Río San Juan.

ships, but few launches or men were to be seen. On the day they arrived they had landed and taken all they could find there, to wit some construction tools that had been buried and a little maize that our people had set fire to, but not completely burned. The same night there came another message from Captain Diego Mendes Torres at Nombre de Dios, reporting the arrival there of a man, apparently a mariner, bringing certain letters from Spanish prisoners in the English fleet and a safe-conduct from the general thereof to bring them to Panama. At once mules, with Manuel de Sosa, a soldier well-known for his dispatch, were sent to collect this man, who was brought to Chagre on the 13th at midday. His name was Gregorio Mendes, a Portuguese, and he had orders and authority to negotiate the ransom of Don Francisco Flores for 4,000 ducats, of two *regidores* of Río de la Hacha and Santa Marta for other sums, and of Ana Gómez, a free Negro of Nombre de Dios, for 2,000 ducats, which offers were not listened to. A statement was taken from him, in which he declared that Drake had died at the entrance to Porto Belo, as has been related above, and that many more of the fleet had died and were dying each day, leaders and rank and file alike. That same day the muleteer Francisco Cano arrived from Nombre de Dios, having been captured near that city, whither he had been sent from the fleet as a guide for the said Portuguese. Both confirmed the death of Drake and said that the fleet was in an extremely weak state, lacking the spirit and the strength to do us any harm or to make any further attempt to reach Panama, the more so because Francis Drake was dead, it being he who had insisted on this.

[Further details of Spanish counter-measures are given.] That day [14 February], immediately after the departure of the men, who, being nearly all citizens of Panama and married, were in good heart, there arrived a soldier, who had fled from the enemy fleet, called Andrés de Yegros, a native of Agudo in La Mancha. He had come in the fleet from England, where he had been a prisoner, having been captured at the fort of Brest in Brittany. He revealed Drake's death and his determination to attack by the Río de Chagre, resolving to take Panama or die in the attempt; and that with his death this project was abandoned; and that there was controversy in the fleet about who should succeed him as general between Colonel Thomas Baskerville and other captains of repute, the outcome of which was that the said colonel became the general; and that the personnel were very tired, weak and discouraged, suffering from hunger and lack of provisions, so that now that Drake was dead they were concerned only with refitting the fleet and taking in wood and water in order to shape their course for England. He also said that among the English there was talk of much discontent with General Francis Drake who, they said, had deceived them and the queen by making them great promises of much wealth to get support for the enterprise, and that it was therefore suspected that they had helped his death, which he affirmed to have been caused by grief at his misfortunes and at having achieved so little; and that he kept to his cabin for seven days.

Hereupon Sergeant-major Hernando de Liermo Agüero was ordered to march immediately to Porto Belo, taking with him Captain Diego Rangel and thirty soldiers, there to join the men under Captain Juan Guerrel and do what damage he could to the enemy. Later there arrived an Englishman sent by Gerónimo Ferrón, who had captured him on the beach at Porto Belo, where he had gone to look for what remained of the maize that had been burned. This man confirmed what Andrés de Yegros had said and stated that all the men were with the fleet, there being no launches missing, while there were only two companies ashore protecting those mariners who were repairing sails and taking in wood and water, and that these companies slept on land covered by the fleet and its guns.

[Further details on Spanish dispositions are given.] Here [on Saturday, 17 February, on his way from San Pablo towards Porto Belo] the general received news that the enemy had burned the huts at Porto Belo and withdrawn his men from ashore to the ships, not allowing anyone to go ashore, because when a shallop with 26 Englishmen had done so, Gerónimo Ferrón had captured two and killed the rest, leaving not a single man, for men had to come from the ships to collect the shallop.[1] And that later Captain Juan

[1] This account agrees with the petition of Captain Gerónimo Ferrón Barragán in an *información* of 1608 (A. de I., Panama, 46), in which Ferrón also claimed that

Guerrel killed six of another seven, who landed in a small boat, taking the seventh prisoner. And the fleet was ready to sail. [At this the general gave certain orders and, accompanied by the camp-master and others, rode towards Porto Belo] where he arrived about nine in the morning [of Sunday the 18th], and on the way he received news that the enemy had put ashore all the Spaniards he had captured at Río de la Hacha and in this kingdom, including Alberto de Ojeda, except two or three from Río de la Hacha who were to be ransomed and a number of Negroes and Negresses;[1] and that he had set sail that very Sunday morning and was sailing away from the port, though still in sight of it. The general and his company therefore pressed on without stopping to Porto Belo, from where he saw the fleet putting out to sea, eighteen sail in all. And he found everything burnt.[2]

[The final dispositions of the general are described. Reasons are given for concluding that the enemy must be making for England.] The enemy is returning much impaired in strength, with many fewer ships and officers, for of the 27 ships he brought from England only eighteen left Porto Belo, the nine having been abandoned or lost as follows:

The frigates from Spain captured one	1
At Dominica they burned another	1
At Guadalupe they burned another	1
Another was lost between Puerto Rico and Río de la Hacha	1
At Escudo de Veragua they burned another	1
Drake sank two at Río de la Hacha	2
At Porto Belo they sank two	2
	9

he came near to ambushing Baskerville and other officers, who were making for the shore in a launch when a shot fired by one of Ferrón's men warned them off.
[1] These were brought to England (see p. 103, n. 1 above).
[2] Dr Çapata had hidden the equipment and supplies in the bush, but Negroes revealed almost all these to the English, who also 'ruined everything we had done and destroyed the defence work' (A. de I., Panama, 44, Çapata, Valverde and Antoneli to the king, Panama, 29 February 1596).

Apart from the *patache* of Captain Melchor Juárez taken at Escudo de Veragua, which they also sank at Porto Belo.

The fleet must have brought 3,000 soldiers and seamen from England, though they gave out that there were 5,000; and now it does not carry 2,000, for more than a thousand died at Puerto Rico and Tierra Firme and of sickness, including many of the officers and persons of quality and high repute, in particular:

Two generals, John Hawkins and Francis Drake, famous corsairs who have done famous deeds, more especially Drake, of whom it is to be noted that he began his career as a corsair in this kingdom, committing various robberies here and knowing the country because he went about it in disguise and visited Panama. And it pleased Our Lord that he should end his days here.

An admiral of Drake's squadron, a person of great estimation and much account, one of the queen's household and of noble birth.[1] Sir Nicholas Clifford, a person of noble birth, lieutenant to Colonel Thomas Baskerville, who is now general and whom they brought back from Flanders, where he was soldiering. Captain Yorke, a captain of infantry and commander of one of the queen's galleons, a soldier of note. Captain Suinter,[2] a captain of infantry and of one of the ships of the fleet, a person of rank and a fine soldier. The sergeant-major, Arnold Baskerville, brother of the present general. Captain Marchant, captain of infantry, an old soldier, who was also killed at the fort on the road to Panama. Another captain, of the queen's guard, a man of authority and a brave soldier. Captain Platt, captain of infantry in Drake's flagship, a soldier of great repute. Captain Fox,[3] captain of infantry and of a ship. Captain Reis,[2] captain of a pinnace, a great corsair who has visited these Indies five or six times. Another captain of infantry, of Drake's guard, who died at the island of Tenerife.[4] Another

[1] Unidentified. In the following list the Spanish renderings of the names are more or less corrupt. The English equivalents are given here when reasonably certain. In other cases the Spanish version is reproduced.
[2] Unidentified.
[3] Unidentified. Possibly 'Rox', which might mean Rush.
[4] Probably Grimston, who was killed at Grand Canary.

captain of infantry called Worrell, a gentleman of Cancar. Angel Drake,[1] ensign of Drake's company. Captain Josias, captain of the *Delight*. The master of the *Elizabeth Constant*. Captain Poore, captain of infantry, who died at the fort of San Pablo. Item, there died many lieutenants, in particular the lieutenant of Captain Barbaclar,[2] called Oncle, who was killed at the fort of San Pablo. He was a brave soldier, and as such was given the vanguard of the musketry. He had been at Coruña, Cadiz, Santo Domingo, Cartagena and many other engagements, and he it was who climbed up to the fort with a pike and javelin. The lieutenant of Captain Rox.[3] Another lieutenant named Rosel,[1] of the *Help*. Another gentleman of the same ship. Another gentleman named Master Liquin,[1] of noble birth. Another named Master Guillens.[4] Another named Master Farar. Another gentleman named Chambar.[1] Another Master Ja-comprador,[1] chaplain of the *Help*. Two other gentlemen, of the *Bonaventure*. A pilot of Drake's flagship.[5] A lieutenant of Captain Platt, a person of account. Another lieutenant of the *Elizabeth*, named Oulten,[1] four other lieutenants of captains, whose names are not known, but who are known to have been important men. Item, two ensigns, whose names are not known.

These 37 persons were expressly stated by the prisoners to have died among those they definitely knew of, not counting all the men taken by Don Pedro Tello in the ship he captured at Guadalupe, and a great many more ordinary soldiers and sailors killed in action and by sickness, together with others of whom we have no report. All this without any considerable damage to us, apart from the burning of Río de la Hacha, Santa Marta and Nombre de Dios, which were vulnerable to boat attacks, being open places of wooden houses and straw huts, for in this kingdom of Tierra Firme only four Spaniards, a mulatto and two Negroes died at the fort of San Pablo, and apart from this not a single man was lost, nor is there report of any other loss elsewhere. Glory be to God.

[1] Unidentified.　　　　[2] Barkley?　　　　[3] Perhaps Rush.
[4] Probably 'Maurice Williams one of her Majesties Guard' (VTD).
[5] Possibly Abraham Kendall.

VII. *Avellaneda*

Although the preparation of Avellaneda's armada was already under way in Lisbon in June 1595,[1] it was probably not decided to send him in pursuit of Drake until definite advice of the latter's objectives was received from the Canaries early in November.[2] The decision had been taken by 3/13 November, the date of Avellaneda's instructions (document 38), which show the value of Spain's intelligence system. Her naval organization was less impressive. Avellaneda did not leave Lisbon with his eight galleons and thirteen armed merchantmen until 23 December 1595/2 January 1596,[3] by which time the English government had learned his intentions and had perhaps sent pinnaces to warn Drake.[4] These never reached the English fleet, and Baskerville, when he took command at Porto Belo, had no precise news of Avellaneda. He did gather from the Spaniards, however, that an armada was daily expected.[5] To reorganize and hold the fleet together in that situation was no easy task, particularly for a soldier among sailors, and it speaks well for Baskerville's ability that he managed it. The eighteen ships that left Porto Belo on 8/18 February sailed with their artillery at the ready[6] and were capable of battle. What remains astonishing, whatever one's view of the

---

[1] Holliday to Burghley, 3 June 1595 (B.M., Cotton MSS, Titus, B. VIII, ff. 176–7); 'Advertisements from Lisbon', 9 June 1595 (P.R.O., S.P. 12/252, no. 58); A. de I., Contratación, 5169, lib. IX, f. 392.

[2] News from Tenerife, received on 22 October/1 November 1595 (A. de I., Contratación, 5169, lib. IX, f. 427).

[3] For the date, see p. 240, n. 2 below. Herrera says that the armada consisted of 21 ships, including the flagship, the vice-admiral and six galleons of about 300 *toneladas* each. The rest were hulks, flyboats and *pataches*. They carried 3,000 soldiers and seamen, most of the soldiers being lads (*mozos*): Herrera y Tordesillas, *Historia General del Mundo*, III (1612), 593.

[4] Document 39.

[5] VTD.

[6] Çuaço's second *relación* (Museo Naval, Navarrete MSS, XXV, no. 66, f. 276: *La Dragontea*, II, 188).

Elizabethan navy, is the fact that Baskerville even then contemplated risking the fleet for some small and doubtful booty at Santa Marta. In the event he ran into bad weather before reaching so far east. The queen's *Foresight* and three other vessels parted company on 15/25 February and on 17/27 February the remainder set course northwest,[1] being sighted from Cartagena the next day.[2] Avellaneda had arrived there on 17/27 February and so just missed a chance encounter with the enemy off that coast. Baskerville for his part did not stay to reconnoitre Cartagena, presumably because he realized the armada might be there and was anxious to avoid contact with it. Avellaneda got his ships out of the harbour on 21 February/2 March and the two fleets met off the Isle of Pines on 1/11 March.

Avellaneda's fleet now numbered twenty, including seven or eight galleons. The officer who reported both ships and men to be in good condition was hardly a detached observer,[3] but it is safe to say that in their two months at sea they had suffered less than the English had in six. On his side Baskerville had fourteen ships, including five of the queen's. As for the battle itself, research has failed to unearth any Spanish account to set beside Avellaneda's inadequate one,[4] but the five main English reports (Troughton, Baskerville, Savile, VTD and 'Full Relation') are now brought together and may be seen for the most part to harmonize. Avellaneda claimed a victory, but in fact Baskerville pursued his determined course without serious loss, inflicted more damage than he received

[1] Munich Log.

[2] Francisco Gutiérrez de la Villa to the king, 1 March 1596 (A. de I., Santa Fe, 93) said that the English were seen six leagues from the port.

[3] Francisco Gutiérrez de la Villa to the king, 1 March 1596 (A. de I., Santa Fe, 93). He was responsible for the maintenance and provisioning of the ships, and said they had incurred no damage whatever on the voyage, which is contradicted by circumstantial details in Avellaneda's letter of 29 February 1596 (A. de I., Santa Fe, 93). Gutiérrez also reported that there had been very few sick, and that only thirty men had died on the voyage out, whereas Avellaneda's letter of 29 February shows that as he approached Cartagena he was running short of water, with his men fast falling sick.

[4] Document 40. His own letter of 27 March 1596 (see p. 240 below) adds nothing to the account of the battle.

and, in the words of one narrator, 'out sayled the Enemy'.[1] Avellaneda was finally content to follow him out of the Caribbean and limped into Havana on 13/23 March 'with many sick and wounded'.[2] His prize, the *Help*, was a consolation prize, won not in the battle but afterwards, for this was one of the vessels that had lost company off the Cartagena coast.[3]

38. Instructions to Avellaneda, 13 November 1595[4]

The King

What you, Don Bernardino de Avellaneda, Captain-General of the fleet I have ordered to make ready to sail to the Indies, have to do in this voyage, with all the diligence and care you possess, is as follows.

[Instructions for inspecting the ships and personnel and for routine procedure on voyage.]

And since it is understood that in September last a fleet left England which, according to the course it was taking and advices received from the Canary Islands that it had reached Tenerife, seems certain to have gone on to the Indies, probably to Puerto Rico and thence to the Main, to do what damage it can there, you with this fleet must set sail and, without touching at the Canaries, pass straight on to Puerto Rico (taking care not to get yourself to leeward of it), to discover whether the enemy has arrived there and what has happened. If he should have gone on from there, you should find out his route and intention and go in pursuit of him. It is thought meet to advise you that it is judged here that he may go to Cartagena and Nombre de Dios with intent to sack Panama, and that the

---

[1] Bodleian Journal.
[2] Summary of a letter dated 1 April 1596 from Don Juan Maldonado, governor of Havana (A. de I., Contratación, 5112).
[3] See p. 107 above.
[4] A. de I., Indiferente General, 2496, lib. v, ff. 129–35. The volume consists of copies of instructions relating to armadas from 4 August 1594 to 25 February 1597. The original of Avellaneda's instructions was apparently signed by the king and countersigned by the secretary, Juan de Ibarra, and by Laguna, the Marquis of Posa and Pedro de Velasco, members of the council of the Indies.

flota bound for Tierra Firme is making ready with all speed and is expected to sail before 10 December, so that if the enemy arrives there first it might fall into his hands, which would be a serious loss. You should take all this into account in directing your voyage as you think best, which is left to your own judgement and decision in the light of the advice of persons of experience in your fleet. Use all the diligence that is expected of you in this voyage, and notify me, by various ships, of what you find out in Puerto Rico and of the course you decide to follow thence.

Since it may be assumed that when the enemy has proceeded to Nombre de Dios his fleet will lie there or in Porto Belo, and that he will have sent troops up the Chagre or overland to Panama (Cartagena having already been advised of this), you are to take your fleet and the galleys of that coast, if they are in readiness, straight to the enemy before he can gain knowledge of your arrival, so as to capture his fleet and subdue him, taking all measures that seem to you best for this purpose and using the help of the local galleys and troops. [He is to use his own discretion and the king is confident that with God's favour he will succeed.]

Should this come to pass, or should you not make contact with the enemy at Nombre de Dios, you are to tell the *audiencia* to transfer immediately what royal and private silver is there as well as what is due to arrive from Peru at the end of March next year or mid-April at the latest. You will then return to Cartagena to refit your fleet so far as is necessary and to recruit the men's health, after which you will return to Nombre de Dios to receive the silver and bring it back to join the convoy of the Tierra Firme *flota*, which will be there, discharged of its cargo. You will then return to Spain with all speed.

If you should have good reason to conclude that the enemy has had warning of your pursuit and has evaded contact by making for Cape San Antonio and Havana, not staying on the Tierra Firme coast or in the leeward islands, you are to seek him out and engage him, forcing him to disembogue through the Bahama Channel and depart altogether from those seas . . . [1] El Prado, 13 November 1595.

[1] Instructions concerning the return of the *flotas* and treasure and other particular commissions make up the rest of the document.

39. Sir Robert Cecil to Sir Horatio Pallavicino, 5 March 1595/6[1]

... I do thincke you may furnishe him with this advertisement. That uppon the opinion of his Invasion wherwith the world was possessed, her magesty resollved of the journey of Sir Francis drakes to make a dyversion of part of his Forces, of whose successe wee have heard nothing but such fragmentes as have ben advertissed from Spaine uncertenly whether it is here Reported That Caravelles of advise have brought some newes of taking of Havanna[2] to which for that her majestie geve some credyt shee doth determyn to provyde that a good strong Fleet shall go to sea to secure his Fleet in the Returne from any suche Fleet of the king of Spaine as might

[1] P.R.O., S.P. 12/256, ff. 240–3. A copy. Extract. Cecil was giving Pallavicino information to pass on to an unnamed intelligence agent. His purpose was to deceive the enemy into the belief that the expedition then in preparation was to meet and escort Drake home, whereas in reality it was designed to attack Cadiz. The ruse was successful and the Cadiz raid took the Spaniards by surprise. The letter must therefore be read as a judicious mixture of truth and falsehood, and the statement concerning the pinnaces is not credible unless verified by other evidence. It is likely, however, that at least one pinnace was sent in January to warn Drake. Raleigh had written to the lord admiral on 30 November/10 December 1595 (*Cal. Hatfield MSS*, v, 477) reporting news of the preparation of a fleet to pursue Drake and advising the dispatch of a couple of small vessels to advise Drake of the danger. He argued that if the armada arrived when the English soldiers were ashore the ships might be lost. In January the *Little Exchange*, owned by Raleigh and Sir Robert Crosse, departed from Plymouth under the command of John Crosse and was eventually captured near Havana by Avellaneda on 12/22 March, ten days after the sea-battle off Cuba. It is nowhere stated that she had instructions to contact Drake, but the circumstances justify this assumption (*Cal. Hatfield MSS*, VII, 232; *Cal. S.P.D.*, 1595–7, pp. 196, 346–7, 375–6).

[2] A false report that Drake had captured the 'castle' at Havana appears to have reached Lisbon by 20/30 December 1595, according to the report of an Englishman who was a prisoner there up to that date (*Cal. S.P.D.*, 1595–7, p. 169). This rumour reached England in January, the date of this prisoner's report. On 5/15 January 1595/6 the casa de la contratación passed the same news to the king, noting a strong doubt of its truth (A. de I., Contratación, 5170, lib. x, ff. 5–6). The rumour continued to circulate until March, when Pallavicino reported it to Cecil (*Cal. S.P.D.*, 1595–7, p. 180, 3/13 March 1595/6).

happely be sent to encounter him. And for the Fleet That went out
of Lysbone in January after him wee doupt not but he had warning
by certen pynnasses which were sent out the xx^th of december to
advise him of that Fleet That was preparing in Lysbone to goe
after him. . . .

40. *A Libell of Spanish Lies*[1]

A Libell of Spanish lies written by Don Bernaldino Delgadillo de
Avellaneda, Generall of the king of Spaines Armada, concerning
some part of the last voyage of sir Francis Drake; together with a
confutation of the most notorious falsehoods therein contained,
and a declaration of the truth by M. Henrie Savile Esquire: and also
an approbation of both by sir Thomas Baskervil Generall of her
Majesties Armada after the decease of sir Francis Drake.

. . . The Copie[2] of a letter which Don Bernaldino Delgadillo de

[1] *Principal Navigations*, III (1600), 590–8 (x (1904), 246–65). The original pamphlet,
*A Libell of Spanish Lies: found at the Sacke of Cales . . . With an answere briefely
confuting the Spanish lies . . . by Henry Savile Esquire . . . And also an Approbation of
this discourse, by Sir Thomas Baskervile . . .*, was printed by J. Windet in 1596
(*S.T.C.* 6551). Hakluyt gives the Spanish text in full, following Savile with only
some spelling variants; both differ slightly, but not insignificantly, from the copy
of the original Spanish text in the Museo Naval, Madrid (Navarrete MSS, v,
no. 11, ff. 81–3). Savile's translation, a bad one, was silently amended by
Hakluyt in various places, but the result is still faulty. Hakluyt also altered
Savile's own contribution in one or two places.

[2] A different letter by Avellaneda, dated Havana, 27 March 1596, is printed in
Tapia y Rivera, *Biblioteca Histórica de Puerto-Rico* (1854), pp. 414–16. This includes
further detail on the Spanish voyage before the encounter, as follows: 'From
Lisbon I wrote to your honour, giving account of how I had prepared this armada
to come to the Indies in pursuit of the enemy, and now I have to tell you that on
the second of January I left that port and ran along the coast of Spain as far as
Cape St Vincent, whence I took a course to pass to leeward of the Canaries,
arriving after good and bad times at Puerto Rico on 17 February. Here I learned
that the enemy had arrived there on 21 November, staying until the 25th without
inflicting damage or loss, though suffering serious loss himself. Then making all
the speed I could, I left that port and arrived at Cartagena on the 27th, where
there was no certain news of the enemy's whereabouts. The following afternoon,
while I was repairing my fleet in great haste and taking in sorely needed water,
there were seen from the city and from the tops of the ships in the port more than

Avellaneda, Generall of the king of Spaine his armie, sent unto Doctor Peter Florez, President of the contractation house for the Indies, wherein he maketh mention of the successe[1] of the English armie, after they departed from Panama, whereof was Generall Francis Drake, and of his death.

From Cartagena I gave relation unto your Worship how I departed from the citie of Lisbone, in the pursuite of the English armie: although for the great haste the Galeons could not be so well repaired as was needfull, and with foule weather one was lost, and a Fly-boat was burnt. And having sayled many dayes in pursuite of the enemie, untill I arrived at Cartagena, and there taking the advise of Don Pedro de Acunna, Governour of the citie, and Captaine generall (for wee had great neede of water, and to repaire our shippes) we stayed in that port: whereas I had intelligence by an Indian that Francis Drake died in Nombre de Dios, for very griefe that he had lost so many Barkes and men, as was afterwards more manifestly knowen.[2] Thus having given you a relation of all that happened hitherto, now I let you understand, that I left this Port

sixteen sails returning from the direction of Nombre de Dios. At nightfall two large lanterns were seen to leeward of the port, and at midnight was heard the sound of a gun being fired. Realizing that it was the enemy and that the shot was a signal, I wanted to give chase at once, although I had not water enough for two days, for what there is in Cartagena is from wells which are quickly exhausted. But that night it was not possible because, apart from the darkness, the wind was contrary, and so continued for the next two days, so that although I made the galleys tow us to the mouth of the harbour I was not able to leave until 2 March. That morning the land breeze freshened and I got away and set course for Havana. Having made all possible speed I sighted the Isla de Pinos and the inlet of Guaniguanico on the 11th, where I found Francis Drake with fourteen ships. . . .'

[1] In modern English the Spanish word *suceso* is best rendered in this context as 'fortune' (neither good nor bad). But Savile probably intended the English word in this sense, just as Baskerville obviously did in three different letters (documents 44, 45, 46 below).

[2] 'By an Indian' is a mistake copied by Hakluyt from Savile. The Spanish has *por un aviso* – i.e. a warning message or (more likely) an advice-boat. However, there is no mention of this receipt of intelligence in the letter of 27 March, where Avellaneda speaks of meeting Drake and his fleet and adds a postscript: 'After making the above report I learned of the death of Drake from illness.' He presumably heard something about Drake's death at Cartagena, but did not give it much credence. Later he seems to have learned the facts from the men of the *Help*.

the second of March, and tooke our course towardes Havana,
where I thought to have found the English fleete. And having used
all the diligence possible, upon Munday the eleventh of the said
moneth, about two of the clocke in the afternoone, at the end of the
Ile of Pinos, in the entrance of Guaniguanico, I met with the
English fleete, being fourteene very good ships:[1] I drew towardes
them although they had the winde of us, and our Admirall who
bore up towards the winde, with two other ships beganne to draw
neere them, and although we thus set upon them, three times with
all their ships, yet would they not set againe upon us, and those
of our men which were farthest off cryed to them amaine, being
both within shot of artillerie, muskets, and calivers,[2] whereby they
received evident hurt by us: They plyed their great ordinance
according to their manner, and especially their Viceadmirall,[3] and
seeing our resolution how sharpe we were bent towards them, they
with all expedition and speede possible[4] prepared to flie away,
hoysing sailes and leaving their boates[5] for haste in the sea: but I

Savile angrily denies that Drake died from 'grief' and points out that the death
was due to 'fluxe'. Avellaneda knew this, but may have thought (as Baskerville
did) that grief had something to do with it, and that for public consumption in
Spain the ascription of the dragon's demise to sheer grief was preferable to a
subtler explanation.

[1] Letter of 27 March has '14 ships, six galleons of the queen's and the rest very good
and very nimble'.

[2] The preceding passage is better rendered: 'and the vice-admiral, which sailed
nearer the wind [than the flagship] with two other ships began to draw near them,
but although she bore down on them three times with all their ships she could not
get near enough to board. We who were farthest off tacked about, getting near
enough to exchange artillery, musket and harquebus fire with most of them . . .'
The letter of 27 March has: 'I made towards them although it was not possible
to get the wind of them, and drawing level with them I called them to battle by
firing a piece, to which they did not reply; the vice-admiral, which with two
other ships sailed nearer the wind, was able to approach them closer.'

[3] Savile had: 'They shot off now and then at us, and especially their Admirall.'

[4] Spanish *con mas diligencia de la que se puede creer* – with incredible speed. As
Bodleian Journal has it, the English outsailed the Spanish ships, and Avellaneda
had a reasonable excuse for his failure to press home the attack. Savile does not
seem to have welcomed this back-handed compliment to the sailing qualities of
the English ships.

[5] Savile had 'oares'.

followed them, with nine ships all the night following, and with foure more the next day, till I made them double the Cape of S. Antonie, and to take the course towards the Chanell of Bahama,[1] according to the instructions from his Majestie. It little availed us to be seene, with lesse number of ships, neither yet all the diligence we could use, could cause them to stay or come neere us, nor to shoot off one harquebuze or peece of artillerie, for they fled away as fast as they could, and their shippes were halfe diminished, and that the best part of them:[2] the rest they repaired in Puerto Bello, whereas they were about fortie dayes,[3] and so by that meanes they were all well repayred; and our shippes were very foule, because the time would not permit us to trim them: I have sayled 2 moneths and a halfe in the Admirall,[4] since we departed from Cartagena, we have not repaired their pumpes nor clensed them: and the same day I departed thence, there came unto me a small Pinnesse in the like distresse:[5] our Viceadmirall and the rest of our ships have the like impediment, but no great hinderance unto us, for ought I could perceive by our enemies: It is manifest what advantage they had of us,[6] and by no meanes was it possible for us to take them, unlesse we could have come to have found them at an anker.[7] Neverthelesse they left us one good shippe behinde for our share, well manned, which tolde me that Drake died in Nombre de Dios, and that they have made for Generall of the English fleete the Colonel Quebraran: and also by meanes of the small time, being

[1] Savile: 'La Canet de Bahamet'.
[2] The Museo Naval copy has: *porque el se dio la diligencia que pudo y la que quiso porque sus navios los habia reducido a la mitad y los mejores* – as fast as they could and as they wished, because they had reduced their fleet by half, keeping the best ships.
[3] Savile had 'fourtie daies before'. The Spanish is *donde se estubo mas de quarenta dias*. Letter of 27 March says, correctly, eleven days.
[4] Savile: 'the Shippe called the Capitana'.
[5] Savile: 'my shippes were all foule with Barnacles'.
[6] Museo Naval copy has: *era muy conocida la ventaja que me hacia, [y el conoce muy bien las mares, como quien ha tantos años que nabega y las egercita,] y mucha dicha sera apoderarse* . . . The bracketed passage (and they know the seas very well, having navigated and experienced them for so many years) is omitted from Savile's and Hakluyt's Spanish texts.
[7] Savile: 'unlesse wee could have come to deale with them with fire and sword'.

straightly followed by us, they had no opportunitie to take either water, wood or flesh, and they are also in such bad case, that I know not how they will be able to arrive in England.[1] The number of men we have taken are about an hundred and fortie, and fifteene noble captaines of their best sort, and some of them rich, as well may appeare by their behaviour: I have no other thing to write at this time. Our Lord keepe you who best can, and as I desire. From Havana the 30 of March, 1596.

Don Bernaldino Delgadillo de Avellaneda.

[Licence to Rodrigo Cabrera to print the above, 15 May 1596. Savile's replies to particular points.]

*The meeting of our English Navie and the Spanish fleete,
and the order of our encounter.*

Sunday[2] the first of March, according to our computation, wee descryed the Iland of Pinos, where haling in for the Westerne part thereof, thinking there to have watered, being within foure leagues off it Southerly, we sent in three of our Pinnesses to discover the harbour, and to sound afore us, about one of the clocke in the afternoone; the same day we discovered a fleete of twentie sailes,[3] and deeming them to be the Spanish fleete, we kept our loofe to get the winde, but their Viceadmirall with divers other ships went about to cut off our Pinnesses: so that our Generall with some other of our shippes, was forced to tacke about upon the larbourde tacke, and so ranne in towardes the lande keeping the winde, so as we recovered our Pinnesses; which forced the enemies shippes to tacke about, and to take the aide of their fleete, and being come neere unto them they shot at us; we still approched, having our close fights up, our flags, ensignes and streamers displayed, our men orderly placed in each quarter, but forbare our fight untill our Generall

[1] Letter of 27 March: 'since the enemy is returning from the Indies so shamed, exhausted and ill-provided, he will lose any desire to return thither, because, apart from the men and ships he has lost (although for our part we are not as satisfied as we could wish), he has received much damage'.

[2] Savile had 'Munday' – correctly.

[3] Marginal note: 'The first discovery of the Spanish fleete.' All the marginal notes given here are Savile's, copied by Hakluyt.

beganne, and gave us warning to come in and fight, by shooting off a great peece, according to his former directions:[1] so being within musket shot, the Viceadmirall of the Spanish fleete came neerest unto us, to whom our Viceadmirall John Traughton Captaine of the Elizabeth Bonadventure gave fight, betwixt whom there was the greatest voley of small shot changed that lightly hath bene heard at Sea, which continued a long halfe houre. In which time the Spanish fleete came in to fight. Our Generall Sir Thomas Baskervill being in the Garland (whereof Humphrey Reignolds was Captaine, being the next shippe unto the Elizabeth Bonadventure) bare up to the enemie, playing with his great ordinance hotly untill he came within musket shot. Jonas Bodenham Captaine of the Defiance, and Henrie Savile Captaine of the Adventure, came likewise into the fight with them. After the Garland being within musket shot played her part, and made good fight for the space of an houre. The Defiance bare up likewise and had her turne; after came the Adventure againe within musket shot, who having changed many a great bullet with them before, renewed his fight, & continued it an houre with small shot. Then came Thomas Drake Captaine of the Hope, who last of all had his turne. Thus had all the Queenes shippes their course: The marchants ships with other small vessels being without the Queenes ships, shot when they saw opportunitie. After the enemie finding no good to be done (being well beaten) fell from us, the Adventure playing upon them with her great ordinance, made three of the last shot at them: their Viceadmirall with divers others of their ships,[2] were so beaten that they left off the fight, and were forced to lie in the winde, for that they durst not lie of either boord by reason of their many and great leakes, which they had received by our great shot. The Generall with the rest of their fleete tacking about, fell in our wake, thinking to get the winde, which in the beginning wee sought to hinder. But our Generall seeing that in holding the winde we should shoot ourselves into the bay, gave them the winde. All that night they kept themselves upon our brode side, notwith-

[1] Marginal note: 'The incounter betwixt the English and the Spanish ships.'
[2] Marginal note: 'The Spanish Viceadmirall can witnesse, what successe they had in this fight.'

standing our Admiral carried his cresset-light all night,[1] having great care of our smallest shippes. This fight continued about foure houres till it was neere night, in the which fight, thankes be to God, there were slaine so few persons of our English fleete, as I thinke the like conflict hath not bene performed with so little losse of men :[2] What harme befell the Spaniards in their fleete I leave to your judgements. Yet our eyes can witnesse their ships were sore beaten and racked thorough, whereby there was such falling backe and lying by the lee to stoppe their leakes, as some of them were driven to haste away, and rather to runne on shore to save themselves then sinke in the Sea : besides within two houres after our fight with them, we sawe one of their great shippes on fire which burnt into the Sea, and all the sterne of another of their ships blowen up : And in the morning a shippe of our fleete was runne so neere the land, that to double the Cape de los Corrientes[3] he must of necessitie tacke about and fall in the wake of the enemie, which caused our Generall in the Garland and the Defiance to tacke about ; which two ships forced the three ships of the enemies (which were put foorth to take our shippe, or else to cause her runne on ground) to returne to their fleete to save themselves, hoysing all their sayles for haste : This morning they were faire by us having the winde of us, being but thirteen sayle of their twentie to be seene :[4] then we stroke our toppe sayles thinking to have fought with them againe, which they perceiving tacked about from us, and after that never durst nor would come neere us : What became of the rest of their fleete wee know not, but true it was that they were in great distresse mightily beaten and torne, by having received many bullets from us. All this day wee had sight of them, but they shewed little will to fight or come neere us, so we keeping our course West, and by North, about sixe of the clocke at night lost the sight of them. And this is a true discourse of our fight with the Spanish fleete. The which the author

[1] Marginal note : 'The English admirall carried his Cresset light, notwithstanding the enemie was upon his broad side.'

[2] Marginal note : 'The English received little losse in this conflict.'

[3] Savile : 'the Cape current'.

[4] Marginal note : 'The remainder of the Spanish fleete were but thirteene sayles.'

hereof will justifie with the adventure of his life, against any Spaniarde serving in that action, that shall contradict the same.

Henry Savile.

[A statement by Sir Thomas Baskerville confirming Savile's account and challenging Avellaneda to a duel.]

41. *The voyage truely discoursed*[1]

As soone as they discried us, they kept close upon a tacke, thinking to get the winde of us: but we weathered them. And when our

[1] Extract from 'The voyage truely discoursed, made by sir Francis Drake, and sir John Hawkins, chiefly pretended for some speciall service on the Islands and maine of the West Indies, with sixe of the Queenes ships, and 21 other shippes and barkes, containing 2500 men and boyes, in the yeere 1595. In which voyage both the foresayd knights died by sicknesse.' *Principal Navigations,* III (1600), 583–90 (x (1904), 226–45). A most interesting and valuable account, this is not republished here in full because it is readily accessible in its only known version. The passage on the sea-battle, however, is particularly important and is reproduced here for convenient comparison with the accounts by Troughton, Baskerville and Savile. The corresponding passage in the 'Full Relation' runs: 'The first of *March* we espyed twenty saile of the Kings men of Warre, we chased them and about three of the clocke in the afternoone we began to fight with them and continued three hours in fight, the Viseadmirall gave us a shot, then the *Elizabeth Boneventure* gave her a shot again, then the *Boneventure* came in and gave him a bravadoe with all her broadside that she shot through and through, then came up our Generall and gave them a brave volley of shot, next came the *Defiance* and she laid on most bravely, next the *Adventure* she laid on that we could see through and through; it was a most brave attempt, but God be thanked we had the upper hand of them, we plying the Viseadmirall so fast that if she had not born up from us she had sunke, and another that was near her; we drove them into such a puzell that with stopping their leakes as we judged, their Powder being loose fired all the Ships as we did behold, within two hours after we had done the fight. The next day we sailed towards Cape S. *Anthony* there following us but thirteen of our gallants, they kept their course and would not come at us, but at length they came somewhat nigh us and the *Defiance* and the *Adventure* bore up to them, but they made away as soone as ever they were able, and so we were rid of our gallants.' Bodleian Journal has: 'The first of march we pased by the Iland of pineris where we descried coming towarde us 20 sayle of the Kings men of ware which lay for our coming and in the after none we fout with them wher captayne

Admirall with all the rest of our fleet were right in the winds eye of
them, sir Thomas Baskervil putting out the Queenes armes, and
all the rest of our fleete their braverie, bare roome with them, and
commanded the Defiance not to shoot, but to keepe close by to
second him. The Viceadmirall of the Spaniards being a greater
ship than any of ours, and the best sayler in all their fleete loofed by
and gave the Concord the two first great shot, which she repayed
presently againe, thus the fight began. The Bonaventure bare full
with her,[1] ringing her such a peale of ordinance and small shot
withall, that he left her with torne sides. The Admirall also made
no spare of powder and shot. But the Defiance in the middest of
the Spanish fleete thundering of her ordinance and small shot
continued the fight to the end. So that the Viceadmirall with 3 or 4
of her consorts were forced to tacke about to the Eastward, leaving
their admirall and the rest of the fleete, who came not so hotly into
the fight as they did. The fight continued two houres & better. At
sunne set all the fleete tacked about to the Eastward, we continued
our course to the Westward for cape de los Corrientes, supposing
we should have met with more of their consorts. In this conflict in
the Defiance we had five men slaine, three Englishe men, a Greeke
and a Negro. That night some halfe houre after, their fleete keeping
upon their weather quarter, we saw a mightie smoke rise out of one
of their great ships which stayed behind:[2] which happened by
meanes of powder as we thinke, and presently after she was all on a
light fire, and so was consumed and all burnt, as we might well
perceive.

The next day being the second of March in the morning by

throughton of the Bonadventure of the quenes shoued himselfe moste valiant,
Thrustinge him selfe in to the middest of them Fightinge tel nyght. The next
morninge the Enemy missed sixe of theire fleet which were spoyled and one other
that fired her selfe by carelessnes to the water, persuinge us past cape currentes
where we out sayled the Enemy suspectinge a greater Fleet of them at cape
Anthony we had fought with them the next morning agayne. But escapinge
without any other losse but with the hurte of captain throughton and captain
Brackly which were sore hurte with shote, the 8 march we were in the height of
Floryda.'
[1] Marginal note: 'The fight betweene the English and the Spanish fleetes.'
[2] Marginal note: 'One of the Spanish great ships burnt.'

breake of day we were hard aboord Cape de los Corrientes, which is a bare low cape, having a bush of trees higher than the rest some mile to the Eastward of the cape. All Cuba is full of wood on the Southside. The Spanish fleete which then were but 14 no more than we were, kept still upon our weather quarter, but dared not to come roome with us although our Admirall stayed for them. Assoone as we had cleered our selves of the Cape 3 of their best saylers came roome with the Salomon, which was so neere the land that she could not double the Cape, but tacked about to the Eastward, & so was both a sterne and also to leeward of all our fleete: But when we saw the Spaniards working, the Defiance tacked about to rescue her: which the Spaniards seeing, and having not forgotten the fight which she made the night before, they loofed up into the middest of their fleete againe, and then all the fleete stayed untill the Salomon came up, and so stood along for Cape S. Antonio,[1] which wee came in sight of by two in the after noone, being a low cape also, and to the Southwest a white sandie bay, where 3 or 4 ships may very well water. There is a good road for North & Easterly windes: there the Spaniardes began to fall a sterne.

[1] Marginal note: 'Cape Sante Antonio.'

VIII. *Aftermath*

On the return voyage across the Atlantic the fleet broke up. With victuals in short supply the faster sailers bore ahead when separated from the rest by storm. The *Elizabeth Bonaventure* and the *Little John* were the first to part company thus, and the former reached Milford Haven on 22 April. The *Hope,* with the *Jewel* and another private vessel, left the rest behind in a second storm and reached Falmouth on 25 April. Wynter in the *Foresight,* having lost company in the Caribbean, made the Scillies on 3 May and Sir Thomas Baskerville, with the *Garland,* the *Defiance,* the *Adventure* and the *Phoenix,* having put into Flores to water and victual on 8 April, sent a message ahead from near the Scillies on 7 May. He had left the rest of the ships behind after the second storm, but they probably reached England before he did.[1]

When the privy council learned of the fleet's imminent arrival, its first thought was to prevent it putting into Plymouth, where the Cadiz expedition was in preparation. The 'confusion and other inconveniences' which it feared might arise from such contact are not difficult to imagine.[2] Orders were also issued to prevent embezzlement of prize goods, but in the event considerable quantities of bullion and pearl were reported illicitly disposed.[3] Various ships' stores and munitions no doubt went the same way and it was alleged that 'the ships which left Sir Thomas Baskerville and came afore was by the persuasion and agreement of the officers of purpose to make up their voyage by embezzling the same'.[4] If by such means some were able to compensate themselves for the miseries of the voyage, many more were reduced to a desperate condition. On 9 June Sir John Fortescue wrote to Cecil: 'if youe saw the numbre being poore miserable creatures hanging at my

[1] VTD; documents 18, 42, 43, 46.

[2] *A.P.C., N.S.,* xxv (1901), 365 (25 April 1596).

[3] *Ibid.,* 367 (26 April 1596); P.R.O., S.P. 12/257, no. 108; Hatfield MSS, 41, no. 63 (Fortescue to Cecil, 8 June 1596).

[4] P.R.O., S.P. 12/257, no. 108.

gate who nether have meat nor clothes it wold pyty your hart'.[1] As late as 31 December 1596 some of the mariners were still demanding their wages.[2] In November the widows of Captains John Marchant and Anthony Platt petitioned for their husbands' pay, and it is unlikely that the heirs of less important men had by then received satisfaction.[3] Sympathy for such claimants could not outweigh the officials' knowledge of their duty to save the queen money. Thus Thomas Webbes advised Cecil how 'her Majesty may save in the payment a round sum with small discontent' by refusing wages for some 23 days in July 1595 and charging the mariners for shoes and clothes issued to them.[4] But the greatest delays in the payment of wages were due to the unwillingness of Thomas Drake and Lady Margaret Hawkins to bear their shares of the expense.[5]

While money matters of this sort occupied the attention of the queen's servants from Cecil downwards, there is no evidence that anyone thought of inquiring into the conduct of the voyage or into its tactical or strategic significance. Baskerville, according to his own private statement (document 47) was accused of fraud, but Troughton's reflections upon his competence apparently evoked no response. It is not known whether Baskerville's charges against Captain Wynter were pursued.[6]

In Spain the news of the success at Puerto Rico was received in February[7] and this was followed on 4/14 April by a report of Drake's defeat at the Isthmus of Panama.[8] On 28 April/8 May it

[1] Hatfield MSS, 41, no. 64.   [2] *Cal. Hatfield MSS*, VI, 542–3.

[3] *Ibid.*, VI, 471; Hatfield MSS, 41, no. 73 (Myddelton to Cecil, 14 June 1596).

[4] *Cal. Hatfield MSS*, VI, 201–2 (Webbes to Cecil, 31 May 1596).

[5] *Ibid.*, VI, 264–5, 542–3. In July Lady Hawkins protested against paying her £2,000 contribution to the wages bill; at the end of the year £1,500 was still due from her and Thomas Drake. The accusation against Thomas Drake (made by Bodenham) that he 'before the breath was out of the body of Sir Francis, fell on to Ryfling and getting together of all such Chiestes, so that he left nothing in any good sort for the gentlemen of Sir Francis in manner suitable to his reputation and ambition' (Eliott-Drake, *Family and Heirs*, I, 145) appears to be borne out by Sir James Whitelocke's statement (above, p. 46).

[6] See document 20.

[7] Museo Naval, Colección Sanz Barutell, 392, f. 34 (art. 4, no. 1254), 19 February 1596.

[8] A. de I., Contratación, 5170, lib. X, f. 31.

was reported that Avellaneda had defeated the English fleet.[1] Less than two months later an English fleet, which included some of the survivors of the Indies voyage,[2] captured Cadiz. The outward-bound *flota* was burned by the Spaniards to save it from falling into English hands. It cannot be shown, however, that the Drake–Hawkins expedition had any important influence upon these events in Europe.[3]

42. *John Troughton to the queen*[4]

Maye it please your moste excellente Maiestie to understande that S*ir* John Hawkins uppon his death bedde, willed me to use the beste meanes I colde to acquaynte your highenes with his loyall service and good meaninge towardes your ma*jes*tie even to his laste breathinge.

And forasmuche as throughe the perverse and crosse dealinges of some in that Jeorney, whoe preferringe their owne fancye before his skill, wolde never yelde but rather overrule him, whereby he was so dyscouraged, and as himsellfe then sayde his harte even broken, that he sawe no other but danger of ruyne lyklye to ensue of the whole voiage, wherein in some sorte he had bine a persuader of your Ma*jes*tie to hasarde aswell some of your good shippes as allso a good quantitie of treasure, in reguarde of the good opinion he thoughte to be helde of his sufficiencie, iudgement and experience in suche Actions; Willinge to make your maiestie the beste

[1] A. de I., Contratación, 5170, lib. x, f. 37.

[2] Hatfield MSS, 41, no. 73 (Myddelton to Cecil, 14 June 1596).

[3] The armada and *flota* of New Spain, which was on the point of leaving, had been in preparation since January 1596. The delay of its departure, however, was not excessive and cannot be attributed to fear of Drake's fleet. The Tierra Firme *flota*, which had certainly been delayed for this reason, had left Cadiz in February, reaching Nombre de Dios in April. See H. et P. Chaunu, *Séville et l'Atlantique, 1504–1650*, IV (1956), 12 and 20.

[4] Hatfield MSS, 48, no. 61, undated. Endorsed: 'The Queenes moste Excellente Maiestie'. Troughton wrote to Cecil (Hatfield MSS, 40, no. 20) from Milford Haven on 22 April 1596 and this letter to the queen was probably written about that time. The letter to Cecil adds nothing of significance to the other Troughton materials.

amendes his poore abilitie wolde then stretche unto, In a Coddicell as a peece of his laste will and Testamente, did bequeath to your highenes Twoe thousande poundes yf your Majestie will take yt, For that as he saide, your highenes had in your possession a farre greater somme of his which he then did allsoe release: Which 2000 yf your majestie sholde accepte thereof, his will is shalbe deducted out of his Ladies portion, and oute of all suche Legacies and bequestes as he lefte to eny his servauntes and frendes or kinsfoke whosoever, as by the saide Coddicell appeareth.

And touchinge my sellfe: I understande to my greate gryefe by Mr Killigrew that your Majestie is highelye offended with mee for my going awaye from Sir Thomas Baskervile, whereof I doubte not but to cleere my sellfe verye sufficientlye, whensoever yt shall please your highenes to cause it to be examyned, Neither did I leave him till we were paste all daunger of the Enemye, (my sellfe beinge then as lykelye to dye as to lyve by reason of my gryevous woundes) nor then without his leave, And that uppon very iuste cause, for that I was in great daunger to have famishte all my companie and so your majesties good shippe muste have perishte with us in the seas. And what I did in leavinge him, the lyke was done by his brother Captaine Baskervile in your Majesties good shippe the Hope, and by others, yet none therein so charged as my selfe.

In the ende I doubte not but my innocencye shall appeare; and that the [?] hathe proceeded rather of malice, then of matter: Otherwise I desire not to lyve. And so moste humblye beeseechinge the Allmightie longe to preserve your most excellent Majestie in all happines to raigne over us.

Your majesties moste humble and ever loyall subiecte
John Troughton

43. Nicholas Baskerville to Essex, April 1596[1]

My honorable good Lorde I have thoughte yt my duty to signify unto your honor my aryvall at famouthe with the hoope and to

[1] P.R.O., S.P. 12/257, no. 50. Enclosed by Essex in a letter to Cecil dated 27 April 1596. Couriers' notes on Baskerville's letter, which is undated, indicate that it was dispatched on the night of 25-6 April.

other marchant*es* . . . [he reports intelligence gained at sea concerning Spanish naval preparations at Ferrol] . . . and am Comminge towardes your honor my sellfe as fast as my weeke body will gyve me leave. farther to Lett your honor knowe what hathe hapened unto us in thys acc*i*on, yt is very Little that we have gotten. yett we have lost noe reputac*i*on. we encountered w*i*th the spanishe fleete and put them to repulse. we suncke theyer Vice admyrall. burnt another. and we Leafte fyve more that Laye by the Lee in greate distres. My Brother is not yett aryved, but her ma*j*esties shipes are all in safety. and I knowe the nexte fayer wynd they will be at plymothe. I hoope to Cume in good tyme to wayte upon your honor in thys acc*i*on my sellfe.

your honors servant duringe Lyfe
nicolas Baskervill

44. *Sir Thomas Baskerville to his wife, 1596*[1]

My dearest frind I send only my fottman to sea thee, and wishe the Charg of this fleett in the comand of some other, thatt I myght have performed the office my self, butt perforce I must see thess shipps in saufty befor I cann Leave them, w*h*ich being donn Nothing cann stay my visiting of the. The sucses of our viag hathe bin very unfortunatt unto us for in Itt I have lost my dearist Brother, w*i*th many other of my frind*e*s and kinsmen (and am retornid w*i*thoutt bringin thatt we went for) w*h*ich Loss I protest hath trobled me very muche and had donn more, had nott thy self bin, whos Love possesid me In such sorte thatt all other Crossis of fortun how greatt soever seme nothing to me. swett malle dispach my fotman with exspedicion, for I long Infynitly to hear from thee, and wryght att Large, send w*i*th hym som of my clokes and dublett and hose, for I hav nothing to putt one when I com to London. I have som Toys to present thee w*h*ich I will send thee assone as I putt fote ashore, godwilling, for all other matters I Leave them till I see the my selfe, only this I wryght I will presently putt your howse In order and send you a coach and then att your pleasure you may go

[1] B.M., Harleian MSS, 4762, f. 33. A draft.

thither. Comend my to my uncle your Brother and sister and kishe
Bess from me a thousand tymes, nother thing I wryght att this
present, butt turne you for the discourse of our viag to your fathers[1]
Letter to whom, notwithstanding I have wryghten, I would have
you comend me, and so kissing you in spiritt more then a million of
tymes I Leave thee swett malle to gods holy protection from the sea
twenty Leagues a seabord the Sillis this 7 of may

send me Lykwise a note whatt
thinges yow would have me by
for yow.

he who only Is thyn
Tho: Baskervile.

45. *Sir Thomas Baskerville to Cecil, 8 May 1596*[2]

Honorable

Sir This day being the 8 I aryvid upon this Cost with only 3 of her
majesties shipps and on pinnas which I have sent apurpos to
plymouth the sonner to advertis your Lordships of the sauff
retourne of the sayd ships, Contraryety of windes having severid the
most parte of the rest from us, which I hope ar allredy aryvid,
tuching the susess of our vyage (I humbly crave pardon of your
Honor) thatt I refer yow to the descourse I send my Lord your
father, and att my Comyng to Courte, If Itt will pleas you to geve
the Loking on of some plattes and papers I have gotten, of the
description of the Indias, portes Havons and fortresis with the ways
from the northe to the southe sea, and richis and Comoditis of
many of those Cuntris, they and my selfe ar allways att your
comandment.[3] No other thing have I to wryght butt only to geve
your Honor this much asurance, thatt ther is no mann more your
servant then my selfe, and so fearing to be over teadious I humbly

[1] Sir Thomas Throckmorton, of Tortworth, Glos. On the 'discourse' see document
20 and pp. 82–4 above.

[2] Hatfield MSS, 40, no. 69. Endorsed: 'To the Honorable Sir Robert Cycyll
knyght one of the Lords of her majesties most Honorable Counsell. Salisbury the
xv[th] day at half an hower past ten of the clock at night. Andover at 4 a Cloke
the 16th of maye in the morninge. at basing stoke 8 of Cloke in the for nowne.
xviij[th] May 1596. Sir Thomas Baskevill to my master.'

[3] See documents 20, 28 and 31 and p. 212, n. 1.

take my Leav resting most redy to be comandid from aseabord the sillis some 10 Leagues this 8 of may.

  he who desires to do your Honor servis
   Tho: Baskervile.

postscript our pearle and sillvar is gotten which is in my possesion the keys of which ar in the Custody of the menn of warr and deputies of the adventurers.

46. Sir Thomas Baskerville to Burghley, 8 May 1596[1]

Most Honorable my very good Lord

 This day being the 8 of this moneth I aryvid upon this Coste with 3 of her majesties shipps and one marchant, the rest some by contraryety of windes, and other quittinge of me I hope are all redy

[1] Hatfield MSS, 40, no. 70. Endorsed: 'To the most Honorable the Lord Hyghe treasurer of England att Courte. xviij. 9. 8 May 1596. Sir Thomas Baskervill to my Lord. His arrivall with iij^ee of her majesties shippes and one merchantman.' Baskerville took considerable pains in composing this letter. Two drafts and a separate short note (evidently intended for inclusion) are to be found in his papers (B.M., Harleian MSS, 4762, ff. 10–11). The following are the points of substance which are not included in the final version: the three queen's ships are named – the Garland, the Defiance and the Adventure – and the merchantman is named as the pinnace Phoenix. After referring to the withdrawal of valuables from places untenable, one of the drafts continues: 'so that ther was nothing to be gotten for us for their towns they would not rannsom, haveing receavid comande-ment to the Contrary from their kyng, and any thing elles we fond nott, and as for those symerouns thatt wer so much talkid of befor we Left England, I protest I hard nott so much as the name of them in the Indies [only this the spanyardes called those their slaves that ronns from them, symerouns which within a weke or a fortnyght are forcid for hunger to come to their masters again]', the passage in brackets being deleted. He asks for instructions about 'whatt shalbe done with this treasur, and Lykwise whatt course shalbe held to the menn of warr, whom I asure your Lordship ar very poore, and have nott means neyther to tary hear Long neyther to retourn Into their Cuntry withoutt order for their Conduction'. In addition to the discourse, he refers to 'Letters and platt taken from the enymy' by which he will show Burghley 'In whatt sorte thoss placis we atemptid wer fortefied and whatt course was taken for the defence of them'. The separate note reads: 'they had so long advertisment of our Comyng att panama thatt the Visroy of peru had send the governeur of Chyla with the forcis of pirue to defend thatt place with munycion and Artelery.'

retournid, of which nomber Captain Winter with her majesties shipp the forsight was the first, for I had no soner Left the Harborow of porte Bella, butt he rann from the fleett, and since, whatt ys becom of hym I know nott, butt this is right certain If he did nott disemboge befor me he hath som greatt hassard with the shipp. the sucses of this Action hath contraried all exspectacion, for in Itt we have Lost bothe the generalls Sir Nicolas Clyford my Brother and many other worthy gentillmen, and gotten no greatt matter som pearle and sillver ther is, which I feare will hardly bear the charg of the vyag, for we found the Indies so advertysid thatt theyr tenable placis wer strengthenid with all thinges nessisary and the other nott to be held all thinges retyrid owtt of them to placis of more surty, as your Lordship may better see by the discourse I send you hear Inclosid. Tuching her majesties shipps I resolue If Itt be possible to carye them aboutt for saving her majestie a further Charg, butt our nessescytis ar so greatt thatt I fear me we shalbe forcid to thrust Into some Harbor to suply our wantes for we have neyther bread nor drinke, nor any other thing butt otmeale and mays, which being donn and god favoring us with a favorable wind I will nott fayle to use all Indevor. so fearing to be over tedious I comend my Humble duty and servis resting in all Humblenis

aseabord the sillis	redy to be comandid
som 10 Leagues this	by your Lordship
8 of may	Tho : Baskervile

47. *Sir Thomas Baskerville to his wife*[1]

My dearist frind, I wronge the excedingly, butt by god Itt is against my will, for If I come yett, as your father will shew thee, I breek my Necke, thinke thy Husband hath myghty Enymys, and those thatt Lye upon the housse to Cach hym att any advantage, butt they cannott, for my Innocensye shall ever bear me owtt, and my consience being free I am carless whatt the divell and they cann do unto me thou artt rych by their saying, for I am acusid of Cussenyng

[1] B.M., Harleian MSS, 4762, f. 22. Endorsed: 'To my wiffe the Lady Baskervile.' A draft.

the quen of thirty thousand powndes. I would we had Itt, for the thankes in this statte is all one to be Honest or dishonest, and no faythfull servis respectid. bribery hath such place, and they abuse her majestie having her eare, disgracing all her Honest and faythefull servantes, and sett upe with all glory whom they pleas be they never so dishonest. I thinke by the tokens I have sent thee, yow may see I am nott com whom as rich as they say, and this I fear me thou shalt fynd thy self to be a thousand pownd poorer att this Howre then you wer att my Leving England I love her majestie, I love her servis and by god I am an honest man to her, and serve her with a trewer affection then the best of them and my Innocensye shall prove Itt, butt I fear me to enter any Into her servis, Lest att one tym or other they Chach me att som advantage, and therfore we must settell our selves to live together upon our fyfty powndes a yeer, for my parte I have mynd contentid with any fortune; fors yours to the same Corse thatt being donn soe will Less Care for them and their greatnis then they for our poverty. Swett mall tak itt nott unkindly thatt I have nott senn the as yett, and thinke this thy absentes is an Infynitt greffe unto me, which I cannot Indure, and therfor If I see I shall nott have a present dispach I will send for the assonn as my house is redy and furnyshid which wilbe within 14 days or 3 wekes. I comend me to thy selfe a thousand tymes, and Leav the to gods protection comend me to thy sisters London this 15[1]

     Thy dearest frend
     Tho: Baskervile

[1] Probably 15 May 1596 is meant.

Februarie 1595

PLATE IV. Munich Log, f. 13v., mentioning Drake's death

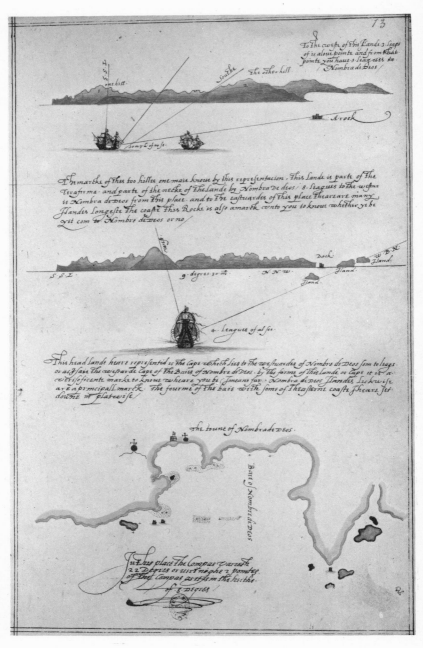

To the weste of this lande 3 leags
of it aloui pointe and from that
pointe you haue 5 leags uus to
Nombra di Dios

one hill   S S E   Southe   The other hill

A rock

Somrk of or se

The marche of these too hilles one maie knoue by this representacion, This lande is parte of the
Terafirma and parte of the necke of the lande by Nombra de dios 8 leagues to the weste
is Nombra de Deos from this place and to the eastuardes of this place there are many
Ilandes longest the coast this Rocke is also amarck unto you to knou whether ye be
yet com to Nombre de Deos or no

land   Rock   W B N

S S E   9 degres 30 m   N N W   Iland   Iland   Iland

4 leagues of at see

This head lande heare represented is the Cape which lies to the westuarde of Nombre de Deos som to leags
or as I saie the westarde Cape of the Baies of Nombre di Deos by the forme of this lande or Cape it is a
verie sufficente marke to knou wheare you be I meane for Nombra de Deos Ilandes Lickwise
are a principall marck The fourme of the baie with some of the easterne coaste theare set
doune in platewise

the toune of Nombrade Deos

Baie of Nombra de Deos

Jut his place the Compas vareeth
22 Degres or uust nee ghe 2 pointes
of the Compas as it is in the heithe
of 8 Degres

PLATE V. Paris Profiles, f. 13, Nombre de Dios

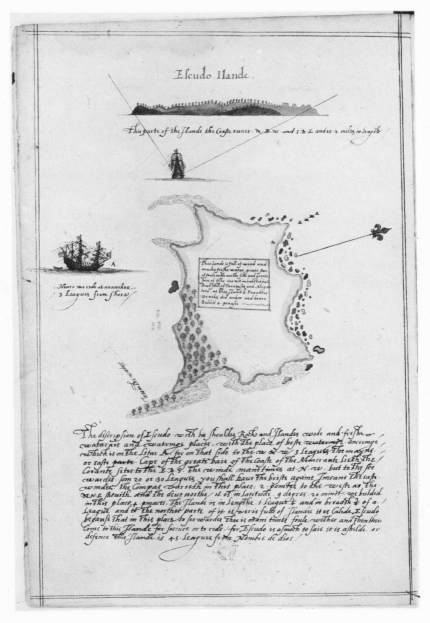

PLATE VI. Paris Profiles, f. 15, Escudo Island

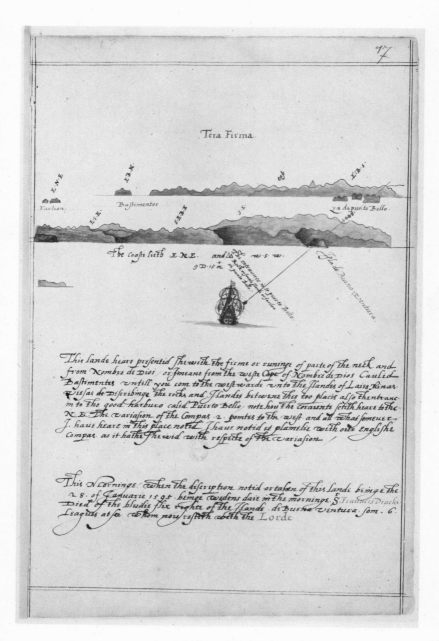

Tera Firma.

ENE · ENE · Bastimentes · Est · EbS · Varlion · va de por to Bello

The coast lieth E.N.E. and N w.s.w. 9D·15m

I la de Buina Ventura

This lande heare presentid shewith the firme or runinge of parte of the neck and from Nombre de Dios or somean from the weste Cape of Nombre de Dios Caulid Bastimentes untill you com to the westwarde unto the Ilandes of L aiss Kinas Viesas de describinge the rocks and Ilandes betweene thes too places also thentranem to the good harburo calid Puerto Bello, note hou the teravents sieith heare to the N E The variasion of the Compas 2 pointes to the west and all what someue r I haue heare in this place notid I haue notid it plainelie with oure Englishe Compas, as it hathe shewid with respecte of the variasion

This morninge, when the discription notid or taken of this lande bijnge the 28 of Januarie 1595 bijnge twedens daie in the morninge S Frauncis Dracke Died of the bludie flix right of the Ilande di Buena Ventura som 6 Leagues at se whom now resteth with the Lorde

PLATE VII. Paris Profiles, f. 17, Porto Belo and Drake's death

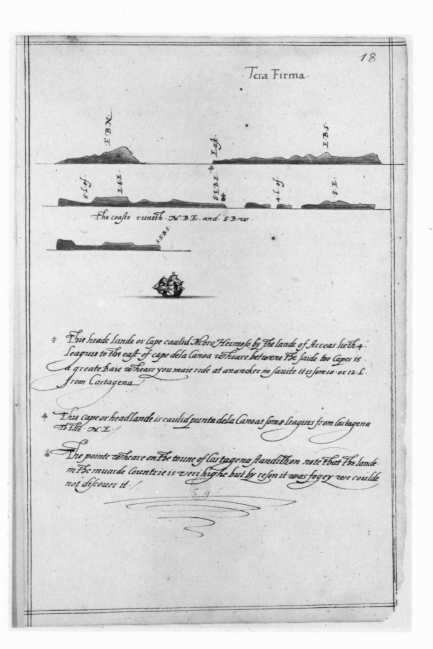

PLATE VIII. Paris Profiles, f. 18, Cartagena

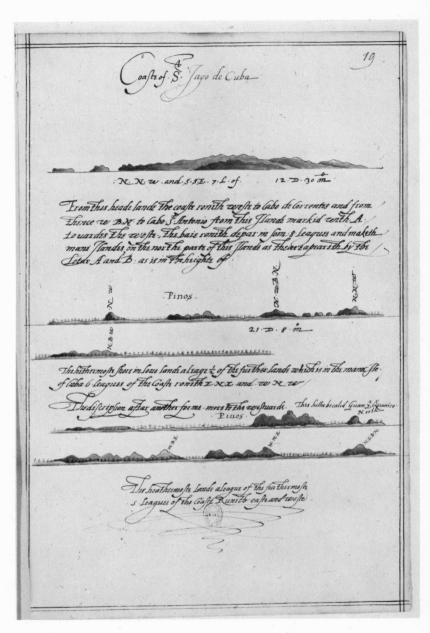

Coast of S. Jago de Cuba

N.N.W. and S.SE. 7 L. of   12.D.30 m.

From this heade lande the coaste ronith weste to Cabo de Correntes and from
thence w. B.N. to Cabo S. Antonio from this Jlande markid with A.
towardes the weste. The baie ronith depar in som 8 leagues and maketh
mani Jlandes in the northe parte of this Jlande as there apeareth by the
letter A and B: as is in the heighte of

Pinos

21.D.8 m.

The hithermoste shoe in some lande a league ½ of the futher lande which is in the mane Jle
of Cuba 6 leagues of the coaste ronith E.N.E. and w. E. w.

This discription after another forme more to the weastuardis. This hillis be calid Guan. S. Joanico
North
Pinos

The heathermoste lande a league of the futhermost
5 leagues of the coaste Runith eastt and weste.

PLATE IX. Paris Profiles, f. 19, southern coast of Cuba and Isle of Pines

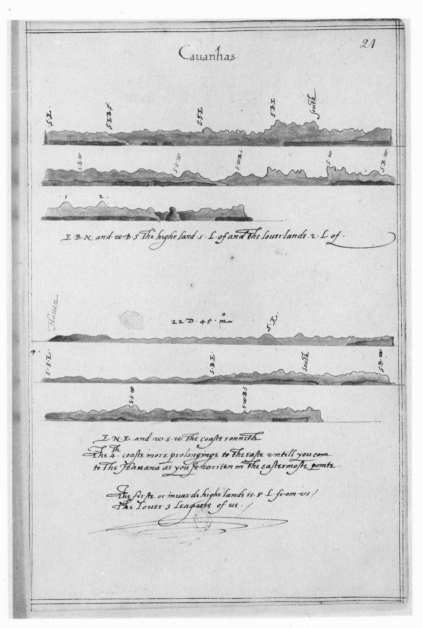

PLATE X. Paris Profiles, f. 21, northern coast of Cuba

The Art of Navigation in the Age of Drake

BY D. W. WATERS

When Drake was a child, the English were only just learning the art of oceanic navigation. Sebastian Cabot had been bribed by the privy council to leave his post of piloto mayor of Spain in 1548 in order to teach them. He had quickly trained a score in the art and in the reign of Mary, when Philip II of Spain was her consort, Stephen Borough, a navigator of the Muscovy Company which Cabot had helped to create, had been shown the Spanish system of training mariners in navigation when he had visited Seville. One result had been the publication in 1561 of the first manual in English on *The Art of Navigation,* which Richard Eden had translated from the Spanish work by Martín Cortés, published ten years earlier to enable Spanish pilots to qualify as navigators. Using the newly acquired art only a year later John Hawkins had navigated across the Atlantic to the coast of the West Indies, being 'the first Englishman' to do so. 'For before he attempted the same it was . . . reported the extremist lymit of danger to sayle upon those coastes. So that it was generally in dread among us', wrote Captain John Davis, in this very year 1595 that Hawkins again set sail for the Indies, adding 'howe then maye Syr John Hawkins bee esteemed'.[1] When Drake, in 1566, sailed on his first voyage to the West Indies (on a trading venture for Hawkins commanded by Captain John Lovell) the Cortés/Eden *Art of Navigation* of 1561 and Robert Copland's *The Rutter of the Sea* were the only two

[1] Captain John Davis, *The Hydrographicall Discourse* (London, 1595), quoted in D. W. Waters, *The Art of Navigation in Elizabethan and Early Stuart Times* (1958), p. 123.

navigational books printed in English. Even so the latter was largely a translation of the first printed French sailing directions and although nearly forty years old (it had first appeared in 1528) was still being reprinted.[1] However, in 1567, when Drake returned to England, William Bourne published his *Almanack for iii yeres, with serten Rules of Navigation,* ten of which were for the aspiring navigator. Bourne began a native literature on the art and science of navigation which enabled Captain Davis to claim in his brilliantly lucid navigational manual of 1595, *The Seamans Secrets,* that the English were now second to none as navigators and that in the art of nautical astronomy and geometrical navigation there were many hundreds as competent as he was himself.

In 1595 Cortés' *Art of Navigation* was still the standard manual; the latest edition had come out in 1589 (the next was to come out in 1596, the last in 1630). But another famous Spanish manual, Pedro de Medina's *Arte de Navegar* of 1545, which had been translated by John Frampton, also as *The Art of Navigation* and first published in London in 1581, was republished this year, 1595, for the benefit of English seamen. William Bourne had followed up his *Rules* by publishing the first original English work on navigation in 1574, his *A Regiment for the Sea;* of this the latest edition, edited by Thomas Hood, had appeared as recently as 1592. The next was to come out in 1596 (and the last in 1631); like the Cortés work it was in the nature of a best seller.

By a happy coincidence the book-seller Andrew Maunsell published, as 'a furtherance to the ignorant desirous of knowledge', his *Catalogue of English printed Bookes* in 1595, the second part of which included '*the Sciences Mathematicall, as . . . the Arte of Navigation . . .*' so that one can gain from it a very good idea of the chief books on navigation available in that year to Drake and Hawkins and their pilots and masters of ships. Besides those already mentioned Maunsell listed, amongst others: Anthony Ashley's translation from the Dutch *The Mariners Mirrour* of 1588, which had first introduced English pilots to the use of plane charts for coastal navigation in the seas of north west Europe; Blundeville's *Exercises* of 1594, designed expressly to enable the sort of young

[1] D. W. Waters, *The Rutters of the Sea* (1968).

gentlemen who flocked to join the expedition of 1595 to learn the basic elements of the art of navigation; Hood's *Vse of both the Globes,* which had come out in 1592 in anticipation of the publication of the first English globes by Molyneux; Hood's treatise on the use of the plane chart, *The Mariners Guide,* also of 1592; Robert Norman's *Safeguard of Saylers* of 1590, which he had translated from the Dutch and first published in 1584 as the very latest sailing directions for north west Europe (unlike *The Rutter* – still on sale – it included woodcut coastal elevations); his *New Attractive,* on magnetic dip, first published in 1581 and reissued in 1592 with the treatise on magnetic variation, *The Variation of the Cumpas,* by William Borough (the younger brother of Stephen) with whom Drake had had such trouble at Cadiz in '87; and Henry Moore's *Almanack ... for 34 yeres,* of 1580. Suffice it to say there were plenty of books available now from which to learn the art.

A man still learned how to become a pilot as Drake had, under the direction of the master of the ship in which he served, by personal experience of the sea, memorizing the appearance of the coasts under the ever-changing light and shadow of fair weather and foul, of sun, moon, and stars and of the seasons. The master taught a youngster how to determine direction with a magnetic compass and to re-magnetize it from time to time with a lodestone;[1] how to judge his speed by eye and to use the recently invented English log and log-line with a half-minute log-glass, and to mark the passage of time with the ship's bell and a half-hour 'running glass'; how to sound the sea bed with a lead and line, when within soundings (100 fathoms) to find the depth of water and the nature of the bottom in order to check his estimated position; and how to use a traverse board to keep a check on the course and speed 'made good' each watch. But to learn the art of navigating over the ocean, to observe the height of the sun or of certain stars to find his latitude, he had need to practice what he had learned from books – Ashley's or Blundeville's, Bourne's or Eden's or Frampton's, Borough's or Hood's or Davis' – under the careful eye of an experienced navigator who would teach him how to tabulate his observations and estimations methodically in a log-book and enter

[1] Drake's is now on loan to the National Maritime Museum.

the logged results in a journal daily in order to record his progress and position each noon.

But to recognize the islands and the 'main' overseas he had only one printed set of sailing directions, Frampton's *Portes of the Weast India* of 1578, translated from part of Fernández de Enciso's *Suma de Geographia* of 1519. For this reason he had to place reliance upon manuscript directions, if they were obtainable, which had been captured from Spanish ships, or upon Portuguese pilots experienced in these waters, if their services could be obtained, or upon the memory of fellow English mariners who had already visited the coasts (such as Drake himself) and might recognize some stretches of it. In fact on his voyage of circumnavigation Drake captured a Portuguese pilot before crossing the Atlantic who was familiar with the coast of Brazil and on whose experience Drake clearly relied for his passage down that coast. On this voyage of 1595 he had two Portuguese pilots, one of whom was Simón Moreno, which may account for the immediate identification of the land-fall made in the West Indies after the ocean passage, in strong contrast to the failure of the Spaniards in the five frigates to identify theirs; all their pilots identified Martinique and Dominica as Deseada and Antigua, lying no less than 2° to the northward – which also says little for their skill (unless the skies were long obscured) in nautical astronomy. The professional pilot, the man who could identify landfalls and pilot a vessel knowledgeably in coastal waters and who offered his services to captains of ships and commanders of expeditions was clearly a key figure in any overseas enterprise at this time. He was, as it has been well put, 'a walking compendium of navigational knowledge and skills'.[1] Early in the next century, with the colonization of Virginia and the Lesser Antilles, the English could dispense with foreigners in the rôle.

We can be confident that the expedition of 1595 had Spanish sailing directions and charts because at the end of the century Richard Hakluyt published some directions in translation in the third volume of his *Principal Navigations,* and Thomas Hood produced a fine manuscript chart of the world.[2] Neverthe-

---

[1] Mr George Naish, F.S.A., in a letter to D.W.W.
[2] B.M., Additional MSS, 17, 938.

less, someone, probably Drake, saw to it on this voyage that all the principal landfalls made should be recorded in colour by some 'painter', such as Drake had carried with him on his voyage around the world (1577–80),[1] so that each should be readily identifiable by other English seamen in future years, for one such book completed on this voyage has survived.[2]

This is a precious relic indeed of Drake's and Hawkins' last voyage because it is the only English 'navigational notebook' of this type of Elizabethan times that has come down to us and because it epitomizes how much hydrographical material was compiled. It included, for instance, not only identified coastal elevations sketched as the ship made her landfall or stretched past the shore but also information on tidal streams,[3] on the depth of water and nature of the sea bed,[4] and on harbours.[5]

Another scarcely less precious document is the journal summarizing the daily navigational record of some navigator of the expedition.[6] Few are those which do survive, and these are made valuable by the loss of every Elizabethan log book, although fortunately Captain Davis showed in *The Seamans Secrets* the lay-out of the log book which he kept during his abortive voyage of 1593 to the Pacific.[7] Fortunately also, Richard Hakluyt reproduced another of Davis' log books, that of his voyage of 1587 to the Azores, thereby transmitting to us the only complete Elizabethan example.[8]

The journal of 1595 gives, typically, the day of the month, the day's run from noon to noon in leagues, and noteworthy events. Thus, on 6 September is noted: ' . . . 12 of the clocke I observede and founde my selfe in 45–30 [degrees North latitude] and we made a south southewest waye 40 leagues'. The navigator observed,

---

[1] Waters, *The Art of Navigation*, p. 535.

[2] Paris Profiles, from which Plates v–x are reproduced.

[3] *Ibid.*, f. 7, 'Curacao' (which, to be in its correct order should precede f. 11); f. 16, 'Veragua'.

[4] *Ibid.*, f. 10, 'Estacia' and 'Saba'.

[5] *Ibid.*, ff. 13 and 14, 'Nombre de Deos'; f. 15, 'Escudo Ilande'.

[6] Munich Log, ff. 8–18, See Plate IV.

[7] Waters, *The Art of Navigation*, Plate LI.

[8] Waters, *The Art of Navigation*, Pl. XLVI, from the third volume of *Principal Navigations* (1600).

of course, the sun at noon when it bore south on the meridian and used a sea-astrolabe, a cross-staff or, possibly, one of Captain Davis' just-invented backstaffs (with which you observed the shadow cast by the sun). This, incidentally, was the only celestial observation recorded on the outward run, for which departure was taken from 'Dudman' on August 31.

The first landfall was 'Forteventura' in the Canaries, which the painter sketched when 'som. 5, leagues from Land'. The next recorded landfall was Martinique whose latitude, not being able to determine their longitude, the ships ran down for 240 leagues before making the land. 'This Ilande lieth in the heighte of 13. Degrees and 15 minots of latitude', the painter noted, as he sketched it from '5 leagues off at see', on that bright October morning. Someone must have observed the fleet to be in that latitude a week before, for since then they had steered 'weste'.

Some of the most interesting navigational entries in the journal occur on the voyage home. At noon on 8 March 1596, the navigator 'observede the sonne and found myself in 23 degrees and 36 minits', between Havana and 'Cape Florida'. Yet he must have been uneasy for that evening he took a star sight 'at 7 of the clocke and founde my selfe in 25 degrees' (only just south of the latitude of Cape Sable). He probably observed *Polaris,* the particular interest being that this is one of the very few star sights actually recorded at sea that has come down to us. Some time during the next 30 hours the ships rounded Florida for, at six in the morning of the 9th they sighted 'Cape Floryda and at 12 of the clocke I observede the sune and found my selfe in 26 degrees and a halfe' – off Palm Beach. The next noon a meridian sun sight fixed the ship in latitude 29° North and they set an East-North-Easterly course for the Azores. On the 16th the navigator recorded another sun sight 'in 32 degrees 12 minetts'. By April 3 he was (by estimation or by observation of some other navigator) in the latitude of Flores for he set course eastwards, sighting that island four days later, where he anchored on the following day and traded for 'vittals', 'watered and had hennes of the Portingalls'. Departing from Flores, sketched by the painter, as was Corvo which the navigator sighted later to 'the northe northeweste of us', he passed by Fayal 'at 2 of the clocke in the afternone' of the 12th, lying 'Southe and by easte' of him and pressed on for the Soundings.

On 4 May they sounded and found '80 fathoms withe sande'; at 3 the next day they sounded again finding '80 fathoms' and the next day the navigator 'observede the sonne and founde myselfe in 49° 50 minutes' – the latitude of the Scillies – 'and caste about to the southeward' to pass clear of them. On the 7th 'we sounded in 75 fathoms ose sande' and on the 8th twice – 'in 70 fathoms ose sande' and 'in 65 fathoms peperye blacke sande', after sighting the islands briefly. By the 9th they had them well in view and stood southwards to clear them before the run up channel the next day, when 'we sounded southweste of Selye 10 leagues in 65 fathoms shelles and sharksteethe'. The painter sketched St Mary's castle and the 'Bishop and Clarks' bearing 'S.E.B.E.' as he skirted them. It was a sad but classic homecoming.

Bibliography

A. MANUSCRIPTS
Public Record Office, London

State Papers Domestic: S.P. 12/250–61.
Chancery: C. 2/Eliz. B.7/26; C. 66/37 Eliz. C. 2/33/96.
Exchequer: E. 351/243, 2233.
Audit Office: A.O./1/1688.
High Court of Admiralty: H.C.A. 13/26, 30–6, 103, 104; 14/33; 24/62; 25/1, 3.

Somerset House, London

Prerogative Court of Canterbury: P.C.C., Drake, Barrington, Kidd.

British Museum, London

Lansdowne MSS, 60.
Harleian MSS, 598, 1162, 4762, 5260, 6997.
Cotton MSS, Titus, B. VIII.
Sloane MSS, 2177, 2292.
Additional MSS, 17, 5209, 11406, 12503, 13964, 14284, 36316–7.

Bodleian Library, Oxford

Tanner MSS, 77.

Hatfield House

Hatfield MSS, 25, 33–6, 40, 41, 48, 172.

Longleat House

Devereux Papers, V.

National Library of Wales, Aberystwyth

Thomas Myddelton, 'A jurnal of all owtlandishe accomptes'.

Bristol Record Office, Bristol

William Adams, 'Chronicle of Bristol'.

Central Public Library, Plymouth

Indenture signed by Drake, 27 January 1596.

BIBLIOGRAPHY

Archivo General de Indias, Seville

Santo Domingo: 51, 81, 128, 155, 169, 179, 180, 184, 187, 193, 207, 232, 584.
Santa Fe: 1, 17, 92, 93, 190.
Panama: 1, 14, 44, 46.
Indiferente General: 1887; 2496, lib. V, VII; 2988.
Contratación: 5112; 5169, lib. IX; 5170, lib. X.
Patronato: 18, 176, 265.
Escribanía de Cámara: 134.

Archivo General, Simancas

Estado Inglaterra: 433.
Guerra Antigua: 432, 448, 459, 469.

Museo Canario

Colección Millares Torres: t. 1.

Biblioteca de la Real Academia de la Historia, Madrid

Colleción Muñoz: 43.
Colección Salazar: F. 19; N. 9.

Museo Naval, Madrid

Colleción Sanz Barutell: 2, 392.
Navarrete MSS: V, XII, XXV.

Archivo y Biblioteca del Palacio de Liria, Madrid (Alba MSS)

'Relacion del viaje de las cinco fragatas.'

Bibliothèque Nationale, Paris

Manuscrits Anglais: 51.

Bayerische Staatsbibliothek, München

Codex Anglicus: 2.

Bibliothèque Publique et Universitaire, Geneva

Collection Edouard Favre: 82.

Biblioteca Nacional, Lima

Manuscritos Peruanos: Espejo historial (1642).

B. PRINTED SOURCES

Andrews, K. R. (ed.), *English Privateering Voyages to the West Indies, 1588–1595* (1959).

BIBLIOGRAPHY

Anon, *Relacion del Viage que hizieron las cinco Fragatas de Armada de su Magestad, yendo por Cabo dellas Don Pedro Tello de Guzman, este presente Año de Noventa y cinco* (Seville, 1596).

Bigges, Walter, *A Summarie and True Discourse of Sir Francis Drake's West-Indian Voyage* (1652).

Birch, Thomas, *Memoirs of the Reign of Queen Elizabeth* (1754).

Boletín Histórico de Puerto Rico, IV, 317–23.

Bourel de la Roncière, Charles Germain (ed.), *Un Atlas inconnu de la dernière expédition de Drake* (Paris, 1909).

Bruce, John (ed.), *Liber Famelicus of Sir James Whitelocke, a Judge of the Court of King's Bench in the Reigns of James I and Charles I* (1858).

Cairasco de Figueroa, Bartolomé, *Templo Militante, Triumphos de Virtudes, Festividades y Vidas de Santos* (Valladolid, 1603; Lisbon, 1615).

Calendar of the Manuscripts of the Marquess of Salisbury (Historical Manuscripts Commission), IV, V, VI, X (1892–5).

Calendar of State Papers, Domestic Series, Elizabeth, 1595–97 (1869).

Calendar of State Papers, Domestic Series, Elizabeth, 1598–1601 (1869).

Caro de Torres, Francisco, *Relacion de los Servicios que hizo a Su Magestad del Rey Don Felipe Segundo y Tercero, don Alonso de Sotomayor del Abito de Santiago* [etc.] (Madrid, 1620).

Collins, A. (ed.), *Letters and Memorials of State . . . collected by Sir Henry Sydney* (2 vols., 1746).

Cooley, W. D. (ed.), *Sir Francis Drake his Voyage, 1595, by Thomas Maynarde, together with the Spanish Account of Drake's attack on Puerto Rico* (1849).

Corbett, J. S. (ed.), *Papers relating to the Navy during the Spanish War, 1585–1587* (1898).

Cordus, Valerius, *Pharmacorum Omnium, quae in usu potiss. sunt, componendorum ratio* [etc.] (Nuremberg, 1592).

Culpeper, Nicholas, *Physicall Directory or a Translation of the London Dispensatory* (1649).

Dasent, J. R. (ed.), *The Acts of the Privy Council, New Series*, XXIV (1900), XXV (1901), XXVI (1902).

Falcó y Osorio, Maria del Rosario, Duquesa de Berwick y de Alba, *Nuevos Autógrafos de Cristóbal Colón y Relaciones de Ultramar* (Madrid, 1902).

Fitzgeffrey, Charles, *Sir Francis Drake, His Honorable lifes commendation, and his Tragicall Deathes lamentation* (Oxford, 1596).

Fox, Francis F. (ed.), *Adams's Chronicle of Bristol* (Bristol, 1910).

Gairdner, J. R. (ed.), *Letters and Papers, Foreign and Domestic, of the Reign of Henry VIII*, XIII (1892).

Hakluyt, Richard, *The Principal Navigations, Voyages Traffiques & Discoveries of the English Nation*, III (1600).

Kraus, H. P., *Sir Francis Drake, A Pictorial Biography* (Amsterdam, 1970).

Laughton, J. K. (ed.), *State Papers relating to the Defeat of the Spanish Armada* (2 vols, 1894).

MacLean, J. and Heane, W. C. (eds.), *The Visitation of Gloucestershire, 1623* (1885).

Marsden, R. G. (ed.), *Documents relating to the Law and Custom of the Sea* (2 vols, 1915–16).

Murdin, W. (ed.), *A Collection of State Papers . . . left by William Cecill, Lord Burghley* (1759).

Nuttall, Z. (ed.), *New Light on Drake* (1914).

Oppenheim, M. (ed.), *The Naval Tracts of Sir William Monson* (5 vols, 1902–14).

Platt, Hugh, *Sundrie new and Artificiall remedies against Famine* (1596).

Purchas, Samuel (ed.), *Hakluytus Posthumus, or Purchas his Pilgrimes, IV* (1625).

Quinn, D. B. (ed.), *The Roanoke Voyages, 1584–1590* (2 vols, 1955).

R[oberts], H[enry], *The Trumpet of Fame: or Sir F. Drake's & Sir J. Hawkins' Farewell* (1595).

Savile, Henry, *A Libell of Spanish Lies: found at the Sacke of Cales . . . With an answere briefely confuting the Spanish lies . . . by Henry Savile Esquire . . . And also an Approbation of this discourse, by Sir Thomas Baskervile* [etc.] (1596).

Sotheby & Co., *Catalogue of Valuable Americana* for sale on 5–6 November, 1962.

Tapia y Rivera, Alejandro, *Bibilioteca Histórica de Puerto-Rico* (Puerto Rico, 1854).

Thomas, Georg Martin (ed.), 'Logbook eines Schiffes von der dritten Expedition Franz Drake's', *Monumenta Saecularia, herausgegeben von der Königlich Bayerischen Akademie der Wissenschaften*, Classe 1–3 (München, 1859), pp. 97–122.

Vega Carpio, Lope de, *La Dragontea* (Valencia, 1598). Ed. V. Fernández Asís, 2 vols (Madrid, 1935).

Vivian, J. L. (ed.), *The Visitations of the County of Devon* (Exeter, 1895).

Williamson, J. A. (ed.), *The Observations of Sir Richard Hawkins* (1933).

Wittich, J., *Arcula Itineraria* (Leipzig, 1590).

C. SECONDARY WORKS

Angulo Iñíguez, Diego, *Bautista Antonelli: las Fortificaciones Americanas del Siglo XVI* (Madrid, 1942).

Alamo, N., 'Drake y Van der Doez en Gran Canaria', *Revista de Historia* (de las Islas Canarias), 35–8 (1932–3).

Alciati, Andreas, *Emblemata* (Seville, 1549).

Andrews, K. R., 'The Economic Aspects of Elizabethan Privateering' (London University Ph.D. thesis, 1951).

Andrews, K. R., *Elizabethan Privateering: English Privateering during the Spanish War, 1585–1603* (1964).

Andrews, K. R., *Drake's Voyages: A Re-assessment of their Place in Elizabethan Maritime Expansion* (1967).

Benavides, Antonio, *Memorias de D. Fernando IV de Castilla* (2 vols, Madrid, 1860).

Brown, Alexander, *The Genesis of the United States* (2 vols, 1890).

BIBLIOGRAPHY

Chaunu, H. et P., *Séville et l'Atlantique, 1504–1650* (11 vols, Paris, 1956–9).

Cheyney, E. P., *A History of England from the Defeat of the Armada to the Death of Queen Elizabeth* (2 vols, 1914, 1926).

Corbett, J. S., *Drake and the Tudor Navy* (2 vols, 1893).

The Dictionary of National Biography (63 vols, 1885–1900).

The Dictionary of Welsh Biography down to 1940 (1959).

Dodd, A. H., *Studies in Stuart Wales* (1952).

Dodd, A. H., 'Mr Myddelton the Merchant of Tower Street', in *Elizabethan Government and Society, Essays Presented to Sir John Neale* (eds. S. T. Bindoff, J. Hurstfield and C. Williams, 1961).

Eliott-Drake, E. F., *The Family and Heirs of Sir Francis Drake* (2 vols, 1911).

Fernández Duro, C., *Armada Española desde la Unión de los Reinos de Castilla y de Aragón,* III (Madrid, 1897).

Henry, L. W., 'The Earl of Essex as Strategist and Military Organizer, 1596–7', *English Historical Review,* LXVIII (1953), 363–93.

Herrera y Tordesillas, Antonio de, *Historia General del Mundo,* III (Madrid, 1612).

Hussey, R. D., 'Spanish Reactions to Foreign Aggression in the Caribbean to about 1680', *Hispanic American Historical Review,* IX (1929), 286–302.

Jal, A., *Glossaire Nautique* (Paris, 1848–50).

Keevil, J. J., *Medicine and the Navy,* I (1957).

Latham, R. E., *Revised Medieval Latin Word-list* (1965).

Marrero Nuñez, Julio, 'Puerto Rico and the Elizabethan Age' (unpublished work in the library of San Juan National Historic Site, Puerto Rico, 1960).

May, W. E., 'The Binnacle', *Mariner's Mirror,* 40 (1954), 21–32.

Ojer, P., *Don Antonio de Berrío, Gobernador del Dorado* (Burgos, 1960).

Parks, G. B., *Richard Hakluyt and the English Voyages* (New York, 1928).

Pollard, A. W. and Redgrave, G. R., *A Short-Title Catalogue of Books Printed in England, Scotland and Ireland . . . 1475–1640* (1926).

Rabb, T. K., *Enterprise and Empire* (1967).

Real, Cristóbal, *El Corsario Drake y el Imperio Español* (Madrid, 1942).

Rey, J. A., *Drake dans la Poésie Espagnole* (Paris, 1906).

Rumeu de Armas, Antonio, *Los Viajes de John Hawkins a América, 1562–1595* (Seville, 1947).

Rumeu de Armas, Antonio, *Piraterías y Ataques Navales contra las Islas Canarias,* II, III (Madrid, 1948).

Simón, Pedro, *Noticias historiales de las Conquistas de Tierra Firme en las Indias Occidentales,* V (Bogotá, 1892).

Sottas, Jules, 'An Atlas of Drake's Last Voyage', *Mariner's Mirror,* II (1912), 135–42.

Torres Reyes, Ricardo, 'The Harbour Defenses of San Juan in the Sixteenth Century' (unpublished work in the library of San Juan National Historic Site, 1955).

Waters, D. W., 'Bittacles and Binnacles', *Mariner's Mirror*, 41 (1955), 198–208.

Waters, D. W. (ed.), *The True and Perfecte Newes of . . . Syr Frauncis Drake not onely at Sancto Domingo, and Carthagena, but also nowe at Cales, and vppon the Coast of Spayne, 1587 by Thomas Greepe* (1955).

Waters, D. W., *The Art of Navigation in England in Elizabethan and Early Stuart Times* (1958).

Waters, D. W. (ed.), *The Rutters of the Sea* (1968).

Wernham, R. B., 'Elizabethan War Aims and Strategy', in *Elizabethan Government and Society, Essays Presented to Sir John Neale* (eds. S. T. Bindoff, J. Hurstfield and C. Williams, 1961).

Willan, T. S., *Studies in Elizabethan Foreign Trade* (1959).

Williams, W. R., *The Parliamentary History of Wales* (Brecon, 1895).

Williamson, G. C., *George, Third Earl of Cumberland* (1920).

Williamson, J. A., *Hawkins of Plymouth* (1949).

Wölfel, D. J., *Die Kanarischen Inseln und ihre Urbewohner* (Leipzig, 1940).

Index

Baskerville, Sir Thomas (contd.)
    character, 8, 28, 34, 82–4, 251,
    254–8; 'discourse' by, 3, 84, 114–24,
    151, 160, 186, 212, 255, 256, 257;
    description of Puerto Rico, 159–61;
    letters by, 2, 3, 15–16, 17, 26, 28–9,
    32, 159–60, 182, 196, 212, 227, 254–
    258; letters to, 21–5
Bastimentos, Isla de Los, Panama, 195,
    212
Bayning, Paul, 49
Bayona Islands, Spain, 155, 177
Becerra, Marco Antonio, 154, 164, 167,
    168, 171
Berkeley, Richard, 82
Berrío, Antonio de, 14–15, 186
Bertie, Peregrine, Lord Willoughby, 82
Bigges, Walter, 79–80
Blavet, France, 17
Bluq, Vincent, 132–5, 138
Bodenham, Jonas, 40, 41, 55, 69, 102,
    140, 245, 251
Bonner, Jonas, 35
Boquerón, River, Panama, 186
Borough, Stephen, 259, 261
Borough, William, 40, 45, 51, 52, 261
Boswell, Captain, 45, 46, 48
Bourne, William, 260–1
Bowster (Bowyer, Boyser), Captain, 45,
    47
Bowyer, see Bowster
Boxwell, Gloucestershire, 82
Boyser, see Bowster
Bravo de Cavañas, Francisco, 181,
    190–1
Brazil, 262
Brest, 5, 83, 85, 230
Bridge, Captain, 45, 47
Bridgewater, 39
Bristol, 31–2, 39, 79, 221
Brittany, 55, 85, 162, 230
Browne, Brute, 45, 81, 91–2, 110
Buckhurst, Lord, see Sackville

Buenos Aires, 183
Burghley, Lord, see Cecil
Bushe, see Rushe

Cabot, Sebastian, 259
Cabrera, Rodrigo, 244
Cabrera, Rodrigo de, 142
Cabrera de Rosas, Alonso, 146
Cadiz (Cales), 15, 22, 39, 45, 47, 75,
    239, 250, 252
Caermarthen, 83
Caesar, Charles, 41, 69
Caesar, Julius, 41–2
Cairasco de Figueroa, Bartolomé, 128,
    129,
Callao de los Reyes, Peru, 201
Camarón Bay, 122
Camarón, Cape, 212, 229
Canary Islands, 4, 18–19, 25, 84, 88,
    89, 115, 125–48, 154, 214, 216, 235,
    237, 240, 264
Cañete, Marqués de, 99, 182, 201
Cano, Francisco, 217, 230
Cano, Pedro, 229
Cape Verde Islands, 85
Capira, Sierra de, Panama, 119, 186,
    195, 197, 201, 207
Capirilla (Capireja), Panama, 2, 50,
    84, 183–6, 203, 204, 206, 213, 224–
    227
Carew, George, 72
Carew, Richard, 49
Carmarthen, Richard, 51, 52
Caro de Torres, Francisco, 3, 181, 183,
    186, 203, 204
Carreño, Captain, 210
Cartegena, 9, 14, 15, 25, 43, 95, 103,
    112, 149, 159, 166, 175, 176, 179–81,
    187–93, 194–5, 202, 205, 214, 216,
    222, 228, 236–8, 240–1, 243
Casa de Cruzes, see Cruzes
Casola, Prospero, 126–7, 129–32
Castro, Beltrán de, 223

Drake, Bernard, 35, 42, 70
Drake, Sir Bernard, 42
Drake, Francis, 102
Drake, Sir Francis, character of, 9, 10,
34, 81, 86, 100–1, 113–14, 127, 133,
191–2, 231; death of, 1, 3, 10, 40, 43,
84, 101–2, 108, 112, 122, 228–9, 230,
231, 233, 241, 242, 243, 251; instructions to the fleet, 177–8; letters
by, 17, 18, 20, 25–8, 31–3, 159,
174–5; letters to, 20, 21–5, 30–1; and
the organization of the expedition,
6–7, 12, 17, 19, 44–50, 51–3, 72,
77–8, 87, 136, 139, 215; relations
with Essex, 5, 16–17; relations with
Hawkins, 6, 10, 86–90, 109, 175, 252
Drake, Richard, 38, 55, 102
Drake, Thomas, 35, 40, 41, 49, 52, 67,
69, 71, 102, 133, 245, 251
Dudley, Robert, earl of Leicester, 82
Duffield, Henry, 35, 42

Eden, Captain, 39, 100
Eden, Richard, 259
Egerton, Captain, 100
Elizabeth, Queen, policy of, 5–7, 10,
12–34, 84, 86, 87, 106, 125; con-
tribution to the expedition, 16, 20, 21,
25, 27–9, 31, 33, 48–50, 51–3, 71, 72,
75, 76, 78, 105, 139, 155, 219, 221–2,
251, 257–8; letters and reports to,
26–7, 31–2, 81, 215, 252–3; letters
by, 13, 20, 21–5, 30–1
Enchanted Islands, see Azores
Enciso, Fernández de, 262
Englesby, Stephen, 70
English Channel, 106
Enríquez Conabut, Juan, see Conabut
Equisman, Daniel, 62, 89, 135–8
Esbran, John, 221–3
Escudo (Escudo de Veragua) Island,
40, 100–1, 112, 122, 228–9, 232–3,
263

Essex, earl of, see Devereux
exchequer, 3, 12, 49, 50, 51–71, 107

Fajardo, Luis, 163
Falmouth, 108, 250, 253
Farar, . . . , 234
Fayal Island, Azores, 264–5
Fenton, Captain, 45, 47, 48
Fenton, James, 35, 70
Fernández de Córdoba, Miguel
Gerónimo, 135, 138, 141
Ferrol (Farolle), 22, 148, 254
Ferrón Barragán, Gerónimo, 182, 231,
232
Finisterre, Cape, 18
Fishbourne, Richard, 39, 67
Fitzgeffrey, Charles, 3
Flores, Francisco Gutiérrez, 102, 111,
118, 188, 192, 193, 230
Flores Island, Azores, 250, 264
Flores, Pedro (Florez, Peter), 241
Flores de Rabanal, Juan, 171, 174
Flores de Valdés, Diego, 183
Florida, 107, 154, 248, 264
Florida, Cape, 106, 264
Florida Channel (Bahama Channel),
162, 238, 243
Folde, William, 67
Fones, Humphrey, 67
Fortescue, John, 52, 71, 76, 250–1
Forteventura Island, see Fuerteventura
Fox, Captain, 233
Frampton, John, 260, 262
Frobisher, Martin, 40
Fuerteventura (Forteventura) Island,
Canaries, 89, 264
Fuller, John, 67
Funchal, Madeira Island, 13

Garrett, Captain, 45, 47, 48
Gasparan, . . . (Gasparian), 131, 139–
141
George, David, 67